MY STORY

HOW A YOUNG BOY FROM CALIFORNIA ENDED UP AN OLD MAN IN FLORIDA

by

ART MYERS

Copyright © Art Myers

All rights reserved including the right of reproduction in whole or in part in any form what so ever.

2015

ISBN 978-1-7357208-4-5

Contact Art Myers: artmyersbooks@gmail.com

For Jeanne

Wife, companion, partner, and best friend.
Who made a major part of MY STORY possible.

PREFACE

This is my story. An auto-biography if you will. As I approach my 80th birthday I muse that it has been quite a journey from the start in Southern California to near the end in Southern Florida. It has been a journey much out of the ordinary after a beginning which was most ordinary for the time. Once underway my life saw many changes in occupations from the start as a graduate electrical engineer to a professional sculptor, with many excursions into numerous other work such as design of a pinball game, a bed and breakfast operation and catering business. Then to home renovation and construction, personal computer design and eventually retiring to a boating life style cruising both U.S. Coasts. There were many automobile trips taken about the United States, Canada and Mexico, including a 12,000 mile trip from the east coast to Alaska and back. A number of trips to Europe and an extended stay in Baja California. About ten years living in the San Francisco Bay area, a year in England, several trips to Aspen, Colorado and later a thirteen year residency there. A couple of years in Lake Forest, Illinois and sixteen years in Loveland, Colorado, followed by nine years living aboard a boat. And now aground in Vero Beach, Florida. Amongst all this was a year or two without a residence, a very good marriage, a wonderful daughter with an approved husband, and two special granddaughters.

As I look back over my life and write these words I come to the conclusion that no other generation has had a better time to be alive than mine. If I present this story correctly you should get a sense of what I mean, from my ancestry, parents, education and opportunities. You do need to have, at least to some degree, "the right stuff" to live a life-style such as mine and occasionally being in the right places at the right times has been helpful. To achieve extraordinary success, however, you need the big three; be in the right place, at the right time, and have the right stuff. This may seem a very simple observation, but it is not a simple matter. The big question is always if you find yourself in the right place at the right time, and most importantly recognize it, do you have the right stuff? I like to think that I have had close calls a few times but never quite put the big three together. As I wander through my story I will expand on this ranging from places and times where I have lived along with the people, inventions, opportunities, schemes and failures with which I have been involved.

A biography has to have some historical context such as father, mother, birth, geography, place and time. I will go a little farther back as I have some very interesting ancestry that may shed light on how, and maybe why, I made this journey. I will also try to be honest and will not claim that I had any great plan. In fact I think this journey was in large part dictated by circumstances that forced me to make course changes that I never fore saw. A good part of my good fortune was due to having a wife, now for over fifty years, who always was a partner and always said lets do it when each change was, or had to be, made. And to a certain degree we had the right stuff to make it all work out quite nicely. I think the true measure of a life well lived is the achievement of happiness which I think I can claim more than my share.

So read on. I expect that there will be many side trips as I put this to paper as I intend to wander into philosophy, politics, finance, education, physics and other subjects I have found of interest along the way. I hope that this time I have right stuff and maybe this is the right place and right time to at least get the story told before the right time for me is no longer available.

CHAPTER 1

Choosing the starting point for the story of one's life is problematic. The birth day is the most obvious, of course, but the moment of conception which starts the chromosomal dance of life sparks the imagination. This is where I will start.

The place, although this is purely a speculation, would have been the Loom Room at Sycamore Ranch in Fallbrook, California and the time a little after 9:00 pm on Tuesday, July 17, 1934. This day was my older sister Nancy's second birthday and the time is the usual time to retire for the night at the Ranch. The assumption I make is that my mother and father would have had a small party for Nancy that day and may have had some romantic feelings later in the evening. They were at that time living with my father's parents on the Ranch and I expect the Loom Room was the room that would have been their bedroom. This therefore may have been the start, the very beginning, of my journey as within my father's contribution was the one in millions that had the right stuff to win the race for me.

My paternal grandparents had moved to California after graduating from Kansas State Agricultural College, a session in the Navy for him, then marriage and one more year with the navy. They then bought a ranch in Fallbrook, which was in some disrepair and cobbled together some outbuildings for a house, planted several citrus orchards, and made a life for themselves. Apparently they did quite well early on. A first son, James, was born and then a second son, my father Frederick Axel Myers. At that time Sycamore Ranch was about 110 acres, about two thirds beautiful, fertile flat land and the rest hillside. Lemons, two types of oranges, numerous other fruit trees, gardens, a cow, chickens and a good well for water provided an income and subsistence. At one time they put in a dirt tennis court and they had ranching equipment and at least one car. I will touch on this later as my grandparents and the Ranch were a very big part of my youth.

My mother and father had both entered Pomona College in 1926, at the height of the Roaring Twenties, where they met, dated, fell in love, and graduated with a group of friends they kept through out their lifetimes. They graduated in 1930, my father with a business degree and my mother with one of the liberal arts degree with emphasis on psychology, Phi Beta Kappa. My mother continued on to gain her Masters degree in 1931. They were married August 2, 1931 and left to start their life together in San Diego at 1624 Meade Avenue. (The small unit is still standing, built in the mid 1920s, and is part of a small complex of units divided in half by a common walk.)

As you might expect, 1930 was not a good year to graduate as the Great Depression was just getting underway. My father had a job with Shell Oil Company driving a gas truck and as far as I can determine was soon transferred to Calipatria in the Imperial Valley, just south of the Salton Sea, an awful place at the time. Sister Nancy was born during this period in Glendale, near Los Angeles, and after her first months spent with family in either Glendale or Fallbrook, mother and daughter returned to Calipatria to rejoin my father. Sometime shortly afterward he was laid off and as the depression had really started to take he wasn't unable to find another job. They returned to live at Sycamore Ranch for several years until he was able to obtain other employment.

Now to be more realistic I must have been conceived somewhere around the time of Nancy's second birthday. In a small house with parents around, a small child, and assorted hired hands that were about, I can only guess at what sort of privacy they had. Whether planned, or in a secret moment such as described above, the deed was done and as nature has it planned on April 7, 1935 I came out to greet the world in

Escondido, California. I was told that it was a fast drive to the hospital down the newly named Highway 395. I was deemed a boy and had all the appropriate appendages. A few days later my Uncle Jim's wife delivered twin girls. The Myers family had grown quite quickly but would only be added to when my younger sister, Carolyn, arrived sixteen years later. I then became the last of the Myers as my wife and I had a single child, a daughter, Janet.

As I look back I had a really great childhood. Norman Rockwell if you will. I have to rely on stories of my very early youth, such as the time I got my head stuck between the wooden arm rest and side of the couch and when, after a difficult extraction, was asked how I managed to get in that situation I immediately demonstrated how it was done with the same result. Once I reached the age five the memories are more first person and there are many and very good ones. I will try to share a number of them with you.

Sometime in my first year or two my father secured a job with Union Oil Company in San Diego and he rented a home in La Mesa, just to the east. The address was 4682 Date Street which is now the entrance driveway to an apartment complex. It was a very small two bedroom, one bath California bungalow. (This was my home and the center of my life until they finally bought their first home, 4133 Lois Street, La Mesa around 1951. It was my sophomore year in high school and the arrival of Carolyn necessitated a larger house.) Around the time my sister and I were discovering that little boys and girls were different my mother sacrificed her dining room to become a bedroom for me. A single bed, a three drawer chest and a Sears Roebuck cardboard closet stored all my possessions and clothes. I had a small work bench outside the back door steps and a basketball backboard on a post in the yard with an orange tree just left the worn spot in the lawn that was the free throw line.

The house to the south belonged to the Riblets, our landlord, and to the north were the Engstroms. There was an alley next to the Engstroms which divided the block between Lemon Ave and La Mesa Boulevard. On that Blvd corner was

4 ~ ART MYERS

Woods Union Oil Station, a lot with a very small house which seemed to be occupied occasionally, and next to it was the La Mesa Movie Theater. Up and down La Mesa Blvd were most of the stores and shops that were present in most small towns, and with our family having but one car which my father needed to get to work each day, made it possible for my mother to take care of the family needs on foot. Our family doctor was about 8 blocks away and when required walking was the means to meet an appointment. Dr. Phiefer was well liked, good, hard working and very fair.

I think I will take an excursion here and write a little about what I assume many of us realize when it has become too late to correct. My parents were very reluctant to discuss personal thoughts and feelings. This in no way saying they didn't show us love, give untold amounts of attention and provided what I will class as a wonderful childhood. But as I think back, I really never thought about or even thought to ask of them personal questions of their relationship, hopes and expectations. I was a self absorbed little boy doing what little boys do and quite happy thank you. Even later I had all sorts of activities, school, summers at my Grandparents, play mates, sports, then high school, more sports, a car, a girlfriend, college, many part time jobs, another girlfriend or two, fraternity, trips, camping, etc. Then on to an adults life of working, marriage, and child rearing. All that time to learn.

What I think most of now was how the depression of 1929 had affected their lives and in turn affected my sister and me. I know from photos and keepsakes from their college years that showed them to be young and attractive, having the good college experience while maintaining their education at a very good college. Neither were from a wealthy family, but they and their group had several cars available and trips to the beaches and parks were taken, parties and dances attended, and stylish clothes worn. To then graduate in 1930 and marry a year later as the depression loomed, having their first child in 1932 and second in 1935 and then not finding suitable work in their studied fields had to be an enormous blow to their ego and self confidence. Then just as some normalcy began to enter their lives World War II started.

One of the few stories my mother ever told me of their early married life was how when in the tiny house they had rented in the Imperial Valley she would start cleaning the house and by afternoon would have it done and a dinner plan underway when the winds would start to blow and the desert sands would start to penetrate the house as they did every day. By the time my father would return from work a fine coat of fine sand would cover everything, her meal would be compromised, and she would be in tears. Here was the new young bride, a Pomona College graduate away from family and friends, with an infant daughter in a unpleasant environment, trying to be the good wife. It is tough to imagine today but it was the way it was then. My father never once made any mention of their time there.

I have very clear recollections of my family life from about age five or six, about 1940 or so. Also, there are numerous photographs and journals in the "Myers History Box" that cover a good portion of my ancestry and early childhood. But other than a photo of my father's gas truck stuck in the mud after a rare Imperial Valley monsoon and another of the house, I have little to go on to know or understand about my parents first few years of marriage. They did have each other and a healthy child, but it had to have been much less than they had expected and hoped it would be. I can only imagine how disappointed they must have been to make a start like that and to then have to move back to my grandparents ranch where they would stay for a number of years.

CHAPTER 2

    I think that I had very much a common childhood for a boy born in this period and economic class. However, I had exceptional parents and grandparents. My maternal grandfather died just days after I was born so I never knew him in person but certainly heard enough about him to make him a real person for me to both honor and respect. My paternal grandparents were very much a part of my childhood and young adult life. I will try to bring them alive in the next chapter. They are worth your knowing them too.

    My mother was my primary guide as a full time parent and my father was there as much as a full time employee of the time could be. He was working six days a week for much of my early life, leaving just as my sister and I were getting up and returning just before our dinner hour at 6:00 pm. After dinner he would read a few chapters to the two us from one of the classics like Treasure Island, Robinson Crusoe, etc., then it was off to bed for us at 7:30 pm. Hard to believe in today's culture. This schedule was modified, of course, as we got too big for sitting on Dad's lap, Nancy first and then me. But I can still remember him reading, smelling slightly of gas from work and smoking a Camel cigarette, doing his fatherly best.

    For us of this generation and class our destiny was somewhat programmed. For me it was go to the Public Grammar School, High School, State College, graduate, get employed by a good company, get married, have children, buy a house, work your way up the company ladder, retire and look back on the good life you have led.

    Well it all started out as programmed and I have no

complaints as to having followed the first part of the script. In school I was a satisfactory student and I think well adjusted. (Although it took my Mother three trips with me in tow to my first class in kindergarten to get me to stay after running home at the first chances offered.) Good grades, the teachers liked me as did most of my fellow students. I had been raised to respect my elders and treat all as friends until given reason not too by their actions. In grammar school I was Captain of the school crossing guards for several years and President of the last semester 8th grade. Lettering in high school football and basketball, President of the Key Club, and Senior Class President. Even a pretty and very nice girl friend for a couple of years. No scholastic honors but easily qualified for college.

College at San Diego State College (now University) was also typical. Enrolled to obtain a Bachelor of Science degree in Electrical Engineering, and was successful. Survived my freshman and sophomore years as a member of SAE fraternity and working part and full time throughout the five years it took to meet the requirements for B.S. in EE, just missing earning a Math Minor. The only scholastic record I have is my Selective Service form that in June of 1958, my graduation year, placing me 37th of 459 full-time male students seeking a B.S. degree. I made the Dean's List only once. Dated a fair share of co-eds and was briefly "pinned" (going steady) until she rightly decided I was not the one.

It was during my last two years in college that I was introduced to snow skiing. San Diego is not known for its snow so many trips to the mountains surrounding the Los Angeles basin and longer ones to the Sierra Nevada. One trip in 1956 to Aspen was to introduce me to a place I would return to in the future.

This has been a rather brief description of my early years, although it covers about twenty-three of them. I will go back in more detail on significant aspects in these years as to the important people and events that were responsible, in part, for what became my journey through life.

I will begin here with some history of my paternal

grandparents. I think that they had a profound impact on me, especially my Grandfather Myers. I will have to start with his father and mother, however, to really set the stage.

Darius N. Myers can be searched for and found on the internet. You will read that he was a member of the 64th Illinois Volunteers, Company D (Yates Sharpshooters) in the Civil War, start to finish, mustering in and rapidly promoted to Sergeant and out as a Captain. He was severely wounded in the battle of Atlanta on July 22, 1864. He was left on the field to die by the medics but refused to do so by walking a mile to get enough medical attention to make it through, which was a very good development for me. After mustering out and a short stint as a policeman in Chicago, but still bothered by his wounds, he then traveled to Iowa and Kansas searching for a new life. As it would turn out, in 1871, part of Kathryn Wynn's family moved from northeastern Iowa to what was to become Marquette, Kansas in a wagon train of which he was a member. The Wynn's then rented a cabin owned there at the time by him. Kathryn, at the age of fourteen, with the rest of her family moved down later that year. She drove a mule team drawn wagon on that trip.

Darius and Kathryn soon married and settled into a small log cabin on a bend in the Smokey Hill River. It may have been Darius's cabin as the Wynn's built a house in Marquette that same year. The cabin and land was soon purchased by a business man to establish a mill. They then traveled back to Iowa with the money from the sale, and with some additional funds from a land sale there, they bought a team of draft horses, covered wagon, supplies, a saddle horse, sixty head of cattle, and a collie pup. With Kathryn driving the team and Darius driving the cattle they returned to Marquette where a homestead on a half section was established about four miles south. Family lore says that Kathryn, now sixteen years old, was left overnight with the livestock, supplies, and wagon box for the two days and a night it took Darius to drive the wagon to Salina to buy enough lumber to build their cabin. This was in 1873. They spent most of their lives there, having 5 children, the third being my grandfather

Fred Myers. (If you want to know what their life was like a very good read is Pioneer Women of the Kansas Frontier, Joanna Stratton.)

After a childhood growing up the son of pioneers Fred Myers was sent off to college to Kansas State AC and completed an engineering degree in 1901. There was some question as to whether he actually got his diploma due to an argument with one of his professors. I can imagine that might have happened. While in college he met the most desirable Edith Perkins who received a Bachelor of Science degree in chemistry in 1900. They became engaged that year. She was the daughter of the editor of the Manhattan, Kansas newspaper but during her college years her parents moved to South Pasadena, California. Their marriage was delayed for five years by my Grandfather's Navy service which included a stint on the submarine Moccasin as the electrician. He was one of the first six navy men to volunteer for submarine service. (The Moccasin, and sister sub the Adder, can be referenced on the web.) They were married March 9, 1905 and spent their first year, as he completed his 6th year in the Navy, stationed in Newport News, Virginia. They then moved to South Pasadena to join her parents where their first son was born. Shortly thereafter both families moved to Fallbrook, the parents to a house in town and my Grandparents to their ranch.

At this point I will inject a little more on my Great Grandfather Darius. He was born in Pennsylvania, one of seven boys and two girls. In 1851 his father, due to an accident that partially crushed his rib cage, had to sell his saw and grist mill. Loading the family's household goods and part of the family into a four horse drawn covered wagon they headed to the wilds of Illinois. The four older boys, of which Darius was the youngest at eight, walked. They settled in Troy Grove, a little over eighty miles southwest of Chicago.

One of the stories my Grandfather wrote down for me was that Darius was given a dollar by his Father and told to go hear Douglas and Lincoln debate on the slavery question. On one of his visit to California my Grandfather recalls his father's description of the debate as he told it to my Grandmother's Grandfather. This would have been about 1906.

"Douglas got up to speak. He was a small man, very neat. Very well dressed, absolutely sure of himself. He was a fine talker and made a fine speech. By the time he was through, I wondered what anyone could say in answer. While Douglas talked, Lincoln sat in his chair with his big hands hanging between his bony knees and his head sunk between his shoulders like a sick turkey buzzard. I felt sorry for him. When his turn came, he got up awkwardly and stood there with a foolish grin on his ugly face. He said a few words in a high voice and stopped. After a long pause he started to speak again. In five minutes I had quit feeling sorry for him. He took Douglas's speech apart point by point and showed where he was wrong. Before he was through, the crowd was wild and would have followed him anywhere."

As far as I can tell this would have been the debate in Ottawa, Illinois on August 21, 1858 and Darius would have been fifteen years old. Since this description of a conversation of an event almost 50 years prior, and described to me some 30 years later, it is probably not totally accurate, but there is no doubt that young Darius was in attendance and his impressions were probably close to those quoted.

As written earlier, Darius and Kathryn started their life together in a small cabin near what became Marquette, Kansas. He would have been twenty-nine and she fifteen. It was just over a year later when they sold the cabin and made the long trip to and from Iowa to homestead their new place and where my Grandfather was born. It should be noted that most of these pioneer homes were very small, maybe fourteen by sixteen feet, which contained their worldly possessions, bed, stove and sitting area. The outhouse was their toilet and the well their water source. No electricity, no lights other than candles and lantern. No telephone, of course, and their transportation was by foot or horse. The nearest neighbor would have been at least a mile away. They lived there for many years and were successful

farmers. In 1929, Kathryn wrote:
"June 9, 1872, D. N. Myers and I were married. Squire Maxwell of Sharps Creek married us. We began our home making in a rough log house with dirt roof and mud and stone fireplace. We have had much better built houses since but have never been more comfortable or happier than we were in the old log cabin where snakes and pack rats often came calling." They were the true pioneers.

This was the environment my Grandfather Myers grew up in. One time he told me he thought he had lived in a most amazing time in that he could remember like it was yesterday when he first saw an automobile in person and he was now watching man go into space on television. He was born on May 1, 1880 and died on November 19, 1958 on his ranch from a heart attack. He was buried in the Naval Cemetery in Pt. Loma. Later Grandma Myers, born May 4, 1879 and passing away on August 7, 1963, would be placed next to him. They were most special people and lived such good lives. I will spend the next chapter describing my memories of them and a few of the many lessons I learned.

CHAPTER 3

My parents somehow worked out an arrangement to off-load my sister and me on my fathers parents ranch for two months each summer. My Dad's brother did likewise with his twin daughters, who were two days younger than me. This meant that Nancy, myself, and Judith and Edith were out of their parents hair for two blessed months each summer. I do think that this was actually equally thought of as a wonderful idea of the Grandparents. I am not exactly sure at what age this all started, but around eight years for me. I think Nancy, who was three years older, lasted only a few years before she preferred the city life. Many holidays and short trips had been made to the Ranch over the years for both families, ours from La Mesa and the Uncle's from South Gate.

The Ranch was located on the south side of Reche Road which runs from what is now I-15 to Fallbrook. On Google Earth you can find it with that address (Reche Road, Fallbrook, CA). Working your way westward until you see a school between Los Cojones and Calmin Dr. and bound to the south by Adaline Pl and Linda St.

Grandfather and Grandma Myers were old school and O'Dad, as Grandfather Myers became known, was in charge of me and Grandma took over the girls. The Ranch was about sixty acres by this time as portions of the larger ranch had been sold off over the years. It was roughly a square in shape, divided by a wash which crossed under Reche Road about one third of the way from the NE corner angling SW until about two thirds of the way down where it veered more westerly to the SW corner. A dirt lane about a quarter of the way from the NW corner went due south from Reche Road to the house.

The house was located about in the middle of the NW portion of the property bounded by the wash. This was all flat land with the lemon groves to the east of the house and the orange groves to the south. Land NW occasionally was used for farming. I remember one year it was in corn and another in squash. The NE portion was also used, the most memorable was for strawberries by share cropping, which is a story I will write about later in this chapter. The rest of the property was hillside, the SE corner having a medium sized olive grove from which some very good olives were harvested and cured.

When they first moved onto the ranch there were a number of out buildings plus a small original house. The story goes that with a little help from the neighbors several of these outbuildings were dragged and attached to the small house to build the home that lasted their lifetime together, until his death, and which I remember as the Ranch. A screen enclosed back porch on the front of the house was the entrance of choice which lead into the kitchen and a hallway to the three bedrooms and a full bath. The kitchen had an electric range that had replaced the big wood cook stove and a small wood stove sat next to it which during the winter months provided heat and always had a pot of coffee heating on top. A sink with wash boards was opposite on the outside wall and a pushed out pantry was next to it. Entrance to the dining room was opposite the entrance from the porch. Not a big kitchen but very efficient and meals of shear greatness came from it, sometimes for two dozen people. Grandma could cook.

From the dining room was an open archway into which would now be called the great room although by today's standards would seem quite small. Immediately to the left was the library and the real front door which faced east with book shelves on either side. I think there was a least one chair and a small table in this room but the big loom was dominant. Between this area and the hall leading to the bedrooms and bath was the living area with the fireplace, several chairs and a small hardwood bench. Opposite the fireplace was a nook with a huge wooden desk, bookshelves, and cabinets which was Grandma's office. She spent much time there, did the Ranch's accounts, wrote articles for the local newspapers, and typed things for Grandfather. I have several of his manuscripts with stories of Navy life, an attempt at a western novel, short stories, and a most cherished letter he wrote to me started on February 9, 1936 and completed and signed on June 24 of that year to be given to me on my 21st birthday. Stories of my ancestry. The best of all gifts. The library was well stocked with really fine literature and some very nice books. No one seems to know where they ended up.

 Directly opposite the door from the living room into the hall was a bedroom which was called the Loom Room. There resided the bed I slept on all the summer nights and the midsize loom, the small loom, and all the storage of weaving material. Also, and not least important, was the wind up Victrola and the box of records. My Grandfather would play his record of Caruso to demonstrate to us that he was better than Mario Lanza, the popular opera and movie star at the time. At the end of the hall were two more bedrooms, to the left the grandparents and to the right the other guest room which the girls would share when we were all there. The bathroom was between the Loom Room and the guest room and had a claw foot tub, toilet, and sink.

 About half way down the lane from Reche Road to the house, on the west side, was the shop. It was mostly a blacksmith shop having a small forge, anvil, and a full compliment of tools. There was a jigsaw, drill press, wood lathe, and work bench and woodworking tools. Across the lane was the well and large water tank fed by a reciprocating pump belt driven by a large electric motor. A big saw, also driven by belt by the same electric motor, was nearby. Near the shop was a sizable corrugated steel storage building and a sizable corn crib. The shop was later moved to a restored barn which was just to the west of the house. This occurred a couple of years after I had started spending the summers. It was much larger, One third for the blacksmith shop and the remainder for the woodworking and machine shop. All the equipment was driven by a single electric motor driving a main shaft that had belts running to each piece of equipment. A large open end garage completed the buildings.

The house was well laid out, comfortable, and for me just the right place. My grandfather was a craftsman, designer, inventor, engineer and great teacher. My skills using all types of tools came from his teaching and I am sure that most of my eye to hand skills came from his side of the family as well as many of the other things that he set examples for me to learn from.

Grandma was of course a very intelligent, smart, and wise woman. She taught the girls things about homemaking and also instilled in them character and moral attitudes that served them well. All adventures and travel off the ranch were under her direction and planning. This included picnics, trips to town, swimming lessons at the high school pool, and even trips to the ocean for days at the beach. Grandma was a small woman and the cars she drove for most of her lifetime were big, the most memorable to me was a Franklin with a huge wooden steering wheel which she would wrestle with to keep the car on the road. Barely able to see over the wheel I am not sure how she was able to brake but obviously she did for not only am I and my cousins here to tell about it but she never had an accident or received a ticket. She was an expert weaver and this skill was one of the few female skills that Grandpa was glad to have me learn.

All the years I knew my grandfather he seldom left the Ranch and only if family obligations demanded it. Once a month he would go to town to have his hair cut. One occasion he made was the trip to town to see all of us swim in the High School pool after we had had some lessons. He was not impressed and took me aside when we got back to the Ranch and told me in no uncertain terms that my flailing efforts were not good enough for a Myers and showed me the proper way to stroke and kick all the while on dry land.

Grandfather also taught the three of us to drive a car. He had my uncle find a car in Los Angeles which he towed down to the ranch. It was a 1932 Chevrolet 2-door which needed an overhaul. At the end of the summer when I was fourteen the repairs were started and by my arrival the next summer it was running quite good. It was to be a sort of ranch truck to haul irrigation hoses around the orchards and had a big hose reel mounted on the back. He took each of us on one trip about the Ranch instructing how to start the engine, use the clutch, shift, brake, and steer. There was much moaning and groaning by him as we lurched about driving over bumps and into and across the small ditches saying his insides could take no more. We were then told to learn the rest on our own without killing ourselves or each other. The girls soon felt enough was learned for them after a few turns each. I of course loved driving and put many miles on the old car both for hauling hose when needed and just for the joy of driving. I still love to drive anything that has at least four wheels.

There were two very important lessons I learned from him that I can clearly remember. One involved the orange and lemon pickers that came to the ranch when a harvest was required. The pickers were organized by the citrus co-op he belonged to and the pickers were all Mexican migrant workers. He had one particular picker he always requested and one time when I was there he sent me out to observe. Grandpa said he was the best picker he had ever seen. Perfect cutting of the fruit stem, an art, and fast. The oranges that day found his sack in a blur and at the end of the day he totaled fifty percent more boxes than any of the others in the crew. At a little gathering at the completion of the harvest Grandfather carefully slip this picker a few extra dollars. As we walked away he asked me if I had seen him palm the dollars and pass it to the picker when they shook hands so no one else could see. As I said I had he told me that any one that good at what he does deserved to be recognized and that if he had given the money to the foreman to give to the picker it would go no farther than the foreman's pocket.

Another great lesson was when in 1945, or possibly 1946, a Japanese man approached my grandfather and ask to sharecrop about seven acres of flatland just east of the lane and on the Reche Road boundary, along with water from the well, to grow strawberries. A deal was reached for a ten percent share of profit with a limit of water such that the Ranch's needs were met first. The contract was a hand shake. I can't be absolutely sure but almost certainly this was one of the Japanese families that had been interned during World War II. At day break, ever day, the family would be there. The first day they arrived with an old truck, a mule, and every member of the family, from a grandmother to a baby. Every evening they would be there until it was too dark to work. After six or seven years having paid for piped in commercial water, a new tractor and truck, and less family working each day they thanked my Grandfather many times and told him they had bought property near Escondido to continue operation. Their ranch became one of the biggest strawberry operations in the State.

Part of the agreement was that after a picking we could go into the field and pick berries left on the plants that were too ripe to pick commercially. Now if you have picked a perfect strawberry off the vine that is still warm from the late afternoon sun and popped it in your mouth you have tasted one of the greatest flavors in the world. We of course ate quite a few this way and would have plenty for the family table and for canning into wonderful jam.

My grandmother, among many other lessons, had me witness another interesting example of human intelligence and skill at the local grocery store she frequented. Babs was the manager (probably owner, or co-owner) and cashier. She would take the basket of items picked out and starting with the first item proceed to add up the bill in her head, including weighing the per pound items, multiplying the weight times price per pound, and adding the result to the total. All this was done while calling out the prices, prices per pound and the total, and the final total. When the cash was handed over the subtraction was made and the change handed over. My Grandmother told me the first few times she came into the store she couldn't believe it could be done but after a number of times checking out her entire purchase by hand at home she never found a mistake and felt no need to check Bab's accuracy thereafter. I witnessed this many times and am still amazed. Babs of course knew the price of every item in her store.

These three examples, of many others, of my paternal grandparents exposing me to positive lessons about human behavior outlined above should demonstrate what a person, or people, can do with the talents and skills they possess. A Mexican migrant worker was able to make half again as much as his co-workers because of his skill and work ethic. A Japanese man, and his family, apparently just released from an internment camp following the end of a long and bitter war was first given the opportunity and then with great effort was able to achieve substantial wealth and a respected place in society. A woman in a most necessary but rather basic position had a mathematical ability that required ones admiration.

My grandparents position was, as was all of the adults in my family, that every person should be met with no bias and should only be judged by the content of their character. This is a good and just tenant to live by. It does have some drawbacks, however. The most obvious is that there are people that lack, or choose not to have any, ethics. Where dishonesty is their livelihood and where lying is second nature to them. To those of us who choose to give each person the benefit of the doubt we often are not only disappointed but often taken emotionally and/or financial advantage of. It seems that in today's world the ethically depraved have become more numerous, sophisticated, and clever and we have now of necessity become a more suspicious society.

Unfortunately this trend of ethical demise has entered all elements of our society. Philosophically, it's basis comes from the concept that the ends justifies the means. That winning the debate is much more important than discovering the truth. That personal gain by any means is more important than achieving it honestly. This has proven over and over to be a plague that is the scourge of mankind.

All this mischief can be laid at the feet of an ethical collapse within those who are supposed to be the protectors of our way of life. Unfortunately our government has reached new heights in this debacle as this is being written. At the same time many of those who are supposed to be casting a light on this behavior have become silent. Our Universities seem to be educating a increasingly number of students total devoid of the concept of reason. And one must also conclude that the young are also reflecting their parents philosophical bias. It is very disappointing to me to see this happening to such an extent over just my lifespan. Such great things have happened during this period that it is sad to see where we are now heading as a society.

I will leave you here with the final paragraph from my grandfather's letter, June 26, 1936.

"To sum up your inheritance should make you at maturity a liberal but not a radical. You should be your own boss if such men still exist. Your word will have to be good and you will be willing to fight for a just cause. Well, young feller, take care of yourself. Your Granddad." Signed by hand Fred Myers.

Two points. This was at the depths of the depression and FDR was on a rampage. The term "liberal" was in the classical sense. Look it up if you, to your detriment, don't know what it meant before it was politicized.

As I mentioned before, my grandfather was an inventor and innovator, not in the context of heroic inventions and innovations, but in more of what was needed in making his life as a rancher and homebody easier and more efficient. These ranged from a multi-size can opener to a fairly complex motorization of my Grandmother's big loom. Many projects were started out by a need for a device,.An idea was developed, a search for the right materials, and then the fabrication of the item in his shop. One of my fun memories was a day in which the search started for the material for something he wanted to make. Between the storage building and the corn crib was a leaf covered area where all metal objects that would someday be useful were buried. Years and years of things. Even what was left of a Model T. In any case Grandfather said lets go find what I need, "I know about where I put it." With a small pitch fork and a rake we started the search. In a fairly short time, and under ten or twenty years of leaves, he found what he was looking for, picked it up, brushed it off and pronounced it was just what he needed and it was off to the shop. I don't remember what was being made but the hunt had been a success and what has always been true, a successful hunt is a joy in itself.

My grandfather wrote a number of short stories, both fiction and non-fiction, and although typed from long hand by my grandmother and sent off to publishers none were ever published. I have most of them in the Myers History Box. Some are both a good read and informative. One of the short stories described the visit by a young lady to his submarine, the Moccasin, which after she boarded the lines were loosened and the sub submerged to the bottom at the dock. The periscope was raised and she got to view the harbor area. Then the ballast was blown and the sub was brought to the surface. As she departed the crew was informed that the young lady none other than Teddy Roosevelt's daughter and I assume was the first woman to have ever boarded a U.S. Navy Submarine.

It was at the Ranch that I was taught about firearms. Grandfather had a collection of guns ranging from a couple of muzzle loaders, a single barrel and a double barrel 12-gauge shotgun, a 410-gauge single barrel shotgun, a .22 rifle, and a .32 pistol. On the 4th of July the muzzle loaders were loaded and he would fire each one off with great trepidation I think because they were very old weapons. My initiation to shooting, after a thorough discussion on gun safety, was to fire the single barrel 12-gauge. This was to be witnessed by the entire family of which all the adult males were in on the lesson. You should know two things. I was a very skinny ten year old and a single barrel 12-gauge is a very light gun and with a full load shell packs a real punch. It didn't knock me over but left an enormous bruise on my shoulder. I didn't cry despite all the laughter and the gentle voice of my grandfather telling me he should have told me to hold the gun very tightly against the now aching shoulder. A right of passage that I think each of the men around me had gone through on their first shot. I did learn to shoot and respect guns and gun safety.

    One last minor story of ranch life humor was the fresh olive, right off the tree. Whenever guests to the ranch were city folks, especially eastern city folks, a trip to the olive orchard was included. This was a nice walk up a gentle incline. An olive orchard is always a pretty sight. The trees are beautiful, nicely spaced, and when bearing olives are really quite impressive. The olives themselves are beautiful, some black and shinny just like they look on a olive can label. The offer is always made to the guest to try a fresh olive right off the tree. There is nothing that grows on a tree that is as bitter and fowl tasting as an uncured olive. All those in the know are watching closely and never disappointed in the reaction. It must be noted that each of us kids were once city folks too and had to go through this initiation.

    I am sure if it were still there I would find the Ranch much smaller than I remember it. A visit some years after the property was sold and the school built I returned with my wife as we drove nearby on a trip. I found the distance down the lane to where the house had been much shorter than I remembered as was the distance to the wash and south property line. When the school district bought this part of the Ranch property one of the stipulations my Grandma insisted on was they not cut down the two big eucalyptus trees and the giant sycamores. At the time of the visit they were still there. Google Earth shows them now gone.

    These summers were such that all the things I learned and experienced cannot ever be even remembered and put to paper. I still have a few things with me that brings back memories as if it were just yesterday instead of seventy years ago. How very fortunate I was to have had this experience and now I regret that circumstance, geography, and life style has afforded me to pass on to my Granddaughters a little more of that which I had by place, time and people with the right stuff.

CHAPTER 4

One more chapter on grandparents, now of my Mother's side. These are different people from that of my Father's, but you won't be disappointed in getting to know them, especially Edwin Hellaby Willisford. He was a true one of a kind. Although very different from my paternal grandfather, Grandfather Myers told me he was one of the finest men he had every known. As I mentioned before he died suddenly, two days after my birth. I therefore have no first person stories to tell you but don't think, even for a minute, that I don't have a tale to tell you.

Edwin Willisford was born in Derby, England April 11, 1866 and was six years old when he, with his parents and two younger brothers and a younger sister, immigrated to the United States settling in Chicago, Illinois. Two years later his mother died in childbirth and soon after on a trip to England his father died before returning. The four children were taken in by an uncle and aunt, John and Harriet Hellaby, living on a farm in Steuben County, New York.

Edwin delayed his formal education for the most part until the younger children had grown. He worked on the farm and attended a rural school during the winters when possible and actually started teaching school at the age of seventeen doing this over a period of three years. He then felt the need to attend the Academy (high school) and graduated in 1891 at the age of 25. Interest in the ministry lead him to Hillsdale College in Hillsdale, Michigan where he met my grandmother, Carrie Ashbaugh. He received a Bachelor of Arts degree in 1895 and then a Bachelor of Pedagogy in 1896. They were married on her graduation day after she received her Bachelor of Oratory in

June of that same year.

They stayed in Hillsdale for three years and he received his Bachelor of Divinity degree in 1898. He served as pastor during this time at a small country church. They then moved to Winnebago, Minnesota as a pastor at a Baptist Church and their first daughter, Carol, was born April 9, 1899. He also taught part time a Parker College during this time. (There is a noteworthy item here in that when the Hellaby's took the children in they were never adopted but they used the surname Hellaby. On Edwin's birthday, two days after his daughter's birth, he formally announced that from that time on he would be know as Edwin Hellaby Willisford.)

Bear with me here as at this point Edwin decided that he needed more and other education and off the family went to Lincoln, Nebraska where he entered the doctorate program at the University of Nebraska. He received his PhD in Philosophy (Economics) in 1906. His thesis, "Some Aspects of the Social Power of Wealth," can be found on-line as a reprint and is an interesting read, much of which seems surprisingly appropriate for today some hundred plus years later. He had various employments during this period to finance his family and his education. I will touch on this life style a little later.

It was then to Mankato, Minnesota to minister at the Baptist Church and it was there that my Mother, Joy Elvira Willisford, was born on October 26, 1909. He then was offered a position as Dean at the college in Oberlin, Ohio which he found once he got there not to his liking. So without a job or prospects it was off to California where they were able to stay with his mother-in-laws parents. By this time he found that the Baptist Church was veering in a direction he didn't care for and went founded the Congressional Church of Glendale, California.

It is a bit unfair in that my Grandmother Willisford does not get featured sufficiently enough during this time period. You can imagine her position as the minister's wife as they were in this time and she was a very active one. She also took very good care of the family although I never recall her being thought of as a particularly good cook. There was a son born that died at birth so she went through three pregnancies, the multiple moves, and the constant changes in positions. My Mother always said that they had very little money and often took in borders and Edwin always seemed to have more than just a single job. I think he was a very hard worker and a very smart one. He felt that education and travel were most important. At one break before he married he spent a summer bicycling around Europe by himself going to and from the U.S. in ship's steerage. He had never been on a bicycle before his first pedal there and one should remember we are not talking about a modern ten speed here. A travel fund was established during their time in Nebraska and upon graduation they left my Aunt Carol with her grandparents and he and Carrie spent ten weeks in Europe. A few years later he guided a tourist group there.

Life had turned quite good for the family in Glendale. The church had prospered and with the help of my Mother's grandfather, who was multi-talented and a very good carpenter, a nice house was built. But then World War I broke out and Edwin decided that he must do his duty by volunteering as a chaplain and minister to the troops. At fifty-one years of age the army would not take him so it was off to the YMCA which accepted him after he neglected to mention his age. He bought his own uniform, helmet (which I have) and gas mask and set off to the docks to be sent over. At first he was refused but I don't think anyone really could say no to Edwin H. Willisford once his mind was made up. He spent thirteen months in France, much of it in the trenches and under fire. He arrived back in the United States on "The Northern Pacific" on New Year's Day, 1919. He garnered many letters of salutation and recommendation for his efforts. He had left his wife and ten year old daughter in a small rented cottage in Claremont where their other daughter, Carol, was attending Pomona College and rented their larger home in Glendale for income.

It was then on to a bigger ministry position in Houston, Texas. It was, as my Mother described, a different world. Think Southern California to South Texas. A few years later Edwin became Superintendent of the Houston Social Services, and later was a representative for Columbia University's Home Study Program. For the first time they had enough income to have a nice house built. The social service's job required a lot of travel about the area and he bought his first automobile at age fifty-five and learned how to drive. By this time my Mother had graduated from high school, with honors, and was attending Pomona College in California. But drive they did. Back and forth from Houston to Glendale, all over the state of Texas, and a big family trip to the northeast and another to the northwest. I have one photograph of the family ready to start east, the four of them in front of a big open touring car with a canvas top, Grandma in her totally covering black dress, my Aunt Carol and Mother in matching brown knickers and long sleeve shirts, and Grandfather in slacks and a white shirt. Many dirt roads, a big tool box for repairs, fording streams, fixing flats, thousands of miles, no air conditioning, and many times questionable accommodations. This is in the late 1920's. Imagine it if you can.

When my parents married it was noted in the Fallbrook newspaper that the brides parents were attending from Atlanta, Georgia. I have no information on what they were doing there but I am sure it was something that would have been interesting. It may have been the Home Study Program just mentioned but at the Columbia Theological University which was in Atlanta at that time.

I think they made the move back to Glendale about the time my sister was born, or shortly thereafter. My Grandfather Willisford died just two days after I was born. My Grandmother received a life insurance award of $2000 and with it booked an around the world cruise for herself, taking my Mother's oldest niece, Barbara, to see the rest of the world. Sometime later, as she had moved into live with my Aunt and Uncle, she decided she would die in her mid-sixties, a few years hence, and distributed her worldly possessions to her daughters and a $250 U.S. Bond to each grandchild. She died at 96 spending her last ten years with my parents. One's plans don't always work out but having a really good family does have its merits.

My memories of my Grandmother Willisford were mainly of a very quiet, rather tall woman, generally sitting and either darning socks, crocheting, or reading her bible. She was always interested in her family and although totally dependent upon my Aunt and Mother, and their husbands, tried not to be a burden. She spent her last months in a rest home in San Diego, died peaceful and I think mentally aware and ready. She had been a good person, mother, grandmother, and the wife and partner to an extraordinary man.

I will now embark on speculation on my Grandfather Willisford. I sense that some, if not a goodly portion, of what has made my life what it has been comes down from his DNA. Maybe I could have used a little more, but maybe a little less would have not been a bad thing. There are two areas that has left me a little bit in wonder. How he conducted his financial affairs and how he followed his pursuit of happiness without seeming to be burdened by his family responsibilities. I think the latter was because of Grandma's love and admiration. For him maybe the excitement of the journey and a fear of being left behind. I never heard from anyone in the family that there was any doubt of his moral virtues, honesty, ethics, or service to humanity.

My Mother always talked of her young life as not being well off, about having boarders in their homes, always watching the pennies, and thinking she was just a little deprived by the standard of her peers. But then she would hesitate just enough to hint that her mother, sister, and herself had always been well cared for and that they had done some extraordinary things and been provided exceptional educations. A great deal of this was, I think, prioritizing what was important and in Grandfather's case that was travel and education. This is what he saved his money for and what he was willing to spend it on. It was how he did it with the type of incomes many of his employments provided is what I wish I knew. The only time a significant income was mentioned was in Houston with the social services position. Interestingly, this was a political appointment job and when the administration changed it came to an abrupt end. I think he must have worked several jobs at all times and managed to make some monies from intellect and ambition. I have no doubt of his honesty and fairness so don't misconstrue what I am saying here. He was some kind of man. I wish I could have known him as I was able to know my Grandfather Myers.

CHAPTER 5

It is now time to spend a more time with my parents. For some reason I find this more difficult than writing about the grandparents and great grandparents. For one thing I have quite a bit of written history provided by my mother about a her parents, the letter my Grandfather Myers wrote me, a document my cousin Edith wrote about our Grandmother Myers, and other items to help layout the previous chapters. Chapter 1 is a start on my parents but more is needed.

I think when one thinks of their parents the first thoughts that to come to mind are, if you are fortunate, that your parents would always be there for you. Until my father died suddenly at the age of fifty-six from a brain aneurysm on April 5, 1964. I had never given much thought that he and my Mother would not be together even as my 29th birthday was but two days away. They both had come up to see their new granddaughter just after her birth on March 8. The last photographs I have of my father is of him holding Janet, standing next to my mother, in front of our rental apartment. And then just a short time later he was gone.

My Grandfather Myers died in November of 1958 and was the first person of my immediate acquaintance to pass away. His funeral was a very sad event for me. He was cremated and seeing his remains contained in a small metal box buried was a very hurtful experience. The passing and burial of my Father was the most devastating experience of my life and to this day still brings sadness.

This is not a very positive way to start this Chapter but I will now try to do better by you. As written earlier, I have no complaints about my childhood, teenage, and early adulthood years. In fact I have no complaints about my life at all. I, of course, do wish I had seen my Father reach old age. He had always said he would like to cheer in the year 2000. The entire family felt that he had been cheated, as were we all, by a life cut short. To describe him in simple terms, tall (six foot one), slender, with thick white hair having turned completely white by age forty. A truly gentle person, honest to a fault, polite and a friend to all who knew him. I remember only once or twice he ever raised his voice to me and can't even remembered now what it would have been about.

He took after his mother much more than his father. As mentioned before he was raised on the Ranch and once he had a taste of life in the city he didn't want to go back. (His brother, even more so.) He was not athletic but as I became more interested sports he showed interest and participated where he could, but I think somewhat reluctantly. We did a lot of tent camping and every summer his vacation time was spent on family camping trips, ranging from short ones to Green Valley Falls, just east of San Diego, to the Yosemite, Sequoia, and Kings Canyon National Parks, and some far longer trips to Grand Teton and Yellowstone. These were great times together and believe it or not very little, if any, rancor. I became addicted to fishing and would wet a line at every opportunity. He would occasionally join in but not with the enthusiasm that I had. He was delighted with my successes and would proudly show off my catches. I remember once he spoke to Mother on what a good sport I was when I lost a particular good fish.

Our early trips were done in a 1938 Chevrolet 2-door sedan. A very small trunk which he would pack with great care and efficiency. All that couldn't be fitted in the trunk would be placed on and about the rear seat. When all was deemed ready for departure my sister and I would be squeezed into the space left, forcing us to lay prone on top of boxes and bedding. We could just manage a look out the small side and rear windows. Later a small trailer was added to carry the bulk of the camping equipment making it much more comfortable for us in the car. In the Myers History Box is a list made by my mother of each trip, the car, destination and dates.

When required he did yard work around the house, with me unhappily helping out, and would work on the car when necessary. He would spend some time with me on small craft projects and had a good hand but I don't think that tools, or using them, were important to him. This is in stark contrast to his father.

My father was an outstanding employee for Union Oil and after driving a truck for a number of years was promoted to the yard foreman, which was a more important and difficult job at that time than it sounds. A few years before his death he mentioned several times to me that he thought he might like to have his own business, such as a Service Station. In retrospect I am not sure if he was looking for a reaction from me but I don't think so. This thought seem to wane and I think he felt that that his best course was to finish out his time with Union Oil until he turned sixty-five and could retire. He seemed very comfortable with that. He didn't make it and I don't think much came my mother's way from the company after his many years with them.

I don't want to imply that my Father was in anyway unhappy. He enjoyed many things with obvious happiness and good humor. The friends of my parents from college were active socially and had a number of family orientated parties, picnics, and camping trips. He actually enjoyed square dancing and for several years they belonged to a group with matching outfits and danced in large competitions.

Mother was our primary guide. Here I refer to Nancy and myself as by the time Carolyn was born, sixteen years after me, there was not much hope left for the two of us. As a boy I didn't pay too much attention to the daughter mother relationship but I can assume it was good as I don't remember any conflicts. As for me she was always there with advice, guidance, teaching and encouragement. Although both my parents let me have many hours of time to myself, either alone or with neighborhood playmates sometimes doing things that may now seem a little risky by today's standards, I survived.

She did want more for her son than just sports and girls. It was understood that all the Myers children were to be well educated and would attend college. None of us ever thought otherwise. As I was slow to pick up reading and spelling flash cards were a daily routine. Other interests were made available, such as piano lessons, drummer lessons, and one last attempt at musical training before she surrendered was the church choir. This I remember clearly. An appointment with the choir director had been made and I was scrubbed up and hauled to where the auditions were held. There was the director, my mother, me, and a piano. I was to sing the scale as he played the notes. As I write this I can feel the tightness in my throat and unpleasantness of the room. The verdict, the right verdict, from the director after just a few minutes was, "Let him play basketball." It was a fine walk home. I still can't sing or play any instrument but truly enjoy music and the other arts.

Her thesis for her Masters Degree was "The Study of the Family." Seven sections, with extensive bibliographies, twenty to thirty pages each. Her original copy resides in the Myers History Box. It was an interesting read for me and provided some both familiar and new insights of her. One in particular was "The Family and Sex Problems." First remember this was being written in 1930-31 by a twenty-one year old daughter of a minister. One part of the section dealt with sex education where it was postulated that it was the responsibility of the parents to thoroughly and openly educated their children on the subject. To the best of my memory neither my Mom or Dad ever mentioned one word on the subject to me. It made for some awkward moments for me as I struggled my way through puberty.

I will share another moment with you and that is when my parents announced the impending arrival of sister Carolyn into the family. This is one of those events that become etched into one's mind and is as real today as when it happened. This would have been sometime in early spring 1950. I had just turned fifteen and my sister Nancy was seventeen. The four us were seated at the breakfast nook at our Date Street home. It had a built in table with bench seats on either side. Mom and Dad on one side, Nancy and me on the other. My mother was very quite and Dad suddenly turned beet red and spluttered out, "We are going to have a little stranger come to our house." After a little more silence, a more accurate description as to what was going to occur in our family was discussed. I don't remember having any feelings other that's fine, what's for breakfast, but I think Nancy took it much harder. Carolyn and I became great buddies.

My Mother was very much like her father in that she relished and valued education. The Myers History Box yielded most of her college transcripts, but unfortunately her Pomona undergraduate one was a copy made in the early 1940's which is now almost unreadable. One can make out the multitude of A's that supports her Phi Beta Kappa award. Her M.A. degree from The Claremont Graduate School shows two semester each of three, five unit courses passed successfully. What surprised me was all the courses she took at San Diego State College, second semester in 1943, 1947, 1954 and first and second semester 1957 &1958. I vaguely remember that she took some courses but didn't realize how many and that she was in SDSC in 1957 & 1958 which was my graduation year. She enrolled and completed thirty-three units comprised of twelve classes and received eleven A's and one B. I am sure she thought she should have gotten a A instead of that B. She was an active substitute teacher for many years in San Diego and most of these classes were related to teaching credentials.

I will end this chapter by acknowledging that I lived at my parents home until I left for my first job after graduation from college. This was both for financial reasons and for my personal comfort. Other than my first semester tuition and books, which in 1953 dollars was about sixty dollars, I paid for all my expenses, except lodging, from earnings made at part time work during school and full time work during the summer breaks. There was never any pressure from my parents to do otherwise and I think they both enjoyed my company and also that I was a very good older brother to much younger sister Carolyn. But every morning Mother would wake me with the message I would never get to my first class on time if I didn't get up immediately. She would have my bowl of Shredded Wheat on the table and my lunch, a peanut butter and jelly sandwich, apple or banana, and six homemade cookies (usually chocolate chip) at the ready. I don't ever recall being late. I still love all of the above for breakfast and lunch.

CHAPTER 6

    I will jump ahead just briefly to get started. I was sitting near the back and on the port side of a four engine commercial airliner at San Diego Airport in mid June, 1958 looking down at my mother and father just beyond the wing tip. Mom was crying and Dad looked quite sad. Their son was off to his first job as an engineer to Milwaukee, Wisconsin. He had on board a small suitcase and a small steamer trunk holding all his important possessions and clothes, had $200 in his wallet, and had given his Dad his 1949 Pontiac two door sedan. It wasn't going off to war in a foreign land but he was leaving the family he was a part of for the last twenty-three years and it was not certain how soon he would get to see them again. Even with letters, postcards, and an occasional telephone call it was not going to be the same. It was a sad moment for all. I had assured my mother I would be able wake up in the morning, fix my own breakfast and get to work on time. Told my father he could use the car, sell it, or trade it in as he chose, and shook his hand. I had said my goodbyes to the rest of the family earlier and then the engines were started one by one and I was off to start what became a very interesting and eventful trip through life to this point as I write these words.
    A few weeks earlier I had my interview with the recruiter for AC Spark Plug, Division of General Motor, Milwaukee, Wisconsin in San Diego. This was my second employment interview and as the Class of 1958 was entering the workplace as the recession of the same year was reaching full force I was a bit desperate. The Class of 1957, the year I should have graduated, had a dynamite employment period and every engineering graduate had multiple interviews and offers. What a difference a

year can make. However, and this is going to be the first of a number of howevers, had I been offered a good position in California all that follows would have been different. The interview went well and as AC was building the inertial guidance system for the Thor Missile to be placed and operational in England the prospect was appealing.

An appointment was set up for me to visit Milwaukee a week later. The recruiter did make the suggestion that I should wear a suit and tie. Now I don't want to be considered a nerd and a dork but I was soon to be a graduate engineer at the age of twenty-three and did not own a suit and hardly knew how to tie a tie. I almost hate to tell you about heading to the near by men's store with Mom and Dad to pick out my new wardrobe. It was a brown, single breasted with white dress shirt and matching tie. The alterations would be rushed and as I sat in the airplane seat described above I was sharply dressed in my new suit. I will only add that for the next six months if someone couldn't remember my name he or she would say , "He's the guy in the brown suit."

I do remember quite clearly the landing in Chicago on my interview trip. I think it was my second airplane trip but the first to the Midwest. It was a typical June early afternoon in Chicago, hot and very humid. In 1958 boarding and leaving the plane was on a outdoor stair ramp pushed up against the plane's doorway. As I exited the plane the humidity hit me like a hot, wet blanket. I almost turned around hoping for a return passage. Entering the terminal was also somewhat of a shock as the building was older and just a little on the run down side. Fortunately the lay over was short and I was soon on a North Central DC-3 headed for Milwaukee. Arrival there was much better. It seemed cooler and less humid and I could see some trees and the terminal was much nicer. I don't remember whether I was met there, but I think so, and I am also not sure which day the interview took place. Two things I do remember are that the interview went well, the offer was made and accepted, and I was given a short tour of downtown Milwaukee (the facility was on Kenilworth in the city center area) and we walked to an overlook of Lake Michigan. It was a beautiful day, the lake was blue as was the sky, and a cool breeze was blowing. Milwaukee would be okay. (I would repeat this scene almost exactly twenty-six years later and will describe it to you in the appropriate time frame.) The second thing was a couple of the engineers took me out to dinner at one of local watering holes and then treated me to lessons on how to play liar's dice and liar's poker. They seemed very satisfied that they had done a fine job as they each walked out of the tavern with half cases of beer under their arms. I am not a good liar.

I was also fortunate that a fraternity brother a couple of years ahead of me was working for AC and he had an apartment with two bedrooms, one of which I could take and split the rent. This worked out well as we had very different life styles and they rarely conflicted. I was to be in training for three months and then would be assigned to the field as a Field Service Engineer. As near as I can judge from Google Earth, the address of 2860 N. Oakland Ave still has the building on the SE corner of Oakland Ave and Locust St.

Since it is at about this time that the things that started the unpredictable part of my trip through life, I will start the story in the next chapter. I have a little more to tell about my life before this point, primarily some information about my close friends, the jobs I had, and one memorable college professor. I will be as brief as possible and hopefully it will be of some interest to you.

My first real friend and playmate was Jimmy Applegate. We were the same age and lived just a few blocks apart. Hours and hours were spent doing the things little boys do and until about 7th grade we were buddies. Later on, for a short time when in high school, we both worked for Woods Union Oil Service Station. After that we drifted off on our own paths. Also during the grammar school years was my first girl friend (or should I say my friend who was a girl) Judy Mannen. She was really cute, had an older brother and good parents who my parents knew. Then Judy moved a little ways away when her father started Mannen Egg Company and later headed up the San Diego

County Fair. One day at College we met again and found a place on the campus lawn to sit and talk. Cute had turned into very pretty, maybe more than that, and all during our conversation it seemed a few too many good looking guys stopped to say hi to her. Maybe I had been spending too much time on my studies.

In high school, which was Grossmont in El Cajon the first two years and then Helix in La Mesa for the remaining two (Actually Helix and Grossmont shared the Grossmont campus the third year.), my closest friend was Bob Anaya, a truly fine person with a great family. I spent much time at Bob's home, almost a home-away from home. We would remain friends through college and kept in contact for a number of years after until my life veered off in both geography and interest. He remained in San Diego and I am sure retired at a reasonable age. He married, and remains married to Cecilia, his high school sweetheart. Another of the boys was Ed Tilling who I lost track of when he left for college. He was a very special kid and I truly thought that some day I would read that he had done some remarkable intellectual achievement or was elected to some high office. I only met his parents once. I believe his father was a mail carrier and his mother a homemaker and was Asian. They were very reserved and I had no sense of their relationship with their son but he was a natural born leader and very smart. Ed was the Student Body President in 1953 while I was the Senior Class President. I had lost the VP position and it was Ed that told me to run for the Senior Class position, that it was much better than being VP. Bob was SB Treasurer. A couple of other boys and a number of very capable girls rounded up the political group, but I think I was the most naive of them all. Hip-Hip-Hurray at graduation was my most memorable contribution.

My high school girl friend was Diane Cassel. A very nice girl with a good family. We went steady for about two years, but a year apart and the separation between college and high school made me realize that I was not nearly prepared to continue our relationship. It was difficult to make and carryout that decision and it would happen to me in reverse later on. I hope Diane found that it was the right thing for her as that in my case it was definitely the right one. Diane's father was a musician, had his own dance band and also owned the soda and ice cream parlor in Spring Valley.

In college I continued my friendship with Bob Anaya and became very good friends with Maury Camillo who was a couple of years ahead of me. Maury's father was part of the tuna fish industry in San Diego and ran a successful fish brokerage business there. Maury and I took a number of camping and ski trips together and one big loop trip with a third person, Dick Emery, to the big National Parks in Wyoming, Montana, Alberta, British Columbia, and Washington. For graduation Maury's father gave him a 1956 Porsche Speedster and he and I made my second trip to Aspen in it. I truly fell in love with a car. (The only new car I have ever owned was a silver with black interior 1959 Porsche coupe. More on that later.) Maury was very active in SAE Fraternity which I joined my freshman year. He and his wife Joyce purchased their first home in Rancho Bernado, just north of San Diego, raised their family and lived there for 53 years. I know I should have kept better contact with Maury, and Joyce, as he was a very good friend for many years. It may be a generational thing, or the fact that my trip has been so different than most of my friends, that this not keeping contact as the years go by has happened in several cases. Rest assured that all the good memories are still floating around in my head.

One member of SAE who you might find interesting was a good friend of Maury's, and I think I can say a friend of mine, was Gary Hemming. He became quite famous in 1966 in mountain climbing circles for a big time rescue in the Alps. Gary took me on a climb to a local outcropping just east of San Diego where I demonstrated absolutely no skill in rock climbing. After a couple of my failed attempts Gary would climb up as if he was walking up a ladder and I would walk around to the trail to the top. Repelling down I did a little better. I probably missed out on climbing the face of Half Dome and El Capitan in Yosemite with him on some of his early major climbs. Well, maybe I could have set up the base camp and done the cooking. There is a book on

Gary's life, Gary Hemming, The Beatnik of the Alps, by Mirella Tenderini and a fictional book Solo Faces, by James Salter based on his life. He made the cover of Life Magazine. He ended his own life at Jenny Lake in Wyoming, a sad way to go, but both books go into some detail on an inner turmoil. I wasn't aware of this although a brief encounter when I dated a girl he was interested in was a clue. Only words were exchanged.

For a brief time I was pinned (fraternity speak for going steady) to Jean Satterlee, an attractive and intelligent young lady who was in Chi Omega. Her father was a doctor and the family, about this time, moved into a beautiful house on one of the hilltops overlooking Mission Valley. I think when I parked my 1941 Chevrolet coupe a good distance from her parent's driveway, as it leaked oil at every stop, and she started driving her new 1956 aqua colored Thunderbird with the port hole side windows about that my days were numbered. To be fair to Jean I was somewhat of a dork. My pride was hurt much more than my heart and her decision was absolutely correct. About this time I decided my luck with women was such that maybe I should concentrate on my studies, work at my part time and summer jobs and go skiing. And that's what I did.

Now you know more than you need to about my friends up to this time. I will list my employment and give no details. Ranch hand, garden service, house work, preparing a softball diamond for play each weekday one summer, working at two different gas stations (Gerald Woods and Son and Andersons), 11th Naval District Facilities Division, General Dynamics, during one school year 5 to 9 pm Monday thru Friday, and as a carpenter's apprentice (Raymond Perrigo Construction) which was the best job of any these. Raymond Perrigo was a quality human being.

Probably the most influential teacher I had in College was Dr. Johnson. I can't remember his first name but he taught English Literature I and II at San Diego State College. I think I enrolled in the spring class in 1955. I imagine I was required to take a least one class of this type and Lit I was chosen. The first day in class Dr. Johnson walks into class, writes his name on the chalk board, walks around his desk and leans back on its edge facing us. At first I thought I am too near the front for Dr. Johnson was a bit overweight, his salt and pepper hair was mussed up a little and he had a couple of large fat bumps high up on his forehead. His attempt at shaving apparently had not gone well that morning. He was wearing a wrinkled white shirt with the collar left unbuttoned to make room for his neck and he had tied his tie loose so little areas of hairy flesh showed in the open areas between shirt and tie. He wore a suit coat open which fit the picture and the bottom button of his shirt was about midway down his rather ample belly. The hairy flesh of his neck area was repeated in the inverted V opening of his shirt until it disappeared into his mismatched pants. The tie was too short to provide any cover. His shoes I don't really recall but I will leave that to your imagination, but don't count out mismatched socks. He then dazzled the class, especially me, in his introduction to what his class would be like and what we would cover. His love of literature was contagious and for the first time in my life I found I really wanted to read.

I enjoyed the class so much I enrolled for Lit II the fall semester 1955. In walks Dr. Johnson and he repeats his trip to the blackboard, writes his name, walks around his desk and leans against it. He first words were, "For those of you that took Lit I last semester you may not recognize me. The Dean of the English Department told me if I was to continue teaching at this college that I would have to make a better visual impression to both my students and the faculty." He smiled his usual smile and started his lecture. His suit was new and fit his new slimmer body, his hair was neatly trimmed, shaving had gone well, his tie was neatly knotted and his suit jacket buttoned, his shoes shinned and I am sure his socks matched. This class was just as good, but I for one missed the Dr. Johnson I had the semester before. None the less, thank you Dr. Johnson.

CHAPTER 7

It could have been the Monday after the 4th of July 1958, which would have been July 7, or maybe it was the week before but it would have been my first day of employment at AC Spark Plug. There were about eighteen of us, all new hires and all coming from different colleges across the United States. On checking in at the security gate instructions were to go to the elevator (a freight elevator) and thence to the third floor. This emptied us into a large room and on my arrival about half the new class was already there. One of the newcomers about my height at six foot three, and similar build, strode over and said, "Hi big man, my name is John Bush and I'm from Maine." I was caught a little by surprise but volunteered my name and shook his hand. This was the start of a friendship that still lasts today, the man who would be best man at my wedding, god father to my daughter, and through how many other future friends would be met and enjoyed.

This is the start of the story I have been promising you. As I described back in the start of Chapter 2, I was bumping along my destiny as planned. I would be at AC for about two and one half years when the first real branch in the road showed up, but that has to wait until I get to it. The trainer for us was a man named Oliver Lewis. I think I have that right, but in any case his quick smile and good nature soon garnered a nickname of, phonically pronounced, Awliee Louiee. He herded us through the three months of instruction, both corporate policy and technical training, saw to getting government security clearances and passports, and gave some personnel guidance as well.

It was a fast few months. A couple of others became

good friends, one Gene Depolo from New York and another Al Metzger from Ohio. (Gene was part of a continuing group that formed when he, John Bush and I later made moves to the San Francisco Bay area.) Another one to be remembered was a Navy Air Force veteran Doug Nygard. A few of the new engineers were married and had their own lives to live but all in all a pretty good group to be with. We quickly found a bar, Vituccis, near the plant that became an after work watering hole and a good place to meet girls. The popular song at the time was "Volare" and I think we all thought by the time we left Milwaukee we had heard it enough for a lifetime. Once and a while I catch it on the radio and it does bring back some good memories.

For Labor Day weekend John decided the thing to do was drive around Lake Michigan. So Gene and I joined in and in his 1957 Chevrolet Yellow and Black Bel Aire convertible graduation present we started off after work on Friday and didn't get very far before stopping to check the local scene. Our second night was in Sault Saint Marie as we wanted to see the Locks. The third night was someplace in northern Michigan and we struggled into Milwaukee around 3:00 am Tuesday morning. Lake Michigan is a very big lake and at least one of us wasn't too bright.

John got me to go out and play golf which I had only done once before as a substitute on the fraternity team. I really enjoyed it and later on in California I got more serious and am still playing, like just yesterday. I in turn introduced John and several others to snow skiing and John ended up living in Sun Valley, Idaho for some years after he retired. Many other exchanges were made as we all had some unique differences in our pre-adult years. It was a good time to be a young, single person.

After our training period was over it was time for assignments. A few were sent over to England with the first guidance systems, a few remained in Milwaukee, and the rest of us went out to Vandenberg Air Force Base in Northern California which was the testing facility for the Thor missile. The two towns where we took up residence were Santa Maria and Lompoc. Not really much to tell about the time there but it was in Santa Maria where I had the chance to introduce a group of the boys to real Mexican Food. John Bush, Gene Depolo, and Fred Zermullen were my students. These were Easterners and when we entered the little restaurant with the red and white table clothes, just a little soiled, and then the somewhat overweight Mexican cook came out to greet us with his apron showing signs of many meals prepared I knew we were in the right place. My friends looked at the menu and at some of the plates of food being delivered to other tables and asked me to order. Tacos, enchiladas, tamales, refried beans and chips with salsa and guacamole. When the table was set I have to mention that in 1958 restaurants like these where not five star in cleanliness. It was the food that made the restaurant and out it came. There were three guys just sitting there when I picked up the taco and took the first bite. It was really good as expected. I looked around and told them each get started which they, if reluctantly, finally did. From that day on it was Mexican at least once a week.

  I was at Vandenberg when my Grandfather Myers died and I made the trip to San Diego on the bus for his funeral. I should point out here that I had not bought a car as I knew I would be going to England shortly and quite frankly I couldn't afford to do so at the time. I was brought up to never buy something you can't pay cash for except a house. Also the only car I wanted was that Porsche and I was saving every penny I could for it. I was assigned to head for England the first part of January, 1959 but by this time I was beginning to realize that something was not quite right with my Field Service Engineer position. On one hand the position was more of a technicians, or maybe even less. Also there was really not much to do and a good percentage of the time was not productive in any way. This of course is very much not my nature. The other was that I was witnessing my first cost plus government contract.

  On January 17, 1961 President Eisenhower in his farewell address warned of the dangers of "the military-

industrial complex" which morphed into a variety of other government complexes but I was in this one and had been over two years by the time he spoke those words. And would be for the better part of ten of my twelve years in an engineering position. Now my exposure was to what happens when a cost plus contract is used to fund the production and installation of military hardware.

A cost plus contract on the surface is a very supportable one when it comes to developing complex and state-of-the-art equipment. The contractor has very little chance to get it right in estimating what it will cost to design, produce, test, deliver, and maintain this kind of equipment. The Auto Industry through years of designing and manufacturing cars has a good idea of what it will cost to produce the next years model. The contractor selected to bring an inter-continental missile to maturity has to make some pretty big guesses, both to secure the contract and make the delivery. There is a logic to this form of contract. The downside, unfortunately, is that the more you spend, the more you make. Most of the ones I knew of were at six and a half percent.

Now add to this that I am talking about contractors funded by the U.S. Government for military hardware and services. You automatically have three tiers of governing, Congress, Military, and (private) Contractor. If everyone does their job with skill and to the best ethical standards it should work. It seems reasonable. The problems immediately surface in skill, ethics, and human nature. The reason that a group of young graduate engineers spent a great deal of time playing the game of battleship while sitting in the company car overlooking the Pacific Ocean was that to insure adequate coverage on site for an unknown testing and maintenance of a sophisticated guidance system was to over specify the requirements in the contract. Once the over staffing was realized, to reduce the staff to the appropriate level would mean less profit to the contractor. And when the Congress, the Military, and the Contractor are joined in one way or another, no action is taken. Votes, Future

MY STORY ~ 45

Employment and Profit. The politician loves to spend the public's money, especially if it is in their district. The military representative enjoys being pandered to and often sees the opportunity for employment in the civil service or private side after his military retirement. And of course the contractor sees the dollar signs in bigger and bigger approved spending. This is one part of the Complex that was warned about by Eisenhower.

I returned to Milwaukee shortly after Christmas which I was able to spend with my family in San Diego. There were two ways to get to England. The first was by commercial air line, at the time it was the Lockheed Constellation or the Douglas DC-6. A nice ride I was to find out on my return trip. The other way was to accompany two or three of the guidance systems and the associated equipment trailers holding the test and launch electronics. Also on board would be an electrical back-up generator to supply the required heater power that was needed for the gyros on the inertial platform. Military Air Transport Service was the transport agency and the plane was the C-130, a four engine monster with the big ramp that lowered down from the rear of fuselage. Myself and one other engineer got the second option for the trip over.

It all started out okay as the MATS plane arrived at the Milwaukee base right on time and the plane had been loaded by the time we had arrived. We had on board for this flight three guidance systems, a backup generator, and two big equipment trailers which pretty much filled up the hold. All were strapped down with heavy duty straps. There was just enough room to walk on either side of the cargo as long as the fold down canvas seats were up. Orders were given to strap ourselves into any of the seats and prepare for take off. The engines were started in sequence and the roar of the engines was loud, the plane was shaking and we taxied for take off. The first leg was to Dover, Delaware which was made in good time. It was noisy and got very hot. The trailers rocked so much that it looked like they would eventually come loose. Dover is home base for MATS so guess what, the next crew was late getting ready and discovered that the #3 generator wasn't working. Out came the mechanics and after a replacement was installed the problem was found not to be the generator but a wire had come loose from the meter in the cockpit. The delay was too long for that crew to make the leg to Newfoundland, so we had to wait until the next morning for another crew. Our job was to monitor the equipment twenty-four hours a day. One of us could leave long enough to use the bathroom and grab a snack. The other meals we had were the ones that the flight crews get when in the air.

  The take off was accomplished early and quickly. Touch down in Newfoundland was for refueling and while this was going on the doors were opened and the temperature went from about eighty-five to forty degrees before we were ready to get back underway. We made the Azores in record time and were to wait until the next crew was available. The next morning we got started on time but one hour out trouble was reported and we started a return to the Azores. The Azores is a nice place and has a very comfortable base. I happened to be walking around up front shortly after take off and I saw one of the crew fiddling with instrument panel. They circled for an hour dumping fuel and then landed. The mechanics came out and the pilot told them the #3 generator was out. We had been on board for three days and nights and I told the pilot to lift that instrument panel up and connect the wire back on the #3 meter and get us to England. They actually did this without too many dirty looks since another crew was to do this final leg because of allotted flight hours. They didn't mind as their objective had been accomplished. Four and a half days to get from Milwaukee to England. I caught a terrible cold and spent my first few days in England in my RAF Officers Quarters bed.

  The work there was a little better than at Vandenberg in that we did get to set up connections of our equipment in the trailers to the guidance system in the missile. This was with several heavy cables which were each tested first and a system test was run. Douglas Corp was the prime contractor and they were responsible for the rest of the installation. Once this was done we had very little to do. Most of the time we sat in the trailers or in the small office for AC.

    On the bright side I found the nearest Porsche dealer and ordered my Porsche. It would be three months before delivery which worked just fine. Our pay in England was thirty-five percent above our base pay and at that time we were exempt from income tax. Our housing cost were very modest. We could stay at the RAF Officers Quarters and use the base mess for meals. We actually had a Batman, a man assigned to bring us tea in the morning, make our beds, and wish us well each day. All this was at very little cost plus a good tip for our man.

    The Thor Missiles were being installed centered around four RAF bases north of London and AC's involvement was over the course of about two years. I think I was there for the second and third installation, and maybe a short time at the fourth as the wind up got underway. The installation was very basic. The missile was on a trailer base that would rotated up to vertical to position it for launching. The missile and trailer were covered by a retractable metal shelter and the equipment trailers were located nearby. think there were five sets of these at each location. The bases were still operational with a very limited staff. There was a large number U.S. personnel and they came in waves and then left. The local economies had a short term boost, and then a more modest gain through out the operational period. At each base there was at least one RAF pilot from WWII who would be at the bar and most nights was very willing to have new ears to bend on what it was like. I don't mean to belittle them as there were still many signs about these bases of the war. Bomb craters, bullets holes and scars on the buildings, and even rubble still left where buildings once stood. I had the chance to visit a hangar that housed both the Manchester and Lancaster bombers, some of which were still being used for flight training. The idea of doing bombing runs over Europe in planes like these struck me as insane. Canvas stretched over aluminum and steel frames, control cables exposed, and turret guns set up where no escape would be possible in an emergency. These were much braver men than I. (In walking around London there was still a lot of damage and destruction left, and many older civilians showed signs of injuries, and a good part of a generation of men were missing. It was even more apparent in Germany.)

An enterprising travel agent had gotten permission to land a passenger plane on the base airstrips and set up excursions to Europe every time there was a three day holiday. I went on four of these trips, one to Lisbon and Tangiers, one to beautiful Copenhagen, one to Paris, and one to Rome. The plane would arrive at 5:00 pm and leave at 6:00 pm and return during daylight hours on the last day of the holiday. These were all great trips. On my own I did one trip to ski in Arosa, Switzerland, a ten day driving trip through central Europe, many trips to London, and toured the local areas extensively. That part of my time in England was great and almost made up with my increasing unhappiness about how my new occupation was turning out.

In September it was time for my return to Milwaukee and this time I flew in style. My Porsche was shipped and would be waiting for me in New York City. The day after I landed in New York I headed down the port to claim my car and had all the paper work in order. There it was looking none the worse for wear and the dock master placed my paperwork on the bottom of a stack of other papers. I stood next to my car, he looked at me and I at him. Occasionally a longshoreman would come to the desk and saunter back into the terminal. After about an hour I noticed the dock master slip my paperwork up a few places. I waited, he looked. Then a little more progress and finally after about three hours he pulled my papers out, stamped them and brought me my keys. No bribe had been offered and he had decided to give up before taking off for lunch. Think unions and think container ships. Times have changed.

The next day I was off on my drive to Milwaukee and somehow had lost a day and thinking it was Sunday instead of Saturday I drove right past the off ramp to Washington DC. I would have to visit there another time, which I have. I drove up South Lake Street into Chicago in late afternoon. It was good this was 1959 as this white man in his small sports car was passing corner after corner crowded with hundreds of black men, women, boys and girls. All non threatening and only out on a warm fall day. I still felt uneasy and each time I had to stop for a traffic light I sensed the crowd closing in on me. I was back in Milwaukee by evening and got a room at the Y.

General Motors at this time had a policy that no white collar employee would be laid off, even if at the time there was no work to be done. Employment for life and a good retirement benefit when you reached eighty-five, the combination of years employed and age. This was the good job as part of ones destiny. AC Spark Plug had secured a guidance system contract for the upcoming Titan II Missile, but it was a few years in the future. IBM was doing the development work as digital computation was just arriving on the scene. For a little history, the Thor Missile guidance was a big piece of equipment in two parts, the inertial platform and the electronics rack. You can find a number of web sites to get a feel what it was like. (Try Thor-The IRBM, afspacemuseum.org.) If your I-pad, or I-phone, has a GPS and Google Earth you could probable replace the several hundred pounds of guidance system built for the Thor Missile with either.

I was transferred to this program although at the time there was nothing to do but study the technology that was coming. AC sent me to IBM in Endicott, New York for a three week orientation but it was too early to learn much. I did get two weekends of skiing in New England ski resorts. I was impatient and sometime in early 1960 accepted a job with Lockheed Missiles and Space Division in Sunnyvale, California. The acronym, LMSD, I would learn later was known as Let's Move Some Desks. This followed some very good social times in Milwaukee at which time much of the original group of engineers had reassembled. The AC Spark Plug operation was moved to a new facility in Oak Creek just south of the city and many of us rented apartments in a new complex about half way between work and Milwaukee. I said my good-byes and then headed west.

This brings us to another however, as mentioned earlier. Leaving GM could be looked back upon as being a mistake, certainly career wise. The new guidance system technology was the precursor to most of the big missile programs that were lining up for the future of space exploration.

CHAPTER 8

I headed west. My employment at AC Spark Plug was over after a very good time but not a full filling start to my career as an engineer. I was a little uncertain about my next position with Lockheed Missiles and Space Division but I was certain about moving back to California and especially to the San Francisco Bay Area.

The drive out was enjoyable as I was zipping along in my Porsche with my possessions inside and my skis on the ski rack. I remember passing through Lincoln, Nebraska at dinner time and learning that it was a dry state. The Rocky Mountains came into view and an hour later I drove through Boulder, Colorado and headed up into the mountains. I felt at home there and that sometime later on it would be.

Gene Depolo had been in the Bay Area for a few months and I was able stay in his small studio apartment at first. It had two single beds that with bolsters were sofas, a kitchenette and a bathroom. We soon moved into a two bedroom apartment in a complex called Del Charro at 151 Calderon Ave, Mountain View. This was only a few blocks from where I was to work at LMSD, was new and upscale. John Bush would show up a few months later and rent in the same complex. A friend I had met in England, Gil Schroeder, also showed up to make third roommate with Gene and me.

The social scene was very active and it was a good group to be with. Stanford University and Palo Alto were NW and San Jose State and San Jose were SE, the Bay to NE, and the Santa Cruz Mountains to SW. San Francisco just a short drive and Carmel and Monterrey just a little farther. At that time each of the towns were separated by orchards of apricots, apples, peaches, cherries and walnuts. Traffic was not bad and the cost of living just about right. The skies were clear and the weather perfect. This was at least ten years before the first inkling of Silicon Valley started to show up, a perfect place to live. One of the favorite meeting places was "Andre's L'Omelette French Restaurant" on El Camino Blvd in Palo Alto. I mention it here as later it will become an important part of my story.

My new job I shall try to cover in two short paragraphs. It was in the test equipment section of LMSD and was for the Polaris Missile, a submarine launched vehicle. Lockheed was the prime contractor and the test equipment was being built by Nortronics in Anaheim, California in the Los Angeles basin. Our job was co-ordination between the Navy, the Lockheed designers and the subcontractor.

It was not a bad position, but not creative and had some politics to contend with. Towards the last few months that I was there a disagreement with the attempted addition of a piece of hardware that would not add value caused me a minor problem with management. Then LMSD had one of their ten percent staff reduction programs. This meant our group of twelve would be reduced by two. Since I was last hire and the only unmarried engineer in the group being chosen as one of the two to be let go was not unexpected. Also my disappointment with the job was starting to surface which didn't help my position. A hiring freeze was put in place for the next thirty days so transfer to any other department was almost impossible. You may also deduce that I was not too happy about this and I wrote a wordy two page letter to whom it may concern. Not the smartest thing I have ever done and it would come back as will be mentioned later.

While at LMSD Edward Pack became a good friend. Ed was several years my senior, married to Peggy, and having four children. He had served in the Signal Corp in WWII and was just to the rear of the front lines in Europe setting up and maintaining the communication equipment as the war ended. From Pittsfield, MA he had moved out to California a few years prior to my meeting him here. I was invited to dinner at his home on a number occasions for some family life and he will show up again in a later chapter.

I was now unemployed and didn't want to start searching for another job in this field. I went to the Unemployment Office in Palo Alto to file for benefits but on entering the building I found a large number of people who looked liked they needed the money a lot more than I did so I turned around and left. I had made some investments with a young stock broker named John Licata and he had done pretty good for me so I had about a years income saved and no debts.

Here comes the first unexpected fork in the road. I drove down to San Diego to spend a few weeks with my parents. I think that it was about the time that my sister Nancy's marriage was falling apart and I was asked to mediate which is definitely not my strong suit. About all I came away with was that I would never get married. I then headed up to the Sierra's to do some backpacking and fishing and discovered another of life's truths, some things are not nearly as much fun doing them alone as they are with companions.

The next stop was Mammoth Mountain, Dave McCoy's ski area. This would have been in July. I was camped out at the local camp ground and for some reason, most likely boredom, I stopped in Lloyd's Lumber Company and inquired about a job. Mr. Lloyd sat behind his desk and after I gave a brief verbal resume (I knew tools and had worked one summer as a carpenter's apprentice) he said, "Do you want to start now, or after lunch?" No paper work (we'll do that later), no security clearance, no home address, no references. Also implied, if you don't work out you will be gone just as fast. I worked, and worked hard, until the first day the ski lifts opened. A great job and good people.

Preparing to spend the winter at Mammoth and ski every day I leased a seventeen foot trailer in the local trailer park and winterized it by enclosing the bottom with boarding to keep the snow and cold from underneath. Ordered the biggest propane tank that could be delivered on a temporary rental and was ready for opening day. Day one of the ski season was Thanksgiving. The snow was good, the skiing great, and the crowds big and cheerful. Then the truth became clear. Mammoth was a weekend and holiday ski area. Monday thru Friday there were no lines and hardly anyone to ski with. Week ends and holidays would have long lines and crowded slopes. Again, there are some things you need to have a little company to really enjoy, but sometimes too much company spoils them. I sublet the trailer and headed to San Diego for Christmas with the plan to leave the day after for Aspen, Colorado.

On December 26,1961, some where around the Nevada and Utah border in the early afternoon an almost surreal peace came over me. My Porsche was humming along and there were few if any other cars or trucks in sight. I was going to a place I wanted to be. I'd saved enough money to live on for a year and I had some investments that were growing. All the material things I would need were in the car with me. I owed no one. My Mother and Father and younger sister seemed content and I don't recall whether my older sister's marriage was still in distress but it wasn't a bother to me at that time. I truly felt totally free. One can say that to have such a feeling is the height of selfishness but at that moment it seemed absolutely right. I was satisfied with my life, where I was, where I was heading, and was looking forward to doing something I really wanted to do. I was happy.

CHAPTER 9

On December 27, 1961 at about 2:00 pm I went into the Aspen Ski Corp office and one Penny O'Negan took my check and delivered my annual ski pass. She said if you hurry you can get a run or two in before the lifts close. I choose to wait until the next day.

I walked around town and thought to myself, "This is the place." I had skied there in 1956 and again in 1958. The town had grown some but I wasn't a total stranger. By four o'clock I had walked into the Holiday House, met Fred Braun the owner, and rented a bunk in the bunk room on a week to week basis. Fred and his wife Renata would become friends. My roommate on a more permanent rental was Michael Ohnmacht who became a well known stained glass artist. He was apprenticing at that time to Herbert Bayer, a famous architect and artist of the Bauhaus School. A few weeks later I found a nice room on the back of a house across the street from the Holiday House with a separate entrance. It was clean, comfortable and at a very reasonable rent. Perfect.

I skied every day except five until the lifts closed the second Sunday of April. Two of the five days was a quick trip to Denver to join a group going to see the USA Hockey team play in a Olympic warm-up game at the Broadamor in Colorado Springs. The other three days were the result of a fall that caused my ski tip to hit the bridge of my nose and head toward my left eye. Dr. Gould fixed me up with twenty-three stitches. 1962 was probably one of the finest snow seasons ever. It was Camelot snowing only at night every third day providing days of powder skiing with the more popular runs lightly packed. Short skis were still a novelty and the moguls were big and perfectly shaped. For me as I wasn't working was to be one of the first on the lift each morning and at the end of the day have a cup of hot chocolate at the Sundeck until the Ski Patrol came in and made the last call. The last run down the mountain with the lifts all stopped and only a few skiers on the mountain is a very nice experience.

During this period I met many of the Aspen locals on the mountain. Ruth Whyte, who became a good friend, made me a house boy for the winter meaning being invited to many of her dinner parties to tend the fire, help in the kitchen, act as bartender, etc. There was often questioning looks but it was just a friendship and lasted for many years after. I met, skied and partied with Bill and Vivian Goodnough who owned and operated the Snowflake Lodge and who were close friends with Ruth. Also John and Helen Kuehlman who were Aspen school teachers, and a host of others.

The four months sped by much, much too fast. National Geographic had an article in the May edition about the area that was proposed to become a national park and Ruth and one of her friends, Carolyn Kerchek, decided that they wanted to do a jeep trip to see the area before it became developed and I was invited to go. Ruth's open jeep was prepped and it was off to Moab and points southwest. The area we explored became Canyon Lands National Park. We met only one other party, a forest service ranger husband and wife team, on a vacation with the same thoughts in mind.

After that was a visit back to San Diego and then a return to Aspen to house sit for the Kuehlmans. This was to look after their house and take care of their dog. The first night that sorry dog came home with porcupine quills sticking out all over his snout. The vet rubbed his nose with kerosene and then pulled them out one by one. The next night the dumb dog did it again and the procedure was repeated. For the rest of the week I put him on the leash and walked him while he did his evening things.

In March of 1962 there was a stock market correction

and my thinking that I would never have to work again had disappeared like a puff of smoke. A change in course now seemed necessary.

It is time to paint you a picture and admit to you that I have some shortcomings, ones that I didn't realize until some time later, but none the less are important to acknowledge. In the preface I wrote about making course changes I never foresaw, some by choice and others by necessity. The picture is as follows:

It is mid May, maybe while I was house sitting for the Kuehlmans, and I am standing in the intersection of Mill Street and Hyman Avenue facing Aspen Mountain. If the streets have been paved by this time the storm drain which would later house the famous Aspen Dancing Fountain (in which I would play a very minor roll in) is directly at my feet. The Wheeler Opera House is behind me over my right shoulder and in front of me on that side is Wagner Park, the grass just starting to push up through the mud. To my left on both corners are businesses whose names I have forgotten. My shoes are somewhat mud covered as this is toward the end of that season. Those that can have left Aspen for a few weeks of sunshine and warmth after a busy and snowy winter. It is very quiet and the town feels almost deserted. It seems time for me to leave.

What escapes me of course is that I am hip deep in the right place at the right time and surely somewhere in my DNA is the right stuff. I have just had a wonderful four months that many would loved to have had and many more are willing to pay a good amount of money for just a week of. Opportunity must be right there in front of my nose. What I see, however, is the last bit of snow disappearing from the ski runs that can be viewed from this point. What I feel is the regret that this part of my life is about over and that it is time to find another engineering job. I don't realize that in another few weeks Aspen will leaf out and flower and become even more beautiful and livable than in winter. How could I leave such a place? How could I not see the opportunities that were here? It had to have been my parents fault since I am missing the smart gene that some have for recognizing opportunity.

    As I drive to Denver I pass a sign that says, "Hiring Trail Crews." Then another sign, "Vail, Colorado." I pulled into the dirt parking lot and walk over the brand new covered bridge that crosses Gore Creek. There are commercial lots staked out on both sides of the street but no one is around. I return to my car and head to Denver.

    I applied for a job at Martin just south of Denver and at Ball Brothers Research in Boulder. The Martin interview was somewhat neutral but the Ball one was better and the job I would have liked. I received only a form letter from each that they had selected another applicant and thank you. At the time I assumed that part of this was that being out of the work force for a full year and having a deep skier's tan did not help my prospects. It was back to the Bay Area.

CHAPTER 10

This may sound familiar to you but much new is about to happen that hopefully will justify my recording it in this way. Please note that at this time I just had my 27th birthday and as I write this I have about fifty-three years left to cover.

As I arrived back in the Bay Area, probably in early June, I called John Bush to see if the offer for a temporary place to stay was still good. He said sure and that his roommate, Neal Shea, would be there before he got home. Sure enough Neal was there and I was warmly welcomed. Neal would become another life long friend and there will be more on this through out the remainder of my story.

John gets home and we get things settled. I am looking in the classified ads and find one from Walter Dorwin Teague Associates looking for a electrical engineer to work in their office at Lockheed Missiles and Space Division. I am going backward but there are not many options at this time so I call for an interview. Dick Najarian, the manager, sets up a interview in the main lobby at LMSD which went well and he said he would call the next day. When he calls he stumbles a bit in getting around to letting me know that I wasn't just the right man for the job, or something to that effect. I had been thinking of the responses I had gotten from Martin and Ball Brothers and had a notion that something was not right with my resume. I took a chance and told him I thought I knew what was going on and that he should call a number of the people I had worked with on my previous job at LMSD, including several in the group, one in the Navy office, and especially Ed Pack. Najarian knew a couple of these and had the numbers for the rest. An hour later he called back and offered me the job. I had been marked Not For Rehire by LMSD. Blackballed. A lesson learned: Never write a termination statement that tells whom it may concern what you really think.

Since Neal was a kindred spirit, and I now was employed, it was decided to get a better apartment situation for the three of us. Before I get to this I have to tell a short roommate story. On one of the first nights after I arrived I offered to provide dinner. Now I still had a few dollars left in savings, but one could say I had gotten very frugal by this time. A trip to the local grocery store netted a big package of chicken backs and necks for a very small price and adding a couple of potatoes and some fresh green beans I set off to make dinner. A huge pile of fried chicken backs and necks, a big bowl of mashed potatoes with gravy, and a pile of green beans all for a dollar seventy-six. I have been razed for years about this dinner and no doubt it will come up at least one more time if the chance permits. Despite all the groans and moans it was all consumed and frankly tasted pretty good.

A very nice three bedroom apartment was found on Pamela Drive in Mountain View which was fairly new and had a good sized swimming pool. We became known as the Pamela Street Gang and many good parties were given there. It was unfurnished, so we divided up the furniture we needed to get. We each bought our own bedroom sets, I bought the Danish Modern chair and ottoman, Neal the couch and chair, and John the dinette set. We ordered the furniture from a small shop just across the famous El Camino Real, about a long block away. There were a number afternoons with one or more of us hauling our new stuff across this busy street as it arrived to the store. It was not a delivery included deal. The apartment was going to be a good place to be at a good time to be there.

John had met a number of people while I was in Aspen and these started to form a large family. Most were employed at Lockheed but others were indirectly employed by outside firms and some in other businesses. A number were skiers and golfers and all liked to socialize and party. It is amazing that most are still good friends and see each often. A few have passed away which is expected at this age. Owen Wade became the fourth in the golfing foursome with John, Neal, and me and a close friend to each of us. Neal, and his wife Patty, and Owen still live in the area. I will try to work as many of the others in as the events come up in the story time line.

As fall approached the upcoming ski season was being anticipated, the Warren Miller ski movie attended, some new equipment sought. We three had become comfortable roomates and life was very good. It was towards early October that my life was about to make one of its biggest changes. I will try to do it justice.

Getting to be the Friday after work routine was the cocktail hour visit to Andre's L'Omelette French Restaurant in Palo Alto to have a martini or two and check out the girls. The girls had a similar routine. As you entered "L'Omies" the bar started a few paces inside with it running to the right. There were a number of small tables and chairs scattered about for waiting for a table in the dining area or having drinks. The bar area was large enough to cater to a respectable number customers. Often behind the bar would be Pierre, Andre's brother, and John and he would carry on quite a banter as drinks were ordered. On this particular Friday night I spotted a couple of nice looking girls sitting against the far wall, one a blonde and the other brunette. With my martini in hand, and most certainly looking suave, I casually walked over to introduce myself. I am not sure I got the blonde's name as another evil guy picked up the conversation with her and the brunette gave me a truly fine smile and Jeanne Bryan, a nurse at Stanford Hospital and from Flint, Michigan made my acquaintance. It may not have been exactly like that, but close.

Now I don't really remember how the first date was established but it was. There were then a few more and as Thanksgiving approached, several more. I then had to explain to Jeanne that I was a skier and that every weekend and holidays would be spent in the mountains and that she should not plan on me being around. She smiled and said she understood and that it was not a problem. I of course thought she would be devastated. Thanksgiving came but no snow had fallen in the Sierras. Jeanne and her room mate Marin were going to prepare Thanksgiving dinner for a small group and would I like to come. No snow, no skiing so of course I accepted. It was very nice Thanksgiving.

As Christmas approached the snow still didn't. The Pamela Street gang were all planning to head to Squaw Valley for the holidays but word came down that it wasn't worth the trip. Christmas morning found John, Neal, and me sitting on the floor opening our presents from home. John got a set of oriental TV tables that evoked laughter from the trio. This was followed by Neal who had asked his family for a slide projector and upon opening the box finding the bottom of the line Argus had our sympathy. My turn was to find a pair of homemade pajamas, blue pants and a top the cloth covered with little skiing figures. My Mother's good effort as a seamstress. And for the record I must mention the Lummi Sticks my younger sister, age 12, had crafted for me. We all started to laugh and agreed this was the worst Christmas ever. By afternoon it didn't get much better as I think we had Christmas dinner at a local at cafeteria. There was probably a lesson in this for each of us.

The winter of 1962-1963 is probably still thought of as the worst snow season in Sierra history, the previous one had been one of the best. That was my Aspen ski year. I later heard from one of the guys that had sublet the trailer in Mammoth that they had twelve feet of snow in the park and they had to dig tunnels to the restrooms and out to the road. The first skiing at Squaw Valley this year was late January and the season ended early.

This of course meant that Jeanne and I had a few more dates than planned. The only time I felt she was annoyed by this was New Years Eve of which I assured her that I wouldn't be there and she got a date for the evening. Spring did come and things returned to normal, or maybe you can say a little more than normal. We became a couple and really enjoyed being together. By summer it was preordained that we would probably get married. I still had a little bachelors remorse, thinking maybe thirty years was better than twenty-eight but the date was set for August 31, 1963. As it has turned out it was a much better day than I could have imagined.

Jeanne, with five other graduates of Hurley Hospital College of Nursing, decided that after working enough to save monies for the trip they would accept the positions offered at Stanford University Hospital in Palo Alto, California. In three cars they packed what was theirs and fled Flint, Michigan. Jeanne waved goodbye to her parents Howard and Dora Bryan, her twin sister Jo and her new husband Carl Franz, and Judy, Jerry, and Janet the rest of her siblings. Jeanne was the only one of her immediate family that had the urge to see new places and that was to be a good thing as we joined up for what was now our trip through life.

Jeanne's parents were not able to attend our wedding. My father escorted her down the aisle as I waited with John Bush as best man and Irene Fyock as maid of honor. All went as planned and a nice dinner for the wedding party and family followed. My little sister at thirteen seemed okay with the marriage, my Dad pleased, and my Mother relieved. Neal had decorated the Porsche and we headed off under the sprinkling of rice and clatter of tin cans back to our newly rented apartment at 1261 Cortez Dr., Sunnyvale, CA.. Not much of a honeymoon, but we would make up for that later.

CHAPTER 11

The morning of September 1, 1963, a Sunday, found me a married man waking up next to a married woman. (The same thing happened this morning and with the same woman.) It was a lazy day. My parents and sister Carolyn stopped by before their return to San Diego. Jeanne and I opened our few wedding presents. John and Neal gave us a nice barbecue thinking that they would get many good meals from it which they did. Monday it was back to work, myself to WDTA and Jeanne to the office of a pair of pediatricians she had been working for after leaving Stanford University Hospital.

Our first Christmas was to be spent with Jeanne's family in Flint, Michigan and since you have to go right past Aspen it was decided we would drive to Denver and then fly to Flint from there. That was probably was my idea, but Jeanne thought it would be fun. My Porsche decided one of its valves had had enough and we limped in to Denver and found a mechanic that would fix it while we were in Flint. I had earlier written a letter to my soon to be in-laws telling them of my virtues and that Jeanne would be a most happy bride. (It has found its way into the Myers History Box.) Now I had to past muster. All went well and continued so for the remainder of their lives. They never indicated having any regrets, at least to me, about this son in law. Christmas was good and Jeanne's family and I got along just fine. On the return trip the Porsche ran perfect with stops in Aspen and Alta, Utah.

Our life took on some routine and our family of friends accepted us as married just as they had as a couple. The fact we were going to have that little stranger arrive in our house was becoming obvious and Jeanne had to reduce her participation in the co-ed basketball and touch football games. Neal and his girlfriend Patty got married somewhere in this time period, Stan and Lynn Peters, Dave and Sally Ewald, and Bill and Joy Rassieur filled out the married couples. The bachelors were all in fine fit. John and Owen, Al Cote, Ray Sluis, and Burt Bloom. I am sure I am missing several.

On Saturday the 7th of March, 1964 Neal and I went skiing for the day at a ski area the closest to the Bay Area and Jeanne had a day to herself after working her usual full day on Friday. Sunday morning Jeanne woke telling me that today was the day. She spent the entire day trying to prove how hard it is to have a baby but came through late in the day with a little gem of a girl with apricot colored hair. Everyone will tell you that the birth your own child is the highlight of their lives and they are right. I may have been a little reluctant to get married but I was in no way reluctant to be a father.

Things in San Diego with my parents had started to be less fine and then get much worse. My parents had purchased a larger house at 4366 Logrono Drive in San Diego shortly after my Grandfather Myers died in late 1958 and had a small one room house built for Grandma Myers. The interior was designed to resemble the Ranch and had one of her looms, their bedroom set, chairs, lamps, small table, decorative items and a small kitchenette and bathroom. It was really nicely done and provided her a great deal of comfort for her remaining days. She died August 7, 1963 just three weeks before Jeanne and I were married. I think she was still alert enough at the time to know that her only grandson would soon have a wife.

Grandma Willisford had moved in with my parents and was living in the third bedroom in the house, my older sister's divorce had occurred, younger sister Carolyn was approaching her teenage years and would later go off to college at University of California Santa Barbara. I imagine my Dad was not having a great time but he did his duty with his characteristic good nature. He was the executor of Grandma Myers's estate and the original sale of the bottom land to the school district had been completed but the sale of the hillside property was a much more complex situation and was dragging on for some time. In fact it still had not closed by the time of his sudden death on April 5, 1964 just after our daughter was born. My mother then became co-executor with his brother who lived in Downey, a southern suburb of Los Angeles. Grandma Willisford passed away in the spring of 1966.

My mother held up fairly well through all this and as I was not able to do much for her from up in the Bay Area my older sister Nancy bore most of the burden. She had her hands full with full time teaching and four children to take care of so I do have some guilt. Mom soon realized that she could not stay in the Logrono house now that only she and Carolyn were there so she sold it and moved into a small apartment in La Mesa. Carolyn was now in high school and my Mother started substitute teaching full time.

I would be remiss without writing more on my Father's death. He was leaving from work on Friday afternoon when he felt a severe pain in his head. He pulled over and stopped near the gate hoping someone would see him and help out. The pain subsided and he decided he could drive home. They made an emergency appointment with a neurologist and an x-ray was taken showing a large depression of the brain on the left side. It was decided an operation to relieve the pressure should be performed the next morning. The dangers were explained but he said he never wanted to have that kind of pain again.

Soon after the operation I was notified that it had gone well and that he was in recovery and looked good. Jeanne and I had been invited to a Saturday brunch at some friends place in the foothills and being the first outing with our one month old daughter we decided to go. When we returned in early afternoon the phone rang as we stepped into the apartment and I learned that he had a major rupture where the aneurism was and had died. You can imagine the crushing feeling I felt after showing off your new born to then loosing your father.

Flying down to San Diego the next day was the start of a

very long week. I think the worst moment was sitting next to my Mom as we packed up his clothes, me holding a pair of his shoes, both of us crying, my Mom asking, "What am I going to do?" All I could offer was I didn't know. Later she asked me if I would mind if he was buried in my brown suit, which I had given to him, as he had always liked wearing it. The funeral was very nice and well attended. So many people were there that Carolyn keep asking, "Who are all these people?" and I would answer, "His friends." That is life, but it still hurts.

While I was in San Diego Jeanne had come down with a staph infection and was quite sick. Fortunately a neighbor was there to help her take care of Janet and during the many calls I made to her during the week she never once let on that she was sick. It was a tough week for us both and continued to be a very sad period for some time. We did have a beautiful baby who was so good and happy that one could not doubt that in time all would be good again.

I will jump ahead just a little as I can't leave you at this point. When my parents were living in the Lois Street house their next door neighbors were Herb and Thelma Meyer. Herb drove a passenger bus for the City of San Diego and Thelma pretty much stayed in the house. They had one child who married and left about the same time I graduated from college. Herb was a friendly person and my parents both liked him.

About seven years after my Father's death, Thelma passed away. A year later Herb called my Mother and asked if she would like to go out for dinner. This would have been about 1972. Mother of course accepted and they had a very good time. They then started to see each other a lot and even began taking a few trips together. Shocking. They soon married and Herb sold his Lois Street house and with Mothers funds from her selling the Logrono Drive house they bought a coach in a very nice park in Santee, just east of La Mesa. I will add to this nice story by telling you that all through my father and mother's marriage they never had sufficient income to do much traveling other than camping and short stay trips. My Father did not particularly like to go out to dinner or dress up, and was not a card player. As far as we could tell Herb's wife did not like to do much of anything. Mom and Herb desires to travel, go out to dinner, play cards (Herb had good card sense and quickly became a good bridge player, my Mother's favorite game.) dress up and go on cruises and long road trips matched up perfectly and made the next twenty-two years of her life a dream. Thank you Herb Meyer for being in the right place, at the right time, with the right stuff.

CHAPTER 12

After our years lease on the Cortez Dr. apartment was up we rented a house on East Estates Dr. in Cupertino which gave us more room and privacy. It was not only nice and clean but had a great landlord. We hustled around for more furniture. It was time for a good stereo system and I set about building, from scratch, a large console with two speaker cabinets and a center equipment cabinet in the spare bedroom. For about a month the smell of contact cement and Danish oil wafted through house. It came out nicely and housed the DynaKit tuner, pre-amp, and amplifier I put together along with a turntable and Sony reel to reel tape recorder and speakers installed in their cabinets.

During this period, about twice a month, John, Neal, Owen and I would set up a round of golf which would be followed by dinner alternating between our place and Neal and Patty's. Dinner was always followed by a game, Monopoly and Risk the most common. Occasionally, when drinks and wine flowed, the competitive spirits would rise and Park Place and it's hotels would find themselves airborne. Not too often, but most memorable. I might add that both Jeanne and Patty were, and are, fabulous cooks.

The next big event is when a year after renting the house we bought our first home at 11860 Brookglen Drive, Saratoga. This was the fall of 1966. And just for historical record the rule of thumb for a house purchase was not to exceed two times your annual salary with house payments not exceing one quarter your take home monthly pay. Also a minimum of 20% down. We stretched just a little as at this time I was the only income producer. It was a very nice 3 bedroom, two bath custom home on one quarter acre. The end of the house with the dining area and living room was all glass with a cathedral ceiling, paneled with heart of redwood as were the walls. A nice fireplace with some built in book shelves completed the living area and an efficient galley kitchen made a very comfortable home for us. It needed some care in the landscaping but I was able to get that in shape in a short time as well as bricking in the area outside the big sliding glass doors around an existing three tier fountain. I then thought Janet needed a play house and constructed the most beautiful A frame Dutch door shake roofed playhouse you could imagine. She played in it about three times. Well it was still a magnificent structure and I suppose could be used for garden tools.

About half way through this period I made a change in employment. Ed Pack had left Lockheed and joined the group with me at WDTA. Ed lasted a couple of years then took another position with Walter V. Sterling Associates in Los Altos. Sterling had one very distinct advantage over WDTA. Instead of being located in the bowels of a giant engineering and industrial complex in a windowless cubicle it was in downtown Los Altos, a most beautiful small town, and was on the main street with lots of windows. Also the job was more fulfilling. I followed Ed in a few months.

Lockheed's Navy contracts were starting to be reduced and of course the first to go were the outside contractors doing ancillary projects and this included both Sterling and WDTA. As this was openly discussed with us it would not be a surprise and we all knew the particular parts of the program we were working were nearing completion. This was around 1968. Two things were happening at that time that are worth noting, one without much influence on our future and the other having a major one which changed the course of our lives. I will deal with the former first.

During the last year with Sterling I had been doing a modest amount of stock trading and thought there should be some way to get quotes on stocks of interest other than having to call your stock broker and having him look them up and recite them back to you. I had just read in one of the trade magazines about a large drum that could be loaded with audio bytes that could be rapidly searched by a computer resulting in audio verbal messaging. Perfect for my needs. I designed a device that could be held on the microphone end of the telephone handset and send a code to a remote receiver, also of my design, which then in turn would connect the service subscribers to their accounts. The accounts would be a list of stock symbols that they wanted quotes on and by combining the stock exchanges computer base on current stock prices with the language on the drum would provide the subscribers with the information they wanted. You must remember this was some years before the touch tone phone.

I started the patent procedure and sent out disclosure information to a number companies I thought might have an interest. This is a very difficult approach in that companies, for legal fears, are very reluctant to even show any interest in an outside the company invention or innovation. So nothing much happened and the idea of venture capital pursuit and starting a company was not in my DNA. (Venture capitalist were not really common at this time, but would become a fixture and stars as the technology explosion hit Silicon Valley in the mid 1970's and 1980's.)

Some years later I saw advertised this almost identical service in a money magazine or the Wall Street Journal. The little transmitter was based on the touch tone system and I am sure the verbal audio would have been much more sophisticated. The idea was the same but as technology was rapidly changing as the personal computer was coming into its own the window for this service's life span would be short. I will touch on this in a later chapter dealing with this rapid change which I became involved in 1984 to 1986.

We now come to the second happening mentioned above. To lay the ground work for this you should know that for several years Jeanne and I had been browsing various arts and craft shows about the area to find something to place above the fireplace in our new home. Jeanne would spot something and I would take a close look, see the price and pronounce "I could make that!" and wander off. Then came a fateful day in the first week of September, 1969.

"Hurry up and eat your dinner. You're enrolled in the adult education metal sculpture class at the high school and it starts in thirty minutes." This was my greeting as I walked in the door and our life was about to take off on a major fork in the road. I did as told, as I always do, and was introduced to metal sculpture. This comprised of a quick lesson in acetylene gas welding, a small supply of sheet copper, and a quick lesson in using a metal shear. The result of the first night was three copper flowers, patina by heat and quenching in water, with stems of welding rod and three thin strips of steel carefully sheared on the shear as leaves. Clutching my first work in hand I proceeded home to proudly display my talent to my bride and mother of my child. These three flowers are at this moment sitting on the mantle not six feet from where I type these words.

I was given my two weeks notice around the first of December and found myself unemployed two weeks before Christmas 1969. This was expected so no hard feelings were harbored. Sterling had been a very fair employer and within a few more months it would close the Los Altos office. Ed Pack had started organizing for his lay off by founding Edward L. Pack Associates, an acoustical consulting firm which today is now being managed by one of his sons. I was experimenting and creating metal art while looking for employment and collecting unemployment insurance. The future was more than uncertain as this time I had a wife, child and house payments and engineering opportunities were again almost zero. Jeanne went back into nursing, the first employment being a very unpleasant job as the nurse at a geriatric nursing home on the night shift. We shared the parenting and things would get much better soon.

A friend and artist, Pat Sedlack, who had painted a large landscape for us saw some the sculptures I was producing and suggested I should show them at one of the Mall shows that she showed at. This was early March, 1970 and I signed up with the promoter and got my assigned space. This was a pay for space and rent display panels. By this time I was doing a variety of table and wall pieces which I will define as metal craft, although officially it was called metal sculpture. Each day of the 3 day show I came home with checks and cash. By the end of the show I had made enough to pay for food and shelter for the month. A light bulb was lit. This was the start of a thirty year career, with a number of interruptions, which will be a good part of the trip that will be described to you in the coming chapters. Jeanne will work during all these years, but her jobs and career will change a number of times and will be much improved over that of her first return to nursing just described.

CHAPTER 13

As 1970 was drawing to the close, my unemployment insurance had run out, Jeanne had found a much better position as a charge nurse at Los Gatos Community Hospital and I was cranking out a goodly amount of metal sculpture. The garage had been turned into my studio and I was ordering the biggest tanks of acetylene and oxygen that could be delivered and going through them much too fast. Welding and brazing rod were being bought by the box. I had all the tools required to make just about ever thing I was producing and was having some of the steel parts I needed produced at a metal fabricator.

There was a problem, however. There is that however again. I was doing two to three mall shows a month and as soon as a show was over I would be back in the studio making the same pieces I had just sold. I had my complete display organized and we now had a Pontiac Grand Safari station wagon, just a few years old, which inside and on the luggage rack on the top could carry everything I needed to make a good presentation. The problem was that the shows were almost always three days, Friday, Saturday and Sunday and you had to be set up at the opening of the Mall and couldn't close up (or leave) before the Mall closed. Add to this driving time of sometimes an hour, or more, meant for very long days. This sometimes left only four days to restock the inventory. The only exception to this routine was an occasional art show like the one in Los Gatos each year which was a one day outdoor show whose patrons came to buy.

I had by this time started to spend my spare studio time trying to do what I labeled welded steel sculpture. These were representational pieces, mostly wildlife, made by welding up a form with welding rod and shaping it into the figure desired. The final surface was made by welding beads of molten steel over the entire surface which was in turn wire brushed to produce an attractive textured and polished steel finish. A protective lacquer was applied and the sculpture was based. The very first one was a deer and given to Jeanne's Dad. It was not very good, think awful, was hidden away and would occasional show up on a family visit as a tease. It was returned to me eventually and mysteriously disappeared.

Jeanne and I had by this time gotten our routine down pretty good. She could arrange her schedule at the hospital somewhat around my shows and we had several baby sitters that were available when that didn't work out. On the weekends I wasn't showing we were able to arranged the golfing/dinners that we all enjoyed so much. Enough income was coming in and by mid 1971 I was selling enough of my welded steel sculpture that I felt confident to slow down on the production of that other stuff. Actually some of that other stuff got to be quite attractive and I was doing an occasional commission in both steel and copper materials.

This brings us another however moment, a really big one. The Bay Area had started to get crowded. The last orchard in our area had been leveled and was being prepared for more homes. The first signs of smog were starting to show on a majority of days. Reservations had started to become the norm and in the mountains the lines for the ski lifts were getting so long you spent more time in line than skiing. You even had to make campsite reservations when backpacking in the Sierras. I was burning out doing the Mall shows and didn't want to start looking like the real old timer Mall show regulars. We decided that as Janet was just completing first grade that maybe it would be a good time for a change.

In June we planned a scouting trip. I wanted to be where we could ski, enjoy the outdoors, have a more enjoyable life experience. Since our camping trips had gone well a trip was planned to visit all the major ski areas outside California. So we packed up the big Pontiac and visited Alta, Sun Valley, and then to Aspen, with side trips along the way. It turned out we happened to enter Aspen in all her glory of Spring. Camping at a beautiful campsite opposite a small waterfall, Maroon Creek a few steps away and the view of Maroon Lake back dropped by a still snow covered Maroon Bells just a few more steps away was more than Jeanne could take. That night the three of us snuggled up in our tent the decision was made, we would move to Aspen.

The next day we went back into town and visited with Ruth Whyte and discussed her plans. She had built a new house for herself and had given the little one, the one I had been the house boy in 1962, to the Aspen Ski Club (which became known as the Whyte House) and in its place was a big hole. She was going to build a duplex as a rental property and it was to be completed by the first of September. The duplex would be on the corner of Second and Bleeker and her house was on the lot just to the west. (Ruth would eventually own the half block between Second and Third Streets. Later she donated the house and lot on the Third Street and Bleeker corner to the Aspen Historical Society.) For us it was a no brainier, as the saying goes. We would rent the hole in the ground and be in Aspen on September 1, 1971 to move into what was to be built there. We chose the unit to the south, 117 N. Second Street.

It was then back to Saratoga to put our house on the market. It had gone up in value at an impressive rate, almost forty percent in just six years. No way could it continue at that pace. As I mentioned before, in one of the side discussions, what part of my DNA made me so blind to the future. In defense, the aerospace industry was still in the doldrums, unemployment was still pretty high, and real estate prices had hit a little lull. The explosion that became Silicon Valley was just around the corner but we were moving to Aspen. No regrets then, and no regrets now.

While we waited for our house to sell, we went to Europe for 4 weeks flying to London and then on to Paris. We then rented VW Bug and drove all over Central Europe. A highlight was seeing one of our best friends, Owen Wade, who was at the time working near Munich for Lockheed. The four of us attended Oktoberfest in Munich. Jeanne still boast of her drinking a full stein of Lowenbrau while we ate the famous fried chicken and listened to the Bavarian bands. Owen wouldn't let us rest and so after three days of intense touring we headed to Salzburg and took a train trip to Vienna for a two day stay to recover. Returning from Salzburg we rented another car (actually it was the same VW) to continue our trip north along the Rhine and finally to Amsterdam to catch our plane home. Janet was seven and was a real trooper. It was a great family trip with memories for a lifetime.

Arriving home to find our house sold the biggest truck we could find was rented and filled to capacity. What was left was stuffed into the Pontiac Grand Safari. One heart breaking moment did occur as I saw the new owner of my silver with black interior 1959 Porsche Coupe go around the bend of Brookglen Drive toward Prospect Avenue and out of my life. Twelve years and 150,000 miles would now become just a memory. Jeanne and Janet don't (present tense) understand my loss. Right after the closing on the house, the engines were started and we headed East. Our journey was now underway.

CHAPTER 14

We have arrived in Aspen very close to the first of September after a two and a half day drive, Jeanne and Janet in the Pontiac Grand Safari and me in the rental truck. Tired but glad to be there. A little sadness in leaving our house in Saratoga but as I headed up the first grade out of the valley the side view mirror displayed a thick blanket of smog shrouding the entire south Bay Area. This was the right thing to do.

The duplex looked just fine except for the several workers who were scurrying in and out with various materials and tools. Not quite finished. Ruth greeted us and quickly advised that just a few days remained until we could move in and that we could stay in her guestrooms until then. It worked out okay and we were able to move in a few days later. Some of the final finishing work was completed over the next week but did not pose any real problems.

The two duplex units were mirror images and were two bedroom, one bath with a living room, dinning area and a modest but sufficient kitchen. Lots of windows and a nice fireplace and hearth and a good amount of closet space and of course were brand new. Probably just a bit less than a thousand square feet. A couple of features that we wouldn't have chosen were the use of barn wood as wall material in the living space and the orange shag carpeting and orange Formica counter tops. But this was 1971! All in all it would prove to be more than satisfactory as the rent was very fair and we would call it home for the entire Aspen stay.

The duplex had a feature that was going to work out very good for us in that the large basement area under our side had three individual store rooms, a laundry area, and a large utility room. Both tenants would have a store room with Ruth using the third one and I would also be able to store some items in the utility room and later set up my welding table in the laundry room.

The move in accomplished we returned the rental truck to the Glenwood Springs drop off location and then started on the relocation list. Ruth had signed us up for a Post Office box and P.O.Box 1458 would be our mailing address for some time until the Post Office forced most Aspenites into home delivery. That was a change that didn't set well with many, including myself, as the daily trip to check for mail was a fun small town experience. The next step was to apply for drivers licenses, car registration and the most important, a library card. We got the billing for utilities done, the telephone hooked up, and a fishing license for me.

Janet was already a few days late for the start of school but the elementary school was just a couple of blocks away and Jeanne got her enrolled and met her teachers. For her first few years she could walk to school. It was all smiles as things were falling into place just right. We felt at home within the first few days. The public school system was very good and Janet would graduate from Aspen Valley High School in 1982. We found no faults to her education.

Jeanne had no trouble securing a job at Aspen Valley Hospital. It was in what was referred to as the Old Hospital as plans were well along for the New Hospital which would be built and open in just a few years. It was in the old hospital where Dr. Gould had sewn up my nose to eye laceration in 1962. One of the nice aspects of a resort town hospital is that many of the patients are there due to accidents and not from illness. Many interesting and fun people are cared for and many stories can be told.

I started looking for a place to open my studio-gallery. The prime locations in town were much too expensive. I found a lower level spot in Dr. Crandall's office building and set up shop. Between the location and fact that few locals or visitors bought much art in Aspen at that time Mostly Art only lasted six months. I did rent a small corner display shelf at Hopkins and Mill next to the Golden Horn restaurant entrance. It resulted in many more sales than the studio gallery at a fraction of the cost and required none of my time.

The Aspen Ski Company had a very good thirty day ski pass which gave a substantial discount and any unused days could be used the next year. Jeanne was given a free ski pass from the hospital and Janet could ski free. We couldn't beat that. As I was in my studio six days a week for this first season, my skiing was limited to Sundays. On especially good powder skiing days I would place a gone skiing sign on my door and take a few hours off. I tried to make up for this lack in ski day numbers in later seasons but due the ever increasing lift ticket prices and limitations on discounts to locals our ski days started to decline as the years went by.

Before we left California John Bush said that one of his friends, Dick Brennan, was spending the winter in Aspen that season and I should definitely make contact with him, that he was a fun guy and a good skier. Contact was made and we, not just me, became very good friends for the rest of his life as he has just passed away few months ago at ninety-two. There will much more Dick Brennan in later chapters.

We had arrived just in time to participate in a Ruth Whyte organized Labor Day picnic. Jeanne and Janet had their first real meetings with many of the people I met through Ruth on my 1962 stay, several of which had children in Janet's age group. A note here about Ruth, she loved to entertain and to take pictures of the goings on. She would always have multiple prints made and everyone in attendance would get photos that they were in. I almost stop taking pictures myself as our albums were well stocked with memorable photos by Ruth.

I find myself having difficulty in how to describe to you this period of my (our) life as so many things happened and so many people were met, several of which had a major roll in what was to come. I suppose a somewhat sequential introduction will be as good as any so I will start with our new neighbors in 119 N. Second Street, the other half of the duplex. Jim and Barbara Wentzel and their two young children. They had moved to Aspen from Ohio and Jim worked for Aspen Highlands. He wanted to hunt and fish, and the rest of the family came along. He asked if I would like to go out on the first day of deer season with him and I jumped at the chance of trying something totally new. We had to put together some blaze orange tape on my cap and jacket to be legal and we set off for Independence Pass. Just on the east side as the sun came up we spotted a couple of bucks high up on the ridge to the south of the highway. A proper stalk ensued and Jim made his shot and I was totally hooked on hunting big game. Another great benefit with hunting with Jim was that he did not like game meat. Our freezer was immediately stocked as it was through our entire stay in Aspen when I started hunting.

Next up was meeting Inez and Chuck Zordel. I am not sure how this happened, but it was through Jeanne. (Please understand that Jeanne meets people like honey attracts bees. I was, and still am, often referred to as Jeanne's husband.) Now Inez and Chuck were old time Aspenites, Inez was a Smith and if you looked in the County phone book back then you could count about twenty-four Smiths and Zordels, each being mostly brothers and sisters. Inez was between a surrogate mother and older sister to Jeanne and they would often have coffee and cookies to chat about whatever women chat about. Inez taught Jeanne how to make pie crust to die for and when the Paonia cherries came to town I won't tell how good the cherry pies that came out of her kitchen tasted. Inez had a butcher shed and when hunting season was in full swing the shed was never empty. She taught us how to hang, butcher and package game meat and we never had any that wasn't delicious. They sold their home as the boom got going, she moved up to Alaska to join her daughter and Chuck went his own way. There's more but that will be in another chapter and a later time. She recently had her 92nd birthday.

Directly across Second Street, if you walked off our porch and went straight across, you will go between Nick and

Maggie DeWolf's back porch and the carriage house. The DeWolfs arrived shortly after we did. Maggie and the five youngest children, Nicole, Quentin, Vanessa, Thalia, and Ivan, along with two huge moving vans (the really big ones) and there was chaos in spades. Jeanne of course met Maggie, et al and was informed that Nick would be coming in a few days as he and Alexander were driving a smaller truck with all of Nicks special stuff. Now Maggie and the kids were of average height and sported dark to black hair and seemed to be most normal in appearance and demeanor. When the day arrived and I had returned from whatever I was doing Jeanne said, "Nick just arrived and what do think he looks like?" I answered as you might expect and Jeanne said, "You won't believe it." It was then I met the six foot five inch lanky man with flowing red hair past his shoulders and a mustache to match. His blue eyes were just a little bit wild and he seemed to vibrate with energy. Nick would become a most interesting neighbor, a friend, an employer of sorts, and a very important person in my future. The whole family would be entertaining in the best sense of the word. I will devote the entire next chapter to Nick and my involvement in a small part of his life as with his major involvement in mine.

  Another person I would meet in our first year or so in Aspen that was important to me in a very personal way was Judge William Shaw. Naturally it was through Jeanne being at the Hospital when Judge Shaw arrived for a brief stay. She immediately recognized that he would be a person I would enjoy knowing and asked him if he would like me to come visit him when he was back home. He and Dorothy Koch Shaw lived on Lake Street just a few blocks away. They were both born in Aspen and I believe he told me it was in 1894, exactly 9 months after the 1893 demonetizing of silver which over night destroyed Aspen's economy. With a wry smile he told me their parents suddenly had nothing else to do. They had both gone to college, the Judge to University of Colorado where he received a law degree and Dorothy to Colorado College and then on to Columbia where she earned a Masters degree in Chemistry. They married in 1921 and he was elected Pitkin County Judge and served as such until 1969. Dorothy ran her father's lumber company until it closed in 1950. They had no children.

On my first visit I knocked on the door and Dorothy answered in a not unfriendly way but somewhat indifferent. I told her that Jeanne had taken care of the Judge at the hospital and had told him I might stop by and she promptly led to the sun room where his bed was located. I think her words were, "there is someone to see you," and she left the room. I like to think over the next two years we became friends. He was bedridden for the most part and on oxygen, which he would set aside when he snuck out a cigarette from their hidden place and lit up. He never asked me to bring him any but he must have had a source.

He was a living history book of Aspen lore and when he found out I was investing in silver we had something to talk about that he never tired of. I would visit once every week or two, for an hour, sometimes longer, or until he got tired. My relationship with Dorothy was much more restrained but I think she always was glad to see me come for a visit. We talked politics, both local and national, philosophy, silver mining, finance, stock markets, and any subject that would come up. His knowledge was broad and he always had a pertinent quote which he would credit, Macbeth, Plato, Adam Smith, etc. Another thing that made our conversations so enjoyable is that he would never interrupt, would let you finish your thought and even when wrong he would wait to comment. I am sure that his many years as a judge would have developed this trait.

Many in Aspen thought the Shaw's aloof and somewhat cold. This was probably mostly a reflection of Dorothy but I think what they did not know that even though the Shaw's owned a number of houses, several along Lake Street overlooking Hallam Lake, they were real estate poor. Dorothy was in charge according to the Judge. During the period he was acting as Walter Paepcke's attorney, when Paepcke was buying up as many properties as he could to build his dream for Aspen, he couldn't buy or own any of the real estate in that it would be a conflict of interest. A slight stretch as many choice parcels were acquired in Dorothy's name. He had several commercial properties in his name but it was my impression that Dorothy did all the accounting. They were renting the houses way below market rates, just barely paying the taxes and overhead. They were both greatly influenced by the early economic conditions in Aspen and by the Great Depression. Dorothy by this time was showing signs of dementia and one time when I was asked to go upstairs to get something for the Judge I saw numerous envelops with cash and checks sticking out that were submerged in miscellaneous papers covering her desk. A visit to the basement one time with Dorothy revealed almost every thing they had bought that broke or was no longer of use ended up there. At least ten upright vacuum cleaners stood like soldiers on one wall shelf.

On October 21, 1974 I received a telephone call from someone saying that the Judge had just died and could I go over to the house to see if I could do anything for Dorothy. I was there in a couple of minutes and Dorothy answered the door. I gave her a little hug and she took me into the sun room where Judge Shaw lay on the floor. He seemed at peace and was stretched out and didn't look like he had been uncomfortable at the end. I asked her if she wanted me to try to get him back onto his bed but she said, "No, help would be there in a few minutes." It was and everyone that came seemed to know what they were doing so I left the house for the last time. I was asked to be a pallbearer which I of course accepted with honor. In my eyes he was a truly great man and I had the privilege of knowing him. Dorothy passed away not long afterwards.

Ernst and Wilma Martens were another couple Jeanne and I had the good fortune of becoming friends with. Our first contact must have been at the Epicure bakery and restaurant they owned and ran on the corner of Mill and Main, diagonally across from the Hotel Jerome. Their history was a whole book in its own. They were in Germany or Holland during World War II and in some very serious situations they did not like to talk about. I think they came to Aspen by some connection to Jim Smith, a combat officer who was a pilot in the Pacific theater, as early employees on his North Star Ranch. I am not sure about that but I do know that later they ran the base restaurant at the newly opened Aspen Highlands Ski area in the late 1950's. They then started the Epicure and later bought the building where they ran their bakery and restaurant up until the building became much more valuable than the business. It was time to retire so they had their dream home built on Red Mountain and did that.

  These were two people that were in the right place, at the right time, and had the right stuff to be a true success story. The right stuff in this case was the ability to bake and cook, the grit to work extremely hard at what they did and to be genuinely good people. A nicer couple I can't imagine. We really didn't know them on a personal basis until after they retired but then shared a number of dinners at each other homes. I don't think I have ever met another couple that were as happy in their relationship with each other. You would catch Ernst glancing at Wilma when she was occupied, as in prepping something in the kitchen, and his face would light up with a smile. If Wilma caught one of these looks she would almost blush and would try, unsuccessfully, to hide a grin. I never heard even a hint of annoyance or displeasure in their speech or saw any in their body language.

  The Martens both passed away many years ago, Wilma first and Ernst soon after. Having no children they left the bulk of their assets in the Ernst and Wilma Martens Foundation and gave very nice sums to the Aspen Music Festival and a few other Aspen organizations of merit. Truly fine human beings

  Jay and Carolyn Diffenbaugh are two that became very close friends, and sadly Carolyn passed away a couple of years ago. They were best of friends, and of course Jay still is one. Jay's college was Dartmouth and Carolyn's was Bennington but we still could be friends. When we met Jay was in the process of selling his construction business, J. D. Diffenbaugh, Inc. in Riverside, California (It is still in business with that name and highly successful.) and they owned a condominium along the Roaring Fork just before the bridge on the east side of town. Carolyn and Jeanne met at an Art auction in the park down the hill from Main Street and off of Mill. We met for cocktails and conversation and our paths have crossed ever since. When Jay retired they bought a house out by Red Butte. Carolyn was an accomplished sculptor. Jay and Carolyn were most interesting people as I hope they found us.

We had many dinners together and visits over the years. Carolyn made a big step in my sculpture career which I will describe in a later chapter. We left Aspen many years before they moved to their new home in Tubac, Arizona. We were going between places at the time they were packing up for this move and stopped by to see if we could help out a little. Five days later after long hours and hard work by the four of us they were ready for the movers which were scheduled to arrive the next day. I would guess there are, as they were on our last visit to Tubac, many boxes still full and unopened in the garage. I don't know how their two children, now well beyond middle age, are going to handle the last move. Maybe the grandchildren will be in charge. The memories of a long and exciting life fill their house with art and mementos from all over the world.

I can't leave the Diffenbaugh's just yet. After Carolyn's passing Jay wrote a very short announcement of her death and although I don't have the one sent to us, it's eloquence I will try to paraphrase and expand on slightly.

> Jay and Carolyn were having their before dinner cocktails. (*He a gin martini and she a scotch on the rocks. If it had been a week day they would have been watching the Nightly Business Report on TV. Carolyn would finish her drink while fixing dinner.*) At dinner Carolyn tells Jay she wasn't feeling well and wanted to lie down. They retired to their bedroom and lay down together. Carolyn looked at Jay and said, "I am going to leave you now." closed her eyes and did.

After the many years of friendship and the many wonderful evenings Jeanne and I spent with them I can visualize everything just described. We miss you Carolyn and as this is being written plans are made to see Jay in a couple of weeks.

There are many more friends and acquaintances from our Aspen stay but I think these were those we met in the first couple of years and the ones that most affected our journey. Our family of friends in California were equally good and in several cases much closer in the sense of generation and background. In Aspen there was this melting pot of the old timers and the new comers with a great range of life experiences. How lucky we were to arrive there in 1971. I will elaborate on this later.

CHAPTER 15

I intend to devote this chapter to Nick DeWolf. It is not as if there isn't enough already written about him as if you do a web search you will find several of pages of links to his history and photography. This is much more about the things we did as the years went by between 1971 and 1986. I have already described our first meeting so I will start on my first visit to his part of the house across the street.

Nick and Maggie had six children, usually three dogs, numerous cats in the house and one or two full time helpers wandering about taking care of that which needed taking care of. I always entered via the back porch, generally with a knock and then opening the door and walking in announcing my presence. After entering the porch the large kitchen was to the right and the living room straight ahead. The front door and entry was opposite and faced Bleeker Street. From the kitchen was a large dinning room that ran at right angles and at the other end was the entry to Nick's part of the house, several rooms that contained his stuff. If it had anything to do with electronics or photography it was in there and I mean anything you could think of.

First I need to describe his work schedule as it varied, as his whole life did, from the norm. He would rise around nine to ten each morning and Maggie would set a very unhealthy breakfast of bacon, eggs and toast with a big mug of coffee to which he would add three or four teaspoons of sugar. The coffee with sugar would be repeated throughout the day although Cokes would also be consumed in large quantities. He would hold council in the afternoon if various people of interest showed up and then he would retire to his place coming out for dinner with the family around six. It was then back to work until two or three the next morning. I think on weekends and holidays this scheduled varied, or if something of interest was happening that he wanted to attend. He definitely wasn't retired.

The first of his projects I was exposed to was his dual projector slide show. His idea that with the Kodak Carousel projectors he would load the carousels with 144 of his slides and project them with fade in fade out, focus in and out, frenzel effect, and normal changing all of them being coordinated by a programmable electronic card of his design. In other words he could orchestrate a rather remarkable slide show planning to either sell or rent it to locations such as waiting rooms, bars and restaurants, airport lobbies, etc. On a periodic schedule he could change the shows by substituting carousels and the program card. It certainly seemed like a good idea. Nick asked if I thought I could take apart the projectors enough to remove the control circuit card and make several modifications to it, removing one part and adding one or two others. This was something I could do and was my start with him.

Nick had worked with photography for years and after he retired from Teradyne (The company he and an MIT classmate started and built into very successful automatic testing equipment business.) he traveled for a couple of years taking thousands of photos. Nick used Nikon cameras modified with large capacity film holders which would allow for hundreds of exposure before needing to reload. He now had a problem with these large rolls of film of how could he find the exposure he wanted and reproduce it quickly. He had by this time been experimenting with the new things called personal computers and generated a program to find a desired exposure on any roll of film. He had a list of the exposures he wanted for his slide show and built a device that when he entered the code for a particular exposure it would quickly run to it, stop with a puff of compressed air to eliminate any dust, adjust filters and with another Nikon automatically make a copy, or copies if he wanted more than one. While this was going on he could be entering the next choice. It was fun to watch.

At about the same time he was working on his slide show project he found a company in Denver, Digital Group, that had developed a personal computer in kit form for hobbyist and small companies that he approved of. This was just around the time that Wozniak and Jobs were readying the Apple II for market. Nick started first buying one and putting it together himself. Installing the parts and soldering, then power it up and connecting it with a monitor and keyboard. He must of liked it as he started ordering a number of boards and the accessories to make complete systems. I then started to do a lot of the assembly work for him.

One thing you should know was that Nick really was a genius when it came to electronics. He could look at a complex circuit drawing, or just the physical board, and understand how it worked. And then he would see a place where he could make it work better, run faster, use less power, eliminate a part or several parts, and tune it up. He could read the music and play the piano. If I practiced I could play chop sticks, maybe. He could also write the music. No one could do it better.

Then came the Aspen Dancing Fountain. Travis Fulton was a local sculptor who had the idea for the fountain and at one of those sessions I mentioned that Nick would have with persons of interest brought forth the idea a fountain placed under the storm grate at Hyman and Mill, in the heart of downtown. I am only guessing at this but I think Travis would have described the jets of water coming up maybe twelve feet and changing heights, cycling and that when not running would not affect auto or truck traffic on Mill. (Hyman was a pedestrian mall by this time.) I imagine at this point Travis would have to have jumped aside as Nick would have leapt from his chair with one idea after another coming forth. I won't say that Nick ran right over him but the fountain was going to be built and it would turn out fantastic. It did and just had it's thirtieth birthday a few years back.

Nick and Travis actually made a good team. Travis had the mechanical spatial sense to layout the plumbing and Nick took over the controls. Their research had shown that a large

MY STORY ~ 91

percentage of fountains failed due to valves, so valves were excluded. Another failure were the pumps, so big industrial sump pumps were used. To get the desired heights they would use speed controllers selected to match the pumps. As I remember the design would use twelve pumps with a pair of nozzles for each resulting in twenty-four jets. Various pumps and controllers were purchased and tests were done in the DeWolf's backyard. I got to witness these on occasion and be part of the joys of experimenting. Think little boys playing in the water. When the right combination was found the orders were placed. I don't know if Nick was reimbursed as he funded the project to this point. My involvement was to make the modifications to the controllers such that a Digital Group computer could control the pump speeds, build a steel rack for the twelve controllers that could be mounted high up on the wall in a storage building which was part of Wagner Park, and a rack for the computer. I then mounted the controllers and helped run the power cables to the pumps down a 100 feet of storm drain. I did the electrical connecting at the controller end but they had a electrician do it at the pump end. Travis took care of all the plumbing which was PVC pipe and bronze nozzles. The grates were modified slightly to provide clearance for the jets. By the time the installation was finished, or long before, Nick had written the program for the "Dance." It was magnificent and a special little DeWolf trick was that it would never repeat a sequence. Nick put out a challenge to anyone to find a sequence. He never had a response. The fountain started up in summer 1979. Check it out on the web.

    From the Digital Group computers the germ for a Nick DeWolf computer sprang to life around this time. He approached a small power conditioner company, Oneac Corporation, in Wheeling, Illinois run by Chuck Pearson, an ex-Teradyne executive, and his partner to build the ON! Systems Computer. You can look it up on the web. (the ON! Systems Computer 1986) One of the photographs you will show you Nick seated holding up something electronic looking.That is the ON! Computer. My part was doing the internal layout and packaging design, parts and component purchasing, working on the metal case design with the fabricator, and seeing that all the drawings and parts list were accomplished. As Nick told me at the start he just wanted somebody at Oneac that he knew would get the thing built. The actual fabrication was done either in house or contracted out. I started work on the project in 1984 in Aspen and finished in 1986 in Illinois. (Our leaving Aspen and move to Illinois will be covered in a later Chapter.) The fancy marketing was done shortly after I left Oneac. I did receive a ON!System Computer in partial trade for an eagle sculpture of mine, which hopefully is still in the lobby. I used the computer for word processing and data base for over four years until I got tired of replacing the monitors. The computer was always on, remember.

It was by far the best office computer of its time. Apple Mac was up and the IBM PC was out but they did not perform as fast or have the attribute of always on, instant boot-up, no fan, complete power conditioning and a power failure protection for your data. Unfortunately, the speed of technical change left us older guys in the dust.

The speed of change. In 1965 Moore's Law became the popular phrase. It stated that because of advance in the new chips that computer power would double every two years. He was close early on but then it accelerated to every year and then got too fast to think about. I will go back to the little design I was building in 1969. I was using a few transistors that were in T05 cans, about the size of a giant pencil eraser with three leads sticking out the bottom, resistors about the size of quarter inch piece of thick pencil lead and diodes just a little smaller. To make any kind of simple electronic circuit would take a circuit board about the size of a three by five postcard. Using these large components to build something like today's I-Phone you would need a very large building, big fans and air conditioning and an enormous amount of power. Chances are you couldn't even do it. You could never afford to do it.

When the ON! Computer was first designed data storage and additional programs were stored on a five and quarter inch floppy disk. Nick had skillfully set up the word processor

MY STORY ~ 93

and data base programs to be loaded in the read only memory. This made opening them extremely fast. I forget the amount of memory it had but the memory chips we started with were 32K and within a year the 64K were available and at the same price. It was soon apparent that the floppy disks were on their way out. Then came the start of the internet and a phone connection, then you could send data over the phone line, then you could drive a printer from anywhere and then the fax machines started to disappear. Technology was making your efforts obsolete before you could get them to market.

    This brings up the question if this speed of change is good for society. You look around today and can see that it has brought a marked improvement in living standards, at least for most. I don't deny that in the least. But like an old man I go back to my childhood and think of racing home to get to listen to the radio for an hour with the Lone Ranger and Gene Autry, even The Shadow, 15 minutes each. After dinner if we got to stay up later Fibber McGee and Molly, all of us waiting for the closet door to be opened. About the time I was twelve it was over to the furniture store to stand around with others to see that new fangled thing called television. You could just see through the snow a man seated behind a desk talking. At age fifteen my parents bought our first TV and we watched the evening news and then George Goble, or Red Skeleton, and on Sundays the Ed Sullivan Show.

    Changes started coming as our generation searched for independence. Instead of listening and dancing to our parents music we started to search for music and entertainment that we liked and soon TV started to provide more programs young people would watch. Advertisers caught on and advertised accordingly. Then advertisers realized that some programs didn't have the same audience as others and their money started to go toward the average. TV realized that to gain larger audiences, they must provide the average and titillate the senses.

    Now comes the internet and the I-Pad and we are just about to the point were who needs television. It will still be a while but it is coming.

What has this done to society. Look at our young people, staring down at their I-Phone, texting their friend who is next to them. Sometimes I think if you take them to the south rim of the Grand Canyon they would search on line and look at a picture instead of the real thing. What have we done to our children plopping them down for hours of watching children programs and then watching the news and adult programming afterward? Does the young mind really develop in this environment?

The excitement of technological progress is so over whelming one can't really fight it. Man on the moon. How could you not be amazed? That little, inexpensive GPS loaded with maps giving you visual and audio directions. I can barely get to the golf course without it. Can I still read and follow a paper map? Can I write this story with out my laptop and spell check? Would I survive a flat tire if my car didn't tell me the tire pressure is low? Even my clock radio that tells me what day it is changes the time when daylight savings come and goes. It is not a question of this progress being a bad thing, but whether it has happened too fast. Would we as a society be better off if we didn't know about and see every tragedy as it happens every where on earth? Would our children be better off if they knew how to add, subtract, multiply and divide instead of using a calculator? And it appears that soon they won't know how to write cursive.

I can't say that it is all bad. How can I as I have had such a good time on this journey, but I suspect that there are a great number of people that have been left behind by all this progress and I am afraid they are about to let us know about it.

Now I don't want to leave you with the impression that Nick DeWolf was invincible. I will mention only most briefly, my apologies the all the DeWolfs, Blue Cactus Mining. A friend and past employee of Nick's brought a story of mystery gold in Nevada sands that they must investigate. They ran into two professionals in Las Vegas, an old prospector and an assayer. Proof was found of micro amounts of gold in vast regions of Nevada sands. From the assay Nick thought that if they could figure out a way to leach it out they could make a fortune. I think they put some money up for the prospector's claims and the assay and headed back to Aspen to plan. I made a small 3-D topographical display of how the mine would look for a talking demo if they decided to try to raise money from investors. All then went quiet and some time later I spotted a letter in the Wall Street Journal about Mystery Gold and not to be swindled by some Las Vegas fast talkers. It was signed Nicholas DeWolf.

Nick DeWolf died on April 16, 2006 from prostrate cancer and a stroke.

R.I.P. Nick.

CHAPTER 16

Aspen in the fall of 1971 was a perfect time for us. The colors came on strong, the weather was gorgeous, and our spirits were high. Janet liked her school, Jeanne was adjusting to her job at the hospital and I had set up my studio-gallery. The duplex unit was proving to be very comfortable for us. We had started to set up a routine that was a comfortable mix of work, school, and social contact. Life was good.

We had come to Aspen with a modest amount of cash in hand, mostly the equity from our house sale, some savings and a few stocks. It was our plan to stay in Aspen as long as we could break even. Not an overly ambitious plan, but I was thirty-six and Jeanne thirty-three, and we were still not exactly sure what our path should be. The thirteen years we spent in Aspen was going to turn out to be quite an adventure and I will try to let you share in a good part of it in the next few chapters.

As winter approaches and the ski season is near the pulse of the town starts to beat faster. The days between the hoped for start on Thanksgivings Day until the second Sunday of April is when the town makes it's money. (As years went by the summer season became more and more economically important but at this time winter was the big earner.) The nice thing about 1971 was that the people who through investment and hard work were now seeing these efforts starting to pay off. The Goodnough's Snowflake Lodge now had many repeat customers and could rightfully expect a profitable season. They had earned it and also their lodge was now starting to have real value as a property. Numerous other business people in town were also experiencing this same earned good fortune.

My experiment with the studio-gallery wasn't working out as planned as I barely made the rent, certainly no profit. A few sales would come later on but after six months it was time to take a different tack. After closing the studio-gallery my routine would change a bit now and then but would be about as follows for a number of years. After making the acquaintance of Mike Strang, a gentleman rancher and owner of the local stock brokerage (eventual becoming a Bosworth Sullivan affiliate) I would after breakfast walk up town to his office and check out the opening at 7:30 am MST, kibitz with a few other locals, read the WSJ and then be home to start working by nine. At noon Jeanne would often be able to join up for a quick lunch, she then returning to the hospital and I would repeat my round trip and then work until about five. This was the weekday schedule. Weekends would vary but Sunday was a particular nice time in that Jeanne usually had Sundays off. Ruth had a reserve at Carl's Drug Store for the Denver Post and the Rocky Mountain News and made a deal with us if we would pick up the papers we could read them first and then bring up them to her place. That we did over a family breakfast, usually waffles with the trimmings.

We started to meet more and more of the locals, Jeanne through the hospital staff and including a surprising number of the patients. The parents of Janet's classmates and most of her teachers through her school. For me it was a combination of people in the stores and businesses which I dealt with in pursing my sculpture and keeping the cars running.

During our first winter season we got both Jeanne and Janet started on skis. They learned surprisingly fast, especially Janet. Within a few days on skis she could pretty much ski all the runs except the expert. Jeanne was comfortable on the beginner runs and could ski the intermediate ones with caution. By the end of the first season they were both skiers. It should be noted that Aspen Mountain is for the most part advanced ski terrain with a limited amount of intermediate on the top of the mountain. The lower half gets more difficult and is crowded at days end making the last run of the day even more difficult. Another factor is that the best skiers favor Aspen Mountain and riding up the lift and seeing really good skiers doing their thing at high speeds is intimidating to the less than expert. Eventually the Aspen Ski Corp had to limit the days season pass holders could ski because the visitors who were paying the much higher ticket prices were being scared away from or not having a good experience on the big mountain. Buttermilk, Snowmass, and Aspen Highlands all provided miles and miles of excellent intermediate and beginner terrain but all visitors wanted, and should have, at least one day on Aspen (Ajax) Mountain.

At sometime early in this first season I met up with Dick Brennan, John Bush's good friend. I don't remember if he came over for dinner or I met him to ski, although I think it was the former. Dick was taller than me, slender, had rugged features and I think I can say not handsome. His real good looks came from his good nature and humor. He was, however, a bleeding heart liberal as opposed to my much more reasonable Ayn Randian capitalistic conservatism. None the less our ski days were most Sundays each month and after the first one where we got used to each other were filled with heated discussions on the ride up and terrific runs on the way down. A full day of skiing was followed by dinner at the Myers's to which Dick's entrance greeting was always, "Oh Boy!, Oh Boy!" He became a close friend to both Jeanne and me. Dick was a little older, about twelve years, and a bachelor. Some time in his sixties he met the wonderful Carolyn, who became Carolyn Brennan, and he must have said or thought, "Oh Boy!, Oh Boy!" every day for the rest of his life. Dick and Carolyn will join us again later in the story. I will add here that Dick was a technical writer and editor. He would later write several books and one I especially like is Heisenberg Probably Slept Here which is a loose biography of the great physicist of the 20th century who shaped the view of our world. An entertaining read and by the way Heisenberg was famous for postulating the Uncertainty Principle. You can look up Richard P. Brennan Author on the web.

By the second Fall hunting season I had purchased a rifle from a younger man who was leaving Aspen for a life in the city and couldn't afford to keep his beloved Ithaca .270. It was a much better rifle than I was a shot. I went all in and bought his reloading equipment too. After several days on the rifle range some confidence was gained and I learned which position I could best shoot from. Jeanne's mother and father came out so her father could go hunting and we all could bond some more. He was a marksman. He could shoot any gun from any position and hit a target. He had hunted, mostly in Michigan, all his life. We had met the managers of Dr. Gould's cattle ranch, just east of Carbondale, and had been invited to hunt there on the BLM property they leased. Opening morning there were about six of us hunting and we scattered about over a fairly large area. I was one of the first to shoot and downed my first deer. (I apologized to the deer, which later I would always do to an animal in my sights. It didn't mean much to them but helped me just a little.)

  As it turned out as I had never field dressed an animal myself I spent a little time getting ready. I carried in my day pack two knives, a small specialty meat saw, paper towels, a cheese clothe to wrap the carcass, my deer tag, extra ammo, a couple of plastic bags, a bottle of water and some cookies. I then laid out the items I would need and was prepared. I positioned the deer to make the first cut. This took a little more planning and I ran the knife up and down tracing the approximate line I would use. Maybe a little more time and a few more practice strokes than necessary. Up walks Pop and says, "What the hell are you doing?" Before I could react he rolled up his sleeves, took my knife and within a few minutes had completely dressed my deer setting aside the liver and heart for safe keeping. I just stood there watching. That was the last time I didn't dress out my own animal.

  I shared with Jim Wentzel a great elk scouting and hunt on the back side of Aspen Mountain. We cooperated in the shots to bag a pretty big bull, dressed d him out and were fortunate to be able to drive my beat up Willys pick up right up to where he lay. The lesson learned was never, ever shoot an elk where you can't get a vehicle or horse close. Even quartered out, two men can hardly lift a quarter. I have carried a deer out on my back in two trips after being three miles from the road and that was doable.

A little more on hunting later but please note, even if you don't approve, our family while we were in Aspen ate almost exclusively game meat. The hunt is exciting, in beautiful country and often at early and late hours where most non-hunters never go or witness. As I write this there is increasing worry in the Wildlife Service that there aren't enough new hunters taking up the sport and that the game herds may become unmanageable. Mother Nature is not kind to animals when they overpopulate and animals like deer and elk can become pests and dangerous in auto traffic situations. Sport hunting is a much better thing than programmed thinning but I am afraid that will start happening more as the years go by.

Another ritual was on Thursday afternoon, at about four, the Aspen Times came out. This was a big event every week and those of us who participated would be outside the Aspen Times building as the first printings were placed on the counter. A rush of the first in line would enter the small area where there was a open container in which you dropped your fifty cents, pick up your copy, and hurry out to make room for those waiting. I would then walk back the few blocks to the duplex and start the thorough reading. Those who were looking for something specific like the jobs classified would be on that page in seconds after making it outside. Jeanne and I followed this routine for most all of our stay in Aspen.

The Aspen Times always had a good variety of local and regional news stories. Mary Eshbaugh Hayes's "Around Town" column on local people and happenings, lots of good and spirited letters to the editor, provocative editorials and Peggy Clifford's "Talk of the Times" column which always annoyed me by its content but was so well written that it was a must read.

She later wrote a book, To Aspen and Back, published in 1980. In it she describes her time in Aspen starting in 1953 until leaving in 1979. The main thread of her story is philosophical and it describes in good detail how a number of younger adults with what can be described as full of youthful good intentions to save Aspen gained control of the local government and made changes to try to achieve that end. She was as one with them and represented them in the press through her column. The pedestrian malls, bike paths, berms hiding anything thought to be unsightly, signs to guide your path and behavior, a bus system to reduce auto traffic, stalling attempts to four lane the "killer" Highway 82, zoning regulations and building codes. This part of her story ends in admitting that it didn't work as planned and in fact made some of the very things they wanted to prevent happen, some even in a worse way than anticipated. It's not that the intentions did not have some merit, it was that age old axiom of unintended consequences keep popping up.

For those of us that thought Aspen was just fine, or even perfect, in 1971 the idea that it must be changed to save itself was hard to take. I am probably being unfair, but the common joke now is that the millionaires came to town and pushed out all the locals and now the billionaires are coming and pushing out all the millionaires. The little duplex on Second and Bleeker is now gone replaced by a mini-mansion, Ruth's house is gone and another mini is there. The lots Ruth bought between her house and the one at Third and Bleeker to protect her view of Shadow Mountain being blocked has the big house she feared. The blue spruce sampling that Janet brought home from second grade and we carefully planted next to the alley, just outside our dinning room window, which grew to an impressive height is no longer there. "It is not true that you can never go back, it's just that you can only stay two weeks."

As a footnote to the above, I went to my bookcase and took out To Aspen and Back and browsed through it since thirty years had passed since I last read it. She still annoys me in her take on almost any subject but it is still so well written you almost believe she was right in her interpretations of events. She ties in much of the national politics of the time and is consistent in her liberal bias. I noted two surprises, one that she questioned the Aspen Mall plans and second that after the first election of some of the young guns she dropped out of support for the second election that really put them in charge of the political game.

At the end of the book she writes, "When people of a certain type arrived ……...and said, "Oh my God, this is it. I am home at last."………This should have been enough, but it wasn't………We began to think more of the idea of Aspen than the fact of Aspen.....The idea overshadowed the reality." The story she tells of the transformation of political control in Aspen from the greedy, money grubbing, mean spirited Old Guard to the New Guard by a lot of truly mean and dishonest rhetoric was the means justifies the ends philosophy so typical in the effete intellectual snobs that we seem to always have around us. Clifford eventually saw what was happening and in 1979 left to go to Philadelphia to finish her book. As far as I can tell she then moved to Santa Monica, California to continue her journalism career and apparently is still writing. She certainly can write.

I want you to understand that by the time we moved to Aspen I had become a big fan of Ayn Rand, read all her books and signed up for her Objectivist Newsletter. I was still a bit humbled by my lay off, not totally sure of my sculpture abilities, and just a little naïve. When we arrived we thought this is it, don't change anything. Change it did, but slowly and all government enforced changes were slow to really take affect. Most of the increase in the cost of living in Aspen was positive for the old timers who owned property and was also national, but not as extreme, phenomenon. Their loss to the community as they sold out and moved away was noticed and one of the nicest experiences for us when we finally had to move on was all the friends we had that offered their regrets. I saw Tom Sardy, one of the true old timers, on the street and he told me goodbye and said , "All the good people are leaving."

CHAPTER 17

Our life was going along very nicely. The first few years the California group came to Aspen and we would have one of the couples stay with us and the rest would rent rooms in one of the lodges. It was always a great week of skiing and parties. As the years went by the distance became a factor and most of them decided Sun Valley was much closer and less expensive.
Halloween was big for the adults, mostly those without children, and just fun for the kids. It almost invariable was cold, and sometimes lots of snow, so the great costumes were usually covered by parkas. Trick-or-treating was still the same as most anywhere else.
Christmas is Christmas but in Aspen those who really wanted the true experience would go to the Forest Service designated tree cutting area with their permits in hand and seek out the perfect tree. Invariably the tree selected was, too tall and looked much better standing in the forest snow covered than it did when first stood up in the living room. Decorating of course solved all problems. Getting the tree posed other problems. On one occasion Nick DeWolf accompanied me in my second beat up 4-wheel drive, a Wagoneer, just after a good snow fall. The Forest Service had dutifully plowed the road but unfortunately they plowed such that the edge of the road on the steep downhill side was indistinguishable from about a foot of smoothly plowed snow. Pulling over to let an oncoming vehicle pass found my right side wheels over the edge and the Wagoneer precariously perched just short of rolling over. The rest of my day was waiting for a tow truck that was supposedly going to come up but never did. A good Samaritan whose jeep, signed Snowmas Coast

Guard, had double winches and its owner had what it took to set up a recovery plan. With cables both front and back, one guided by a pulley affixed to a tree and me in the car, we gently winched it back onto the road. Nick had his tree, a particular bedraggled one, and Jeanne, Janet, and I selected one from a lot in town as I think we did from then on.

Another great event was the Winterskol parade held towards the end of January each year. The various restaurants, bars, and businesses all have floats, as well schools, clubs and especially the Hospital. The Hospital float usually is centered around some sad patient in a hospital bed with legs and arms in casts elevated in a most uncomfortable position. Nurses, aides, and a doctor or two wander around with clipboards, giant syringes and bed pans while drinking beer of the appropriate color from urinal bottles. Jeanne did not usually participate but most were friends and we cheered them on. One year the very attractive Bunny Early, a nurse from New Jersey, was a particular favorite. (Jeanne fixed Bunny up for a date with John Bush and even though they hit it off with some good times it didn't take and John remains a bachelor.)

The next big holiday celebration was the Fourth of July. The Volunteer Fire Department, which was excellent, was the organizer. It was held with the fireworks at the end of Wagner Park nearest to Aspen Mountain and the crowds were positioned about half way back. Funding was mainly done by donation at the park as the fireman walked through the crowds passing their helmets. At dusk the first bombs were set off, God Bless America sung and the display started. Always a great happening until one year one of the rockets went into the crowd instead of were it was supposed go. From then on the fireworks were moved up on the mountain side, and since the crowds had grown to fill the entire park, it was just as well.

Memorial and Labor Day were the important bookend celebrations, mostly private picnics and parties, for the summer season. One Labor Day, maybe 1980, John Kuehlman talked me into joining him for his annual climb of Pyramid Peak, one of the 14,000 foot peaks in Colorado. This was a walk up climb, not the highly difficult rock climb on the face side. We were joined by another who I am pretty sure was Jon Seigle, later killed in a avalanche accident in 2006 while skiing in France. Understand a walk up means just what it implies. John walks up just as he would stairs in a high rise. Jon was a little more cautious as we got towards the top but still followed John with ease. I got very cautious as when using hands and looking back under my arms all I could see was a distant wall of rock and what looked to be a several thousand foot drop off directly under my feet. I took a break and told John I thought I should stop there. I was getting a little altitude sickness, which I had expected, and a bit of hypothermia, which I had not. John told me it was just a few hundred feet more to go, was much easier and with this encouragement I made it to the top. After some tang and a candy bar and putting on my down vest I recovered quickly. We signed the registry that was placed in a can tucked into the rock carrion and then enjoyed the view from on the top of our world. And what a view it is. What was interesting was that as we started down, I could see exactly where I was going and where I should step, all uneasiness left me and I walked down. Jon on the other hand reversed places with me and became overly cautious and extremely nervous until we had gotten back to a normal incline. I have climbed only one "fourteener" and it was this one and only once. (A little research on the web describes the route taken not quite as easy as I have just described. Maybe I had a right to be a little apprehensive as we neared the top and Jon had the same right on the way down. John Kuehlman was on his 13th climb and maybe was not as accurate in describing what we were about to do as he could have been.)

  We were now about to face our first major change. We had been in Aspen for about five years when one of Jeanne's fellow nurses was planning her up coming wedding and was worried about the cost of having a small reception party. Jeanne had been tiring of the nursing grind and the shift from the old Hospital to the new Hospital had gone very smoothly. The facility was much better but the romance was missing. After almost fifteen years in nursing Jeanne's pay was about what first year baggers were making at City Market. (This would all change in a few more years as the Florence Nightingale syndrome finally left the nursing profession.) Jeanne made the offer to cater the party at one half the best price she could find and the offer was accepted. Jeanne, with my help of course, was deemed a great success and very soon the next request to cater came. Jeanne gave notice to the Hospital, our catering business was underway and would provide a good portion of our income for the next five years. The last big push was over the Christmas Holidays and we did twelve functions over the fourteen days, concluding with a birthday dinner party for John Denver on New Years Eve and hors d'oeuvres for one hundred for Maggie DeWolf's New Years Day party.

There was one dinner I remember the best and that was the one where I meet Jill St.John. Yes, that Jill St.John! You should know that this was a few years after Tiffany Case hit the big screen with James Bond in Diamonds Are Forever and Tiffany, a.k.a. Jill St.John, had moved to Aspen in 1972. My description to my non-Aspen friends was that she would be dropping by my studio to talk art and have a glass of wine, etc, etc, but of course by this time I was working in the laundry room at the duplex and didn't have a bottle of wine and two glasses anywhere nearby. The dinner was at Elizabeth Paepcke's home and the guests were two 20th Century Fox executives, D.R.C. Brown and his wife Ruth, Mrs. Paepcke, the young mayor of Aspen Stacy Standley, and Jill St.John. (This was associated with the sale of Aspen Ski Corporation on December 16, 1977 but not necessarily that exact day.)

When Jeanne and I arrived we entered the kitchen and set up our meal preparations. I think it was rotisserie brazed tenderloins, wild rice stuffed tomatoes, started with a salad and followed by one of Jeanne's special desserts. The bar and drinks were in the dining room and served by someone there. I never entered the dining room and as dinner neared its end was busy washing the dishes in the large sink with my back to the dining room door. At Jeanne's request Mrs. Paepcke had brought Jill St.John into the kitchen to introduce us and I sensed something going on behind me, I turned, and there she was just a few feet away, approaching with hand extended. I want you to understand that she is just as remarkably beautiful in person as you have seen in the movies and I am turned with both hands still in the dishpan full of soapy water. There is no towel within sight, Jill St.John is getting closer, and more beautiful, with her hand still extended and I do the best I can do. I quickly wipe off my hand on my shirt and shake her hand. She shows no reaction to what must have been not the best handshake she ever experienced and we have a short glad to meet you and hope you enjoyed dinner conversation. Jeanne, to this day, says she didn't do this on purpose but maybe I had told the Jill St.John in my studio story a few times too many.

I don't want to gloss over the preceding Aspen years as they were very good ones other than we were just meeting our stated goal of breaking even financially. We were learning to live at the poverty level, discovering garage and yard sales, and even more important the Aspen Thrift Shop. We had found a number of ways to make some extra income, one of which is worth mentioning here. That was that at the end of the ski season used skis, boots, poles, and clothing were being sold at garage and yard sales at very low prices. In the fall the Ski Swap, which was an annual fund raiser, was becoming one of the Fall's big events. We bought in the Spring and sold in the Fall, Jeanne in charge of clothes and I did the equipment. By the second year we were classed in the commercial division and were able to make a few extra dollars each of the next few years. Competition for this niche became too strong to make it worthwhile for us so from then on we only shopped for our own needs. We did ski on some very good skis and were always dressed to match.

I had begun doing a number of jobs for Nick DeWolf and had a few quickies thrown at me by ones who knew someone who needs someone. By this I mean installing insulation in the new employee housing apartments that were under construction and cleaning soot off rock fireplaces in a large condominium complex. These were a paid on a per piece basis and I worked fast so for a few days I made really good money. I didn't pursue it as a vocation, however.

Several other big changes will happen before we make our fond farewell to Aspen but those will be covered in later chapters. Janet was progressing towards High School which when she becomes involved in athletics alters Jeanne's and my life considerably. Somewhere in here, I think the fall of 1976, I get drawn for a Big Horn Sheep hunting license. This is a big thing as very few permits are given and the Sheep herds are very carefully managed. The Fish and Game Department, with help from the Rocky Mountain Big Horn Society, does a lot of herd management including using medical antibiotics and trapping and transplanting, even trading with other states to advantage the health and welfare of the herds. It may seem some what at odds with hunting but this not only provides funding it also help dispersal within the herds.

I had helped Jim Wentzel scout and hunt the year before on his try for a Ram in the Tarryall's just west of the Continental Divide and he was obliged to help me in the area just east of Marble. Opening day found us wet and cold in the clouds with six inches of snow on the ground. August 26 for crying out loud. I then started to hunt alone, which is not a good idea but something I preferred. The area I picked had not been hunted before and the Game Department will give you no help other than say that they are in that 100 square mile area. I made about six overnight outings covering about ninety miles of hiking off trail. As it turned out I got my Ram not three miles from one of the back roads above Crystal and except for the very steep terrain where he was it was easy hiking.

The following year a friend got his license for the same area and knowing my position got his on opening day. A few years later John Thorpe, who co-managed Aspen Sports, got his license for the area directly behind Aspen Mountain and I accompanied on a scouting trip, one hunt, and helped him pack out his camp while he walked in front of me with his much better trophy than mine staring me in the face. A few days later during a dinner of perfectly cooked sheep at John's home, with another good friend that had helped him out, M.J. Elisha, John presented each of us a beautiful custom hunting knife.

I will only convey one story of my hunt. I was walking the ridge which runs due south of Mt. Spohris (if you go north you start to climb it) towards Capital Lake and Peak. As evening approached I was still on the ridge and not wanting to hike down to level ground at timberline I found a group of elk beds which they dig out on steep grassy slopes to give them a good place rest and sleep having good visibly in all directions except from above. I found a good sized bed and put up my two man tent mostly in it and spread out my down bag, had a little dinner and watched the sun go down. Crawling into my bag and just getting comfortable I started to hear a commotion going on in the trees below. It was definitely elk and I could only imagine that they were going to come up to bed. I was by now comfortable and warm and very tired, so I waited. I had my rifle and could fire off a shot if they got too close but all quieted down and I fell asleep. The next morning the commotion started up again so I slipped out of bed and watched as a cow elk came charging out the trees racing north with a sizable bull chasing after her. A loud bugle came from ahead of her and the chasing bull stopped. I had just watched an unhappy cow make it back to the bull she wanted to be with. Sounds some what familiar, doesn't it.

CHAPTER 18

We are several years into our Aspen adventure. Still breaking even financially although my investment in some silver bullion was starting to look promising. The 1974 recession had been felt in Aspen but since my sales of sculpture had just gone from slow to slower and the catering business was starting to give us some income we were able to enjoy our life with a little less economic stress. During this period Jeanne published the Coloring Book of Skiing with the drawings done by Dan Shook, who I think worked at the Hospital. It was distributed locally, in a few shops down valley, and one or two in Vail. She would check with the shops on a regular basis and re-supply as needed with invoice attached. Several printings were done but as sales slowed down it was shelved.

Another product she developed were Wine Sacks. We had often thought carrying your gift wine bottle bare, or in a paper bag, was not very sophisticated so she put together a few neatly sewn cloth bags with ribbon ties and was off on another project. I am not certain a claim can be made that the ones you now see in stores sprang from her original designs but it was fun and profitable for a few years. We did amass an extraordinary amount of cloth remnants and she made a lot of very nice bags.

There was another idea from our dining room table. Guests at one of our dinner parties, whom I cannot remember at all or the circumstance of their being there, was the reaction to Jeanne's and my idea that a game based on the Monopoly format (I bet we were playing Monopoly at the time.) with the buildings of Aspen, and other points of value, could be developed and prove popular. His, of the couple, eyes got that look and after a few minutes he asked if we had any plans to follow up and produce it. We said no and he then asked if he produced it would we mind and we said no again. A few months later The Aspen Game arrived, autographed with an inscription of thanks and hope you enjoy the game. Later a whole series of similar games showed up. There is even a Missoula-opoly on E-Bay along with other -olopys.

And then there was the Shampoo Shower. Jeanne and I were snuggled up in bed one weekday morning as Janet readied herself for school. At the time she had long, very pretty blonde hair and the fashion was to have it shampooed into golden lightness each morning. This morning she had her head in the kitchen sink making more than the usual grunts and groans along with the sounds of water splattering about. I thought there must be a better way and on my morning walk up town I stopped at Sardy's Hardware and picked up a faucet snap on coupler, both ends, a cheap shower head, a length of copper tubing, and 2 brass threaded fittings. At home some bending, a little soldering, connection of the shower head to the top end and the female coupler to the bottom, followed by a trip to the kitchen to replace the aerator on the sink faucet with the male coupling (also an aerator) and snapping them together and there was in place the Shampoo Shower. Turning on the faucets provided just the right shower at just the right height.

Janet's shampooing the next morning went perfectly and everyone thought me a genius. Janet, Jeanne, and of course me. I submitted a patent application, not expecting any success at it being granted but to show patent applied for protection and recorded my invention in a bound note book with proof of date and witnessed. A friend of the California family group, Dave Knudson, was at dinner one night and thought he might have a business contact that might be interested. I put together several units, both in plastic and in chrome plated copper and made a small suitcase display with a mounted faucet that allowed for demonstration of ease of use. Dave made the presentation and an agreement was hammered out. The business was a marketing firm that thought if they could get some small products in house that it would be more profitable than just marketing other peoples inventions. They were developing a first project at this time. It was a measuring device that placed on the top of a jar containing sugar or coffee, and the like, could with a very easy adjustment dispense precise measures such as a teaspoon or tablespoon. They were at the point where the working model pattern was ready to be sent to make the special molds necessary for production. The Shampoo Shower would be their next product. The breakdown was presented with me getting twenty-five percent of any profits with no risk. What a deal!

It was not a month later that when browsing through a Sunset magazine I spotted a full page color add for almost exactly the same type of measuring device, in function not design, and immediately knew that this was going to make my new business partners think twice before venturing into a next product. Unfortunately I was right so as I write these words there is a Shampoo Shower model in a box in the garage, almost 40 years old that still looks new. Besides, the idea of washing your hair every day long ago changed to doing it in the shower that is now taken almost as often.

We had been close but didn't have the right stuff to go it alone on any of these ideas. It takes a different mindset and different talents to get into the position to make a profitable venture from one's ideas and inventions. Most often is the combination of talents of another, or several others, to bring out a new product and successfully market it, and of course timing is everything. We didn't have quite the right stuff to pull it off alone and really didn't have the drive to approach others for help.

I have always liked the story of Apple. Steve Wozniak was a happy Silicon Valley nerd building small computers and programming them to do fun and interesting things. He had just designed a unique computer board that incorporated a new microprocessor and which would eventually be the basis for the Apple 1. Steve Jobs was on the scene when Wozniak was about to pass out his design to the Homebrew Computer Club members and he convinced Wozniak that they should make the boards and sell them instead. Which was what they did with good success. Before the dust had settled on this scheme they formed their company, Apple, and the design, building, and marketing of Apple 1 was under way. The rest is history. This is probably not totally accurate but you must see that the two needed each others talent to make it all happen. Steve Jobs would have found something to run with and Wozniak would have designed a number of things of merit, but it wouldn't have been Apple. Each of them were in precisely right place, at the right time, and with the right combined stuff.

In Walter Isaacsons's new book, The Innovators, he describes the two. "They made an odd but powerful partnership: Woz was an angelic naïf who looked like a panda, Jobs a demon-driven mesmerizer who looked like a whippet." I think most would concur with this and what a ride it has been for all of us to watch.

Two things are about to happen around this time. Jeanne had left the Hospital and we were fairly busy with catering. I think in order the first had to have been about 1978 and the second about 1981-1982. I will start with the first. Carolyn Diffenbaugh was preparing to teach a life sculpture class at the Anderson Ranch in Snowmas. Anderson Ranch was like a school for adults centered on the Arts and had a number of other programs through out the year. My welded steel wildlife sculptures were selling about as fast as I could make them, the problem was I couldn't make them fast enough to really make a decent living. The amount of welding I was doing was also starting to give me back problems and even though I felt I was starting to do some pretty good work I didn't see a good future using this process. Carolyn first tried the logical approach to convince me to take her course and then used the, "I need one more student," one. She was a very good friend and I really needed a break from what I was doing so I agreed and signed up.

I arrived on time at the classroom and there four women and another man and myself made up the class. Carolyn gave us a little talk on the class organization, we got our materials and tools, and were assigned a stand for our work. All was very positive and it is at that point that two things happened that changed my career as a sculptor. The first was one of those events that is important but fleeting, the other a part of the whole but which lasted for the rest of my career in sculpture.

    A very pretty young lady came into the room dressed in a bathrobe and Kelly was introduced to us. Carolyn spoke for a few minutes on the protocols of modeling, that the class would select a pose that we all liked and over the next two weeks we would try to finish and fire our clay sculptures. We would also do a number speed sculptures, which would have Kelly strike a pose and we were to quickly sculpt a small work. All well and good and Kelly was ask to position herself on the platform so we could get started. I have to be a little careful here but to say that she had the most beautiful body I have ever seen would not do her justice. Even Carolyn let out a little gasp of appreciation. The two weeks would fly by was my immediate thought. There are two points I will make here. First it was Kelly's first time as a model. She had a considerable amount of ballet training and although slightly uncomfortable at first turned out to be an excellent model, mainly because she was able to pose in exactly the same pose position and hold that position for each of the many 30 minute posing periods. Secondly from the sculptors point of view, believe this or not, when in the pose she became an inanimate object and all concentration was on the work at hand. As Kelly became more comfortable she would not always cover herself at each break and would sometimes stretch to relax. This was not inanimate. I had to turn away and pretend to continue sculpting or take a short walk. I of course did not comment on this or make any suggestions to Carolyn or the rest of the class.

    The other thing I discovered from the class was the joy of sculpting in clay. It was pleasant to the hands, very malleable, easy to make corrections, to remove and add. After years of working in the rigid metal of steel it was a dream media. I was quick to decide that this was the route I would now pursue and the finished product would be a bronze casting. A new world had presented itself and I was ready to take it on.

As I started to sculpt and cast a few pieces in bronze another event would occur that really sidetracked my sculpture career, but just for one year. Dixie Rhinehart and Al Gross had a small company named New Product Development People, NPDP, in Aspen and they had received a contract from Stern-Seeburg Corp to design and build a prototype pinball game with a contoured playfield, 3D pinball. Dixie had some craftsmanship skills but Al had little. I am not sure but I think Dixie had been talking to Nick DeWolf the morning he showed up and asked me if I might be interested in a job. Nick was a good enough friend to know both my skills and that things weren't too bright on our financial situation. (Silver had been great, past tense. You have to sell to make a profit.) I went with Dixie to meet Al and see their small facility. Sometimes you walk into a place and know immediately that it's the right place. I hired on.

Stern-Seeburg was looking for a way for their pinball division to compete in the arcade business with the new electronic games that were flooding the market. It turned out that Gary Stern, son of the original Stern and now president, had a condo in Vail and Dixie and Al had made a presentation of their idea for a 3D pinball game there. It was a go and by the time I had my visit to NPDP it was crowded with boxes of pinball hardware. My first day as an employee was to drive to Denver and pickup several hundred pounds of sheet plastic cut to size to form the play fields. Thus began a year of fun engineering and construction of Orbitor 1. (If you want to read about the history of Orbitor 1 on the Web search for Orbitor 1 pinball and look for the link to Flippers. Click on this and then scroll down to the history of Orbitor One and click on it.)

I won't spend much time on the construction of the proto type. The early design and construction was done by Dixie and me. Later another craftsman, John Kantana, joined us. Stern Seeburg accepted this first game and went into production and it was introduced at the 1982 Coin Operated Game Show in Chicago. Shortly there after Stern-Seeburg closed down their pinball operation and later declared bankruptcy. My job had lasted exactly one year. It was a very good year. It reminds me of that famous line in the movie Back to the Future where the good Doc Brown says to Marty, "You know what this means Marty, something I invented actually works!" It was not my invention but I think I played a major roll in its making and it was, and still is, a good pinball game and the only one ever made with a contoured play field. It also is now considered "vintage."

CHAPTER 19

We were now entering our last years in Aspen. Janet became very active in sports and was on the Volleyball and Basketball teams and was particularly good in the former. She played all positions and played all summer on both sand and grass, two man, three man, six man, and also coed. She was good enough to try for a college scholarship and we had tryouts at San Diego State, UCLA, Stanford, and Colorado State. She was always encouraged to try out as a walk on with some indication she could make the team but no scholarships. Later that summer a scout from Rice arranged for her to have a try out in Houston and after she was offered a full ride scholarship. For a number of reasons such as heat, humidity, and lack of housing available at that late date it was declined, and rightly so. Janet went to CSU and played lots of intramural volleyball; play til you drop, then have pizza and beer, and never practice. Fun! Fun! Fun!

I have gotten ahead of myself here so let me go back a bit. Jeanne had opened a small shop naming it Mostly Art, just off the main shopping center, but close enough. Business through the first winter was OK but not really profitable. She then found a much better location when she struck a deal with Stephen Kalen who's ski shop was not open for the summer months and she could rent it for a very reasonable amount. It also included use of all his store fixtures. This resulted in a very good first summer and a like one the following summer which would be our last one spent in Aspen. This would have been the summers of 1983 and 1984. She had a variety of crafts and woven goods, pottery, gift items and a little sculpture and small paintings, all from locals and all on consignment. If the rent hadn't been five to eight times as much in the winter months it would have been a profitable business year round. We might have been able to have stayed in Aspen longer but the time had come.

    A little more detail of this period of our life at this time is necessary. Janet's sports required much of our attention. Attending games twice a week for almost four years became our main social activity. Aspen's away games were always a long distance away, from the closest at about twenty-five miles to Steamboat Springs and Rangely at around one hundred miles. One other father and I went to every game, sometimes the only Aspen fans in attendance. Another father who had children in school playing sports over a nine year period told me as his daughter played her last basketball game that he would never, ever attend another high school game. A confession I have to make was that I was a coach's and referee's worst nightmare. Before every game I solemnly swore I would not yell or criticize any call or decision and at every game I failed. I am still embarrassed about acting that way. One of the fathers having two daughters playing who was a retired NFL player was as calm as could be and never showed any concern on what happened on the court. There was one Dad who was banished to sit alone and occasionally I was asked to go join him. Surprisingly I was President of the Booster Club Janet's senior year.

    The winters were getting longer and the beautiful summers seemed to be getting shorter. Janet had left for college and our social life seemed to have left with her. The lack of any ski ticket discounts and the steep increase in prices made skiing almost unaffordable. My entry into bronze sculpture was slow and very expensive. It was becoming apparent that our goal to break even was slipping away. Then Nick DeWolf sauntered across the street and made the offer to me to work full time on his latest venture, what would become the On!Computer. In Wheeling, Illinois. Wheeling, didn't he know where that was? Aspen, Colorado to Wheeling, Illinois! The skier, fisherman, hunter and outdoors man in Wheeling? Well, he said, the headquarter were actually in Bannockburn, just south of Lake

Forest, and only the manufacturing was in Wheeling. Maybe.

    The next week I was to be interviewed by Chuck Pearson in Bannockburn and Nick had laid the ground work that for the first few months I would spend to two weeks in Aspen and two weeks in Wheeling until the program got to the point that my time would be full time there. Chuck is a really good person and the interview went well and an offer was made. I was sure that it had been already decided that the offer would be made as Nick was heavily involved in the financing and would actually be in charge of the design and operation until production could commence. I will add that after the interview Chuck took me down to the nearby shore of Lake Michigan which on this day the water was blue as was the sky and a cool breeze was blowing. This was early June 1984. In the earlier June of 1958 I had my interview with AC Sparkplug, a Division of General Motors, in Milwaukee, Wisconsin and stood about sixty miles north of where I now stood, twenty-six years almost to the day later. At the first one I was twenty-three years old and now I was forty-nine. I had almost no money at my first interview and was approaching a similar situation here.

    Jeanne had already agreed that the time had come so the decision was made to accept the offer and we started to plan for our departure from Aspen. It was much harder than when we left the Bay Area. With the exception of financial success, Aspen had been good for us. Many too many good times to count, our daughter had a very nice time growing up and a good education, we all had made numerous good friends and had met many interesting and even some famous people. We had lived the Aspen dream but recognized that Aspen was changing faster than we could adapt and that if you wish to phrase it in this way, was leaving us behind.

    The summer was a flurry of activity. Jeanne was very busy with her shop and was again having a successful summer and Janet had some sort of job in Ft. Collins and was playing volleyball with friends in tournaments all over the state. I was spending my days in Nick's place and the initial design was firming up. Understand I was the packaging designer, all the computer electronic and electrical design and programming was done by Nick. My time in Illinois was setting up my office, making contact with parts suppliers, a metal fabricator (who was very helpful in the cabinet design and continued be helpful through the entire project), and in constant contact with Nick.

Sometime in August I started looking for a place to rent and found one in Lake Forest which turned out quite good for us as I will describe in the next chapter. We were almost ready for the move and then the day came.

CHAPTER 20

By my third two week stint at Oneac it was apparent that I would become a full time employee on the On! Computer project and that we would be moving to Illinois from Aspen in the near future. Janet was now entering her fall semester of her Junior year in college and through an opportunity Jeanne had found and researched, she enrolled for the Semester at Sea college program on a student-work scholarship. Semester at Sea was a one semester college accredited program on a small cruise ship sailing around the world. This semester it would leave from Seattle, Washington and return to Ft. Lauderdale, Florida. With her on board work credits and all of the profits from Jeanne's summer business it was financed. It is her story but was a once in a life time adventure for her and we happily paid the balance and were rewarded by having her have such an experience. One photo of her standing on The Great Wall of China is reward enough.

With Janet safe, Jeanne and I were making our plans. Ruth would allow us to sublet the duplex furnished for six months as I was a little concerned about this move and change of life style and we might have to make another change in plans sooner than expected. I contacted a local real estate broker in Lake Forest as this was the kind of place we would like to live in and it was close enough to commute to work. The rental market was very limited but he came up with a six month rental from an older man who went to Florida each winter. Old Bill was a recent widower and the home was dated, the furnishings likewise, but it was not a bad house and was in a very good neighborhood. The rent was quite acceptable. I was taken over to meet Old Bill and we immediately liked each other and the deal was made. He said he was going to head south driving his aging Oldsmobile sedan towards the end of September so the timing was good for us. Old Bill didn't look too healthy, but he was the stubborn type and all went as scheduled.

Jeanne was to close her shop the end of September so on the last day of the month we packed all our personal possessions and my sculpture equipment and supplies in a small cube van, and with Jeanne driving our car and me the van, we headed for 1140 W. Deer Path Rd., Lake Forest. Not two weeks later Old Bill dies in Florida. He had a son in Florida and an estranged daughter in Milwaukee which leads to a story I won't elaborate on but which resulted in our being able to stay in the house for our entire two year stay in Illinois. It couldn't have worked out better for us but not so for Old Bill, of course.

My job on the On! Computer was designing the interior packaging so that all the components and circuit boards that Nick DeWolf designed and needed would fit in the cabinet dimensions selected. I designed the floppy disk drive cabinet, ordered the parts, established the parts and vendors list, and oversaw the drafting of the manufacturing drawings and specifications. My office was a small cubicle and I was allowed to work alone and co-ordinate with Nick. This was a perfect fit. My technical knowledge was long outdated, I worked best by myself, and my skill level on building something of this type was very good.

At this point I will attempt to describe how sudden technological change can affect employment and to which I was a witness. The development of a circuit board, as late as 1983, was a very high skilled and labor intensive work. Just a brief review is that the designer presents a wiring list to the circuit board designers and they start laying out the "traces", which you can think of as wires, to connect each point to point for every component on the list. Unlike wires, the traces cannot cross each other. Complex boards can have traces on both sides of the board but the same rules apply. This was done on a scaled up mat, maybe 4 to 8 times the size of the board, with various pre-cut templates placed for the components having the arrangement of pin locations for each. The pin locations must be connected by following the wiring list and following the trace rules. The completed drawing is reduced photographically and that photo is then transferred to a prepared circuit card that is etched in a manner leaving the traces and template pin connections in perfect scale. The holes for the pins and mounting locations are drilled and the board loaded with parts soldered in a way to make all the connections.

    This procedure was used for a number of years and those doing the lay ups were skilled and highly paid. It was also time consuming. The mother board for the On! Computer took about thirty days to get from the wiring list to a functional board. This was fast at the time but very slow in modern computer time. It also had a serious defect in that if any mistake had been made, or if a change was necessary, it essentially had to be redone. (You may remember me saying that Nick would always find a way to improve or enhance an electronic circuit and that included his own.)

    Now at this same time, and I will guess it was as the first circuit board was being laid out, Nick purchased the new IBM Computer Aided Design (CAD) program for circuit card layout and a high resolution plotter. He hooked his new system up and proceeded to enter his wiring list. D1 to R5, R5 to M22, etc, etc, one after the other. At each entry the computer would grind away and find the best route for that trace and this would be repeated for each connection. At the end some of the grinding took a long time, several minutes or more, but eventually the COMPLETE, or DONE, would show up and Nick would click on the PLOT icon and in a few minutes a perfect layout would appear for both sides of the board. He would overnight mail these to the circuit board manufacturer and they could have a board to us the next day. Within another day it would be loaded, soldered and in testing. Any changes needed could be done in just a few days and a new version would be ready.

    Practically over night an entire circuit board layout industry was made redundant and disappeared. High skilled, high paying jobs were gone. The drafting department at Oneac was three people and when the young manager saw this he enrolled the three of them in CAD courses. He could see the future and the drafting table, parallel rulers, angles and templates were on the way out. This would go into every area were pencil meets the paper in design, even to some extent into the highest creative level.

It hasn't just been robots welding or painting in the automobile industry, computer controlled lathes and milling machines costing both low and high skilled labor jobs. As I write this 3-D Printing is emerging so maybe even sculptors may become redundant.

Chuck Pearson had set up my last scheduled trip to Aspen so I could fly out, get whatever work needed to be done and then drive back with Janet's little VW Rabbit. This worked out nicely and I would use it for my commute car. Part of the deal for Janet's Semester at Sea was that she would give up her car for the year. We flew to Ft. Lauderdale just before Christmas and met her ship as it came into port. The holiday was spent with Jeanne's parents as they had moved to Florida, and then it was back to Illinois. Some where in here we ended up with a Plymouth Horizon hatch back and Janet got her car back

We joined the Lake Forest Newcomers. It had several divisions, such a bridge group, a gourmet group, a literature group, etc. We tried a couple and ended up primarily in the bridge group. Now you may think this not a really good way to meet new people but you have to understand that Lake Forest is sort of a temporary residential area for mid to high level executives which are putting their time in Chicago with the major corporations on their way up the ladder. It was quite a group to get acquainted with and we made friendships with a number of them. Jeanne also belonged to an organization that promoted education for women called P.E.O. and one of their fund raisers is a Bed and Breakfast for traveling members. We spent our first two weeks in Lake Forest with Lois and Laroy Meyer and were very good friends for many years. It was nice to be able to develop so many friendships in a such a short time.

I still had a number of sculptures available from our last couple of years in Aspen and showed at the Lake Forest Art in the Square shows in the fall of 1984, 1985, and 1986, the last coordinating with an eventual move back to Colorado. There were also a couple of high end Art and Craft shows in Highland Park. I manage to make a few sales and also made a few sales several years later from contacts from the shows. I wasn't doing any sculpting, however, and it would be a little later when I started back full time. One of my best sales occurred at the garage sale we had as we downsized a little for our next move.

Work on the ON! Computer progressed rapidly and after about a year and a half it was ready to go into the first production runs and a marketing group, maybe two people, was formed. My work was mostly getting loose ends tied up and our life in Lake Forest was actually becoming comfortable. The house we had rented was sold to the couple across the street who bought it for their son. He wasn't going to need it for at least another year so our renting could continue if we would let them fix it up, one room at a time. In a month it was like a new house. Jeanne had taken a job at Aimee's, an upscale women's clothing store in Highland Park, just south of Lake Forest and very Jewish. She was on commission and all the little ladies loved her.

Our last days in Illinois were starting to become clear as the On! Computer project for me was nearing an end and our house rental was almost over. We started to look at buying a house as I had been offered another position to continue with Oneac. Jeanne had decided to look into getting into real estate sales and was taking a class in Chicago. Everything then happened at the same time. The position I was being offered was okay but not what I wanted to do. I think it had more to do with Chuck Pearson's philosophy of treating his employees right than an actual need. The date we had to vacate our rental was almost upon us and we couldn't afford any of the houses we liked. Jeanne's test for her Illinois real estate exam was just a short time away. I wanted to get back into sculpture and it was a very cold, cold late winter day. We looked at each other and agreed, as we always do on the big things, lets go do our own thing.

I gave notice the next day. Chuck said he understood but wished I would stay and I think he really meant it. I asked him if I could have four weeks more as this was the time everything was going to come together and I also thought I needed about that much time to get everything tied up so what I knew about the On! Computer that hadn't found its way on to paper would be there. He said that would be fine and I was very busy for most of that time. I had everything well documented and organized when my good bye luncheon was given me. It had been a good experience and I had no regrets.

All our furniture which had been transported to us from Aspen after the six month sublet was over and all our bulky personal items, my sculpture equipment and supplies, and a number of thing we had bought over our two years here were put into a storage unit nearby. Our family car had been sold and the little Plymouth would be it for a while. Jeanne had just been notified she had passed her real estate license exam with very good marks.

Jeanne and I were sitting in the now empty house packing the last few items to put in the storage room on the morrow and had all the things we would need for a month or so ready to put in the hatchback when the phone rang. It was a man's voice and he said his name was Craig Blankenship and could he marry my daughter. I paused a little and then told him I only had one requirement of him, that he make her life a happy one. He sighed and I think he said he would. As of today I think he pretty much has. We told Janet that this wasn't a particular good time to plan a wedding but it wasn't to be until February, 1987 and this was late April. Lots of time which sped by way too fast.

We then headed back to Colorado by first going to Washington DC , Williamsburg, and then New York City. Not exactly the shortest route but a pattern we had started to develop in our travels. Before embarking on this little side trip Jeanne made contact with several of our acquaintances of the last few years that were in Washington DC. The first was Supreme Court Justice Harry Blackmun whom we had met at a party while in Aspen (which we may have catered) and after a very cordial conversation over cocktails he mentioned that if we ever came to Washington please let him know and he would arrange for us a tour of the Court. Jeanne wrote him a nice note saying we would be visiting and he wrote back that the Court would not be in session but to bring this letter to the receptionist and she would take care of everything for us. Jeanne's sister and brother-in-law were visiting with us and did the four of us get a first class tour. The Chamber, Library and all adjoining rooms not private. I suppose the signature on the letter was machine written but we have kept it any way and the results were enough for us to claim it authentic.

Another contact was with a lobbyist that had something to do with the Israeli military, or some such activity, whom Jeanne had met in her hospital duties. He offered, "if you ever visit Washington, etc," and she wrote him a similar note with a similar reply but to call him when we arrived. We met him at his town home for cocktails and then he took the four of us to dinner at his Club in Georgetown. That was followed by a driving tour of Washington DC by night. Spectacular.

While in Lake Forest Jeanne played bridge with a group and one of the ladies was a Jean Hegarty who's husband was Edward Hegarty, the head of the Chicago division of the FBI. This resulted in VIP treatment on the tour of the FBI in the J Edgar Hoover building. Not as big a deal as the fore mentioned but after the public tour the Myers's and Franz's were asked to wait and we were given a tour behind the stage to a room that housed a collection of confiscated weapons. A group picture taken with the boys holding Tommy Guns looking like idiots. An 8X10 black and white glossy arrived in a couple of weeks.

Another stop on this round about trip was very special to me. I had admired the sculptures of Charles Cropper Parks for some time and had purchased one of his fine brochures. We had stopped for the night in Wilmington, Delaware and I knew his studio was in the Brandy Wine Valley and was nearby. The telephone directory listed his address and the next morning we headed in that direction. As if guided by that invisible hand I ended up parked in front of his studio at 9:00 am on a Sunday morning. I rang the doorbell, the door opened, and there stood the man himself. I introduced myself and Jeanne and told him I was going to start back into sculpture and he invited us in and gave us a wonderful tour of his studio. He encourage me, even at fifty-one, to go for it with gusto. He passed away October 25, 2012 at ninety. A truly fine gentleman and sculptor, one I admired and had the privilege to meet.

    Our final visit before heading back to Colorado was in New York City where my nephew Art Sandy and his charming wife Jan were both doing their residencies, Art in radiology and Jan in psychiatry. Art became our tour guide and we did the all out walking tour of downtown with world famous deli corn beef sandwiches for lunch. Jan joined us for some of the tour but I think she had covered the route before. They now live in Birmingham, Alabama and have three grown up daughters. How time flies.

CHAPTER 21

We arrived in Ft. Collins, Colorado in good time to be there for Janet's graduation from CSU and proudly watched her receive her Bachelor of Arts diploma in Graphic Arts. We had a chance to meet and get to know our prospective son-in-law and he met our approval. I am not sure but I think we found a bed in the house that Janet and her friends had rented. We had been on the road for several weeks and would be heading to California in the next day or two so it wasn't a long stay.

The trip to San Diego went smoothly and a few days with my mother and Herb were fun and gave us a chance to see most of my family. Again this period seems to be a little bit in the I can't remember area but surely we went north to the Bay Area via Highway 1 with quick stops in Carmel and Monterrey and on to the Bay Area to visit all our friends there. I know we were back in Ft. Collins in July and rented one of the student apartments for a month at a very modest rent. It was time we landed and we needed a base to start a search for the right spot.

Loveland was becoming a sculptors town by this time having one of the best foundries in the country, Art Castings of Colorado. Also a number of well known sculptors and many of the artisans and craftsmen needed in the production of bronze sculpture lived there. If I was to really restart my career as a sculptor this was one of the best places in the country to do so. My first stop was to George Lundeen's studio on the southwest corner of Fourth Street and Jefferson Avenue in downtown Loveland. I had seen a show of his work in Aspen some years before and liked what I saw. George was there and set about to make me feel not only welcome but encouraged me to join the group in Loveland. His enthusiasm was real and when Jeanne and I had left the studio it was not that we wouldn't be here but whether Loveland was the place to reside. Fort Collins didn't seem to be a fit and Boulder didn't seem quite right either. Both are college towns and Boulder was much more expensive as far as rentals were concerned. Berthod was attractive but not too different from Loveland. It seemed that the best choice was to choose Loveland. It turned out to be the right choice.

We secured a town home at 1100 Taft Avenue, #39, that was new with two bedrooms, dinning area, a well equipped kitchen, good living space and a two car garage. We made the first and last month rent and the damage deposit. It was then to make the trip to Illinois to retrieve our stored furniture and other belongings from the storage unit. We combined that with my participation in the Art in the Square show in Lake Forest. We stayed with our friends the Meyer's for several days, always valuing our friendship. I then rented a moving van and spent a day loading the contents of the storage room and the next day we headed home.

A few days later I had my first chance to try out the prospective son-in-law. Craig proved he could be in the family although a big and very heavy TV console was put on his, "I will never help you move this thing again unless you cut it into three pieces list." Actually he did once more but by that time they were married and I had a little more leverage.

We were now starting to worry more about our financial health as the start up costs kept mounting. I was going to use the garage as my studio which would help. We had to buy another car and settled on an inexpensive, and bad choice, Buick station wagon. Next was what Jeanne should do and that her prospects to return to nursing would require a six month refresher course at an adult education facility. We drove up to Ft. Collins and she enrolled and paid the modest tuition. Half way back to Loveland she told me, "I don't want to do this!" and an immediate U-turn was made and the check retrieved.

Jeanne found that her real estate license from Illinois

was transferable to Colorado and that she was only required to pass a Colorado real estate law test which required a one week super class. The week went by and she passed her test and received her Colorado Real Estate license. Unknown to either of us at the time she would turn out to be an excellent agent and after a couple of years would become a partner in The Group in Loveland. For our stay in Loveland she made it possible for me to pursue my sculpture career and lead us into another venture which will be described shortly.

Before Jeanne started to receive some sales and listing commissions my income was almost zero. Any of my sales money was quickly put back in casting expenses and show and travel costs. Having two incomes that could vary from nothing to a good amount month to month is not the most reassuring way to live. After selling several of our emergency gold coins and embarrassingly having to borrow a sum from my Mother, we were still in pretty tough shape. This was the late fall of 1986, I am fifty-one and Jeanne is forty-eight, and we are starting over with very close to zero in financial assets. Fortunately VISA never discovered this as we always paid our bill in full each month.

February 7, 1987 was approaching much faster than we were ready for and this was the date set for Janet's marriage. Jeanne worked with her in planning and the two of them found a very nice wedding dress at a good price after several tries. We three went on a scouting trip to Denver and found the Grace Methodist Church as a fine choice and secured it and the minister for the service. One of Craig's friends lived in an apartment and town home complex and the Spyglass Hill Clubhouse was reserved for the reception. Jeanne and I would cater the event and another of Craig's friends would bar tend. Janet's bridesmaid's brother was the DJ. On the big day Denver provided the best February seventh on record with blue skies and seventy degree temperatures. The ceremony went off without a hitch and the reception was agreed by all to be one of the best parties ever.

Most of the family stayed the night in a local hotel and

we all met for a late breakfast in the lobby restaurant. I think we all were happy and satisfied. We went out to the front of the hotel and witnessed a young man, smiling, drive off with my daughter next to him in a red Toyota pick-up truck. As I write this over twenty-seven years later I think Craig has done, and is doing, what I asked of him in our first conversation.That was to provide my daughter with a happy life. The two granddaughter's they have given us are a blessing and following their growth is a continuing pleasure.

I was accepted into the sculptor community immediately and received much good advice and help. There were about fifteen or twenty sculptors who, although working solitary, were socially and business wise companions. Loveland's Sculpture In The Park show was in it's very early years and co-operation between the sculptors and the Chamber of Commerce led it to becoming one of the biggest and best sculpture shows in the country. The Rotary Club was involved and also put on a winter show of both painting and sculpture which, although smaller, was first rate and very prestigious.

In October of 1987 Jeanne's parents, Howard and Dora Bryan, celebrated their 50th wedding anniversary in Flint, MI at a nice party put on by their children. At this time they had moved down to Florida full time and the party was held a few months prior to their actual December wedding date such that the whole family and their many friends could join them for the event. It was a very good time and Jeanne and I enjoyed it with all the rest. Pops, as Howard was called, wasn't feeling his best and would discover a month later that he had pancreatic cancer and sadly passed away at seventy years of age on June 14, 1988. He had led a good life, he and Mom raising five children while both worked full time. His last few years were spent in pursuit of the elusive snook, a top Florida game fish, at all hours of the day and night depending on the tidal conditions.

Jeanne and I were right in the middle of our next change of direction and we were not able to attend his funeral although later would go with Mom to help her put their house in Florida on the market so she could move back to Flint to be among family and friends. What had happened was that Jeanne had secured the listing for 342 E. Third Street from the owners, Mary and Charlie Gibbs. The Gibbs had this building, the parking lot to the west and another house to the west of that, for an office complex for their design and graphics company. As the business declined in the rather severe recession following the oil boom and bust in the early 1980's, and their interest trended more toward owning a nursery, they were selling off the properties. The last to be put on the market was the John Hahn House, built in 1893. John Hahn was an early, and very successful, business man and rancher in Loveland. At the time the house was built and the Hahn family moved in it was considered the finest and most modern house in town. Over the years it had some aging issues and an architect who bought it in the 1970's made the modifications to make into an office building. The Gibbs had bought it from him for their expanding business.

  By June, 1988 the business climate on the Front Range, which denotes the Eastern slope of the Rocky Mountains, was still poor. Real estate prices were still dormant and office properties like the Gibb's were almost impossible to sell. I had by this time rented a studio space from George Lundeen just a half block away on Jefferson Ave and would go over when Jeanne had an open house. We would tour the house together and could see what a fine home it had once been and how it could be restored. It had a fully finished attic with lots of under eave bookcases and storage and a little room with plumbing for a sink. A perfect studio space for me as it had a quirky raised cupola centered on the roof with windows on all sides providing great light. It had four rooms and a half bath on the second floor, and rooms that had been a living room, parlor, dining room, another half bath, and what was where the kitchen had been on the first floor. All the rooms had been converted into offices. Also a back porch with an entry room to the kitchen and a large veranda porch fronting the house. It was red brick with an appropriate amount of gingerbread in the many cables.

  The owner in 1970 had rewired the entire house with

surface mounted conduit painted bright blue. All the outlets were placed at desk height and the conduit was extended on the ceilings for overhead lighting. It would all have to be replaced. The worn carpeting would require new carpeting through out. Under it was unfinished soft wood flooring, and upstairs linoleum under carpeting covered the same material. The many squeaks would require re-nailing all the flooring. The existing bathrooms would have to be completely redone with the upstairs one converted to a full bath and a master three quarter bath would have to be added to the master bedroom. An entirely new kitchen would have to be designed and built in the original footprint and a variety of other tasks would require a good amount of time. The air conditioning was an older model heat pump with gas backup furnace and would need replacement at a later date. What was there in landscaping was minimal and would need some care to make it presentable. A big task, but I of course said, "I can do it!"

    The immediate thought was it would be perfect for a bed and breakfast upstairs with one room for us that had enough space in the closet to put in the bathroom. A few more weeks went by with no interest shown in the property and then we approached the Gibbs. It went like this in fast time. "We are interested in buying the house but can't afford the asking price. Make us an offer. We made the offer and the Gibb's said okay. We then said that since at this point we have no income history we may not be able to get a loan. The Gibbs say they have a balloon mortgage due in three years and will finance it for us using their mortgage. We shook hands." The contract was accomplished and the closing date was on August 5, 1988. Jeanne got a sales commission and we got the house.

    Estimate for me was do the restoration in three months at a cost of $15,000 (1988 dollars). Jeanne's sister and brother-in-law agreed to loan us the money and I took a temporary leave from sculpture. I was very accurate in the dollar amount, but the next six months were almost seven days a week, at least eight hours a day. The project was to turn the upstairs half bath into a full bath, add a master bedroom three quarter bath, and put in a new kitchen in the foot print of the original one. Also, all the wiring, outlets and switches were to be replaced. We added a washer and dryer to the back porch. All the woodwork was cleaned and varnished using two gallons of varnish and all the walls painted using twenty-two gallons of wall paint. I hired a plumber to do the plumbing and had limited help in designing the kitchen cabinets and hanging them. There was some floor flattening, adding a wall between the master bedroom and the adjacent bedroom to provide closets. A large roll of carpeting was ordered and carpeting was installed by a carpet layer as we progressed in the restoration. The kitchen floor and counter top, the bathrooms, including the floors and the tub and shower surrounds, were tiled. The result was a beautiful and comfortable home, the Jefferson House Bed and Breakfast was opened, and the Art Myers Studio occupied. There was also an exhausted Art Myers.

CHAPTER 22

One of our first customers at Jefferson House was Stephen Beal who had just arrived in Loveland and was working at Interweave Press as an editor and writer. He would stay a month until he could find a house or a rental and became a delightful friend. He published a small book of his poetry in 1995, The Very Stuff - Poems on color, thread, and the habits of women. Our copy is inscribed, "For Art and Jeanne Myers, Thank you for making me feel so warmly welcome in my first Loveland home. Stephen." If you like lightly written, humorous poetry and color, find a copy for your own enjoyment. Stephen joined us on our flight over to Italy as he was headed to Naples via Milan which was also our starting point. We had rented a car to start our tour to Lake Como spending our first night in Varenna. Stephen joined us and then took the train to Naples the next day. He eventually bought a small house were he lived with his cat named Red. He passed away a few years back, but will be remembered by us as a good friend and good person.

Loveland Sculpture Works was a second foundry to add to the increasing production of bronze casting and a little later two more foundries would start up. Eventually the sculpture community taken as a whole would be considered the second largest industry in Loveland. Sculpture Works started an Art School and artist supply store, and later the School would become independent. The school had a constant series of quality instructed classes which were well attended. Jefferson House became a very popular place for students to stay for their three to five day classes. We provided nice, clean, comfortable and safe lodging at very reasonable rates. We served continental breakfast and change of linens every three days, make your own bed and share the bathroom. At most there would be four guests, but that was rare. Downstairs they could use the dinning room and parlor, and share with us the living room. (Later we would add a sun room as our private space and the living room became available.)

Our life was now starting to take some form. The B & B was profitable and was paying our monthly living costs. I was starting to sell a little more sculpture and had gotten to the point that there was a little monies left over, and Jeanne was starting to make real progress in real estate. The market had finally started to turn up and sales picked up accordingly. The bulk of real estate agents had been forced out during the big slowdown and hadn't returned yet. Jeanne was in the right place at the right time, with the right stuff. One year she was in on twenty-five transactions. This would seem much bigger in today's market but at that time the average sale was around $85,000. She did manage to develop an ulcer, however. We were able to pay back the sister and brother-in-law and later re-finance and pay off the Gibbs, and within a few years pay off our mortgage.

As the mid 1900's approached our life developed a routine that would continue until early 2002. Jeanne would continue working hard and long hours at the Group as housing prices continue to modestly rise as demand increased. As this became more of a sure thing the number of real estate agents also increased. More competition also meant more stress. The Group had a number of very good attributes. The management were very experienced realtors and managed accordingly. They also set up the organization as a partnership structure which you had to buy into and which Jeanne did at the first opportunity. Also an IRA vehicle was established such that a percentage of the commissions could be invested and taken with you when leaving the partnership. Again Jeanne took advantage of this and put the maximum allowed of all her commissions into her account.

For the Bed and Breakfast we divided and shared the duties. Jeanne did the reservations unless she was not available at the time and I would fill in. She took care of the breakfast preparation and serving, laundry and bed making. I would do house cleaning and yard work. We both did the social graces. I think we made a good team and the business was steady and profitable.

My sculpture career was maturing and began to produce some income. I did a few life size sculptures and started to specialize in golf related works. This led to a series of trophy and award sculptures, a number of which became annual sales. I had several galleries and did a few shows each year. Unfortunately a large amount of time is spent in marketing and on average a little more than the actual sculpting. The sculpting I enjoyed, the marketing I didn't. There is also a lot of time in the management of the production end. All told only forty percent of my time was spent on the creative side.

None the less, things were improving on the financial front to the extent that we could afford to do some traveling and went on trips to Italy in 1996, Great Britain in 1998, and France in 2000. These were driving tours following the Rick Steve's guide books for lodging recommendations. We never made a reservation in advance and only once or twice were disappointed in where we slept. There were many highlights, but one was a little out of the ordinary. As we approached Cambridge about noon thinking about finding a place to have lunch we stopped at an intersection to allow a man slumped in a wheel chair with an attendant cross just in front of us. Jeanne and I both said at the same time, "That's Stephen Hawking." His female attendant could see our expression and read our lips and waved with a nice smile. Hawking never noticed the admirers in their rental car acting as if they had just seen royalty or a movie star.

And this brings me a chance to discuss nothing with you. Stephen Hawking has spent the better part of his life in search of how the universe works and how it was created. I have no background nor the intellect to offer anything to this search. Newtonian physics I can understand at the most simplified form of $F=MA$. Then comes Einstein's $E=MC*$ plus a cosmological constant or two. And then quantum mechanics comes along and I am lost among the quarks. What I am interested in is the concept of nothingness and the singularity. These are the basis for the Big Bang Theory, the creation of the Universe, the start of everything and are so anti-intuitive that I can offer only an opinion, which is only for one to ponder.

What is most annoying about quantum theorists and cosmologist is that they keep coming up with all these seemingly unbelievable theories and then keep finding evidence they are true. In 2012 the Higgs Boson particle is detected at CERN in Switzerland. The God Particle, as theorized in the Standard Theory, exists. Alan Guth's thirty year old Inflation Theory of the first micro micro seconds of the Big Bang that there was an expansion which was at a speed much faster than the speed of light and that if true a gravitational wave should exist in space time. That's one of those theories that stretches the imagination but this year (2014) physicists have detected that wave and the Inflation Theory is possibly verified. (Maybe, as other physicists are now questioning the measurements.)

Before the Big Bang, 13.9 billion years ago, all the mass, everything we think of as real, is now in a space of zero dimension and is in the form of energy, a singularity. To make it worse, it is then said to be flittering about in this nothingness which has no boundary, dimension, no space, no time, etc, and where there are no laws of physics. It simply doesn't exist. It is truly nothing except for this pesky singularity which can be there, and not be there, because it has no dimension. And then that singularity decides to spectacularly transform itself into mass. As far as I can tell no one has really made the case that this is really the true start. Only mathematically working backwards does this theory look probable. It seems to me like an enormous jig saw puzzle with most of the pieces now in place but this large, ungainly Big Bang piece is on the table and really doesn't look like it will fit in anywhere.

It's only just before the first micro-micro second, and it is a very big and old universe, but it seems nothingness and the singularity just don't seem plausible.

Roughly 2450 years ago a Greek, Epicurus, and some friends came up with the atomus theory that an infinite number of indestructible atoms, flying about in an infinite space, over an infinite time would occasionally swerve, collide, and stick together and eventually form all that is, and will be, and before that all that had been. It is a simple theory but surprisingly accurate in describing the attributes of the atom. Not bad for that place and time.

The book, written by Stephen Greenblatt, The Swerve- How the World Became Modern, tells the story about Poggio, an unemployed scribe to a 15th-century Pope, and his wandering search for ancient manuscripts. He comes upon Lucretius's poem, On the Nature of Things, in which among other subjects is found the description of the Atomus Theory. The rest of the story is how this discovery makes the world become modern in as how it affects the teachings of the Catholic Church and civilization in general. A good read and one that got me to think about nothing again.

CHAPTER 23

February 2, 1994 became a very important day for us. Devin Blankenship, our first grandchild, was born. Her birth was three months earlier than it should have been and Janet was flown by emergency helicopter from Emporia, Kansas to the Wesley Medical Center in Wichita for the delivery. Janet had a earlier miscarriage and also had developed post gestational diabetes so this pregnancy was being closely monitored. Devin was just over three pounds and was in intensive care for three months. We raced over the next day to see our first grandchild and try to be of some support for Janet. She was of course pale, worried, and tired and Devin looked so small and helpless in the incubator it brought tears to her grandparents. Remembering Janet's birth of this chubby, full sized baby moving around and ready to go home after just two days made us both feel that Janet and Devin were being short changed on what should be one of life's great experiences.

A few weeks later there was more bad news in that the geneticist at Wesley posed that Devin was born with Beckwith-Wiedemann Syndrome. The indicators were an enlarged tongue, small ear creases, and some facial structural signs. On our visit a few days later, with Janet, we were given a thorough explanation of BWS, what could be expected and what would later need to be done. The first was, of course, to get through the next three months and then get through the next sixteen years.

BWS is fairly uncommon in that there are only about one case in 13,000 births in the Untied States each year. Mostly it is sporadic, meaning it is not handed down from the parents as is in less than fifteen percent of the cases are the genetic defect found in either one. It is located in the short arm of chromosome eleven and referred to as 11p15. In Devin's case it was a trans-location of the 11p15 and in layman's terms had the code reversed and when mated to the partners causes the BWS unusual results. The enlarged tongue causes problems in eating, speech and breathing and is usually reduced in size to more closely match the mouth in the first year by an operation which was Devin's first surgery. The ear creases are not really a problem and usually not enough to require any cosmetic correction. In Devin's case a number of major surgeries were required to correct a too small palate to make room for her tongue and for orthodontic considerations, as was at sixteen years a lower jaw re-alignment and some facial bone correction to aid in breathing and cosmetic improvement. Along with all this surgery was the removal of her tonsils and adenoids.

Jeanne would spend the first week with Janet and Devin on her first week home in Kansas. As most of the major surgeries were done in Denver after Craig was assigned a position there we could spend much more time with them. By the time Devin was approaching her sixth month I began to feel I could be a real grandfather and carry her about outdoors and have her touch leaves and flowers and have her looking at birds and squirrels. After she first came home from the hospital she seemed so small and fragile that I was uncomfortable trying to hold her but that was soon remedied as she caught up in size.

It was a rough go for Devin as it wasn't until her final surgery that everything really got properly fitted and in place and that her speech became clearer and the cosmetic improvements lent themselves to a more attractive appearance. She has come through it all with remarkably good nature and is now a little over six foot tall, slender, very pretty, and a really fine young woman.

Six years later, October 12, 2000 Andie Blankenship would join the team right on schedule and at fighting weight and height. The two girls are best friends and Jeanne and I count ourselves as very proud grandparents. They are very different, have individual personalities but are happy and well adjusted.

I will now jump into subjects that I think demonstrates the best of human endeavors, one being the Human Genome Project, as you might expect I would have interest from the above, and the other Stem Cell Research. Both these have been and are now occurring and in just the last few years the magnitude of their importance is starting to be witnessed. They are equivalent of sending man to the moon and bringing him back safely and one can make a good case much more important of an achievement for the betterment of mankind. Why there is so little coverage of these achievements is both surprising and disappointing. Occasionally there is a little mention of an event resulting from the HGP and most of the coverage of Stem Cell Research is on the political side of right to life aspects in growing cells instead of the discovery of the fantastic potential for the use of stem cells to aid curing and recovery of man's many serious ailments.

In the case of the HGP probably the first steps were in private research and can be dated to 1953 when the famous double helix of DNA was first discovered. The very first mapping of genes goes back to 1911 with research on the lowly fruit-fly being done but that was primitive to what was to come. By the mid 1970's research really started to take off and government funding entered the picture and around 1987 the HGP was underway.

The first formal announcement that the majority of the human genome had been sequenced and mapped was in 2001. It was announced that there was probably fewer than 30,000 genes containing the three billion base pairs which defines human beings. By 2003 it was established that the number of genes was much closer to 20,500, surprisingly less than anticipated and comparing in number to the lowly fruit-fly mentioned above.

The discovery of stem cells, cells that can self-renew, was in the early 1960s and by the 1970s religious organizations and government stepped in on the moral and ethical grounds of the use of embryo cells in research. Numerous laws were passed and much posturing and preaching done to prevent and control *their use. Despite all this by the late 1990s and early 2000s the possibilities of the use of stem cells in treatment of disease, organ failure, and injury was being researched. Today a number of tests in humans are being conducted and the list of possible breakthroughs are growing.*

Two of the possibilities are the regeneration of the pancreas for diabetics and another, even more exciting, is regeneration of the spinal cord for paraplegics. This may be far off, or maybe not even be possible, but think what it will mean if it is.

I have already exceeded my knowledge and grasp of these two subjects, and won't get into the moral and ethical debate on the use of genetic information or the use of stem cells to cure and repair living human beings. The debate should be continued and one can see that there is merit to both sides but at some point the benefits to those that are should be weighed against those that aren't and never would be.

CHAPTER 24

Sometime in 1996, probably on a cold winter evening while watching TV in the living room, a decision was made. The living room was on the NE corner of the house and on the corner of the lot, shading this room, stood one of Loveland's biggest blue spruce trees. The air conditioning was all registered on the interior walls and this room just didn't heat enough to be comfortable. We had been thinking of adding on a sun room on the south side of the house or building a garage with a second level apartment or studio. The south end of the lot was a asphalt parking area so landscaping would also need to be done. A garage would be nice but a sun room with a fireplace, over looking a gorgeous garden, would be much better. Again I uttered those fatal words, "I can build that!" And I did.

After laying out the foot print, which would be just under 400 square feet, several very important calculations had to be made. To achieve the high ceiling to match the house it would have to be two steps down. The entry from the house would be through the south wall of the dining room to a landing requiring matching the house floor level. The small half bath window would be closed in and the kitchen window would be open as a pass through. The south wall would consist of high Anderson patio doors, with matching sets of non-functioning doors on either side all capped with transom windows. The east end would have a gas fireplace with book cases and windows on either side and a fine mantel capable of housing a large TV. The west end would have two windows, one on the landing and the other centered to the room. All the wood work would be varnished yellow pine routed to match the original woodwork in the house.

The floor would be tile.

With my design we had an architect do a drawing with the footing and slab requirements and obtained our building permit. All the asphalt was removed and the trenches for the footing dug and another dug so I could run the sewer pipe far enough out to clear the building. From that point on I did almost all the construction except for pouring the slab and several parts I felt better done by others. The rafters were ordered which with a little help were put in place and the sheeting laid. I had roofers do the shingles, which were matched to the shingles we had put on the house earlier. A brick layer did the west wall, not really happy about using used brick that we had purchased to match the 1893 ones on the house. I ended up laying the rest as he seemed always to have too much work to come back. I did have the dry wall done, but did all the electrical work including stereo, telephone, and TV hook ups. After picking out the perfect tile I had a better back lay the tile but did the grouting myself. The work was done over several months as breaks were taken to do some sculpture work. When we settled in, now with a private space from the B & B, pardon my modesty, it couldn't have come out any better.

We now had to landscape the remaining yard with fence, parking slab, rose garden, grass, trees, flowers, and a row of prolific blackberry bushes. A large storage building was placed between fences next to the alley on the south end. The storage building was needed to house all that garden equipment I now needed and my master molds which were taking up more space every year.

Life was now going along pretty nice. The Group was starting to grow larger as real estate sales kept increasing and a lot of new construction was happening. Jeanne was doing better than ever and I was actually starting to show some measurable progress. The B & B was now a consistent income producer. One discouraging happening was some major problems I was having with galleries. The first was with the Wildlife of the World Gallery in Aspen in 1990 when the owner skipped out and declared bankruptcy (in Hawaii) owing a long list of creditors, including me at $2895. The second, an even worse situation, was in 1992 with Galerie d'Arte in Palm Desert, California where I was defrauded of what would have been close to a years income. The operator was a con man, liar and cheat that left town leaving a host of creditors and got away with it. This was followed in 1995 by a non-payment of $1440 at Royal Palm Gallery in Palm Beach, Florida due to a management failure and lack ethics by the owner. Finally, in 2000, was an unique twist of solving a galleries financial problems when Westside Gallery in Del Ray Beach, Florida was stripped of all the artwork in an overnight heist, including $7825 of my sculptures which would have amounted to $5216 in income. This particular situation was almost laughable if it hadn't hurt so many artists. I am not sure if the owner ever got his just rewards but his claiming he had $8,500 in cash in his cash box taken sort of makes you suspicious. How I managed to be connected in this many bad situations is a wonder as the majority of gallery owner's are pretty decent people. It is, sadly, amazing how vulnerable you are in situations like these. The law does not really serve you well when recourse is extremely expensive and collection is next to impossible from people like these.

  On September 11, 2001 sometime just before 7:00 am Jeanne and I are on Highway 34 a few miles from home heading to I-25 to go to Chicago to the Danada Sculpture Show. We are in my Chevy Van towing a trailer with both loaded with sculpture of mine and several other sculptors who would be flying two days later. I heard something on the radio about a plane flying into the World Trade Center building and at first thought it was a replay of a small plane that hit one of the New York buildings years before. A second announcement didn't sound right for that and then came the second plane strike. We turned around and headed back home. The television coverage was underway and our spirits were crushed.

  The decision was made not to leave until we could get more details. By the end of the day it was decided not to go. None of the sculptors who were planning to fly could get there and we really weren't feeling like there was any enthusiasm to show. The Danada group went ahead with the reduced show and it was surprisingly well attended and had some sales. It was a good sign that people would not be cowed by the attack and tomorrow the sun would rise. It changed us all and unfortunately the problems are still with us. How humans could do such a thing is still incomprehensible to me. But one should never underestimate the depth men will go to when following false prophets. A sad commentary on human nature.

This would be the last sculpture show I would enter as I was tiring of the time and effort required and in many cases the long travel and expenses that often resulted in not selling enough to be profitable. I had done most of the Danada shows between 1991 and 1998, several of the Lake Forest shows after moving to Loveland, a few others in the Chicago area and a long trip to do a Golf Expo show in Charleston, SC. Locally in Loveland I showed in Sculpture in the Park from 1987 to 1992 and in the Loveland Invitational in 1993 and 1994. I made the invitation to the Colorado Governor's show in 1993. Before leaving Aspen there were a number of Wildlife Art Shows that ranged from Spokane, WA to Minneapolis, MN and places in between. It was not always fun and games to be an artist.

Just eleven days later on September 22, 2001 my Mother died. She was ninety-two, had been in a rest home and then a care facility for a period of two years and had dementia to the point of not recognizing any of us and was, I think and hope, ready to pass over. Jeanne and I went to San Diego for the memorial service. She was laid to rest next to my Father as they had planned. Herb had died on March 8, 1995, and what was an interesting and complimentary decision of his own, choosing a plot very near my Mother's and Father's.

We are now getting close to the next big change which is about to occur. Again it is Jeanne who is the catalyst.

CHAPTER 25

Soon after the holidays and the new year 2002 was just getting started Jeanne comes home from work at The Group office, or an open house, and announces, "I quit! I don't want to do this anymore." I, in my infinite wisdom answered, "How about we sell the house, buy a boat and live aboard?" She says, "Let's do it!"

Now this requires a little history. With a couple of very minor exceptions neither of us had ever been on a boat, much less know anything about operating or living on one. At a time many years earlier, when things weren't going too great in a wintry Aspen, I happened on a Sail magazine at the library and there were these beautiful boats, in beautiful waters, with beautiful people on board. What could be better than that? I read a few articles and thought this might be fun to try someday. Although I was now just a couple of months from my 67th birthday, and Jeanne was keeping up with me, that image was tucked away in my brain and just popped out when she indicated it was time to make a change.

Jeanne was starting to burn out in the real estate game. The Group had combined several offices and it now had about ten times the number of realtors as when she had first joined. Pressures had increased, housing prices were much higher, and contract problems were becoming more common. We had closed down the B & B about two years earlier as it was starting to wear on us. We also wanted to remove that use of the house from the IRS recapture requirements when it was sold. (As it turned out the rules were changed such that the recapture part for home businesses was removed. Then the capital gain exemption was raised well beyond what we could expect. Add to that for some unfathomable reason the county decided to forgive fifty percent of property taxes for seniors who had lived in their current residence for the past ten years for 2001. Talk about breaks.)

For me, I had been working very hard at sculpture and still not getting over the hump to the real money side of the mountain. The problems with several galleries I depicted in the previous chapter had bothered me more than I liked to admit. We were ready to retire. So we set about to do so.

We prepared a brochure for the house. Jeanne establish the listing with The Group and by early May we had a For Sale sign in front of the house. There were a lot of things to get ready if a sale materialized. Jeanne would resign her partnership and I had quite a bit of small sculptures to have cast and finished, including trophies for Castle Pines, Cordillera, and Catamount Golf Clubs. We would have to prepare to store all our furniture and possessions and all my sculpture equipment and molds.

I was also starting to prepare for life on a sailboat as that was the kind we would start with. It so happened the Sail Expo held each May in Oakland, California was beckoning. We had just enough frequent flier miles to get me an airline ticket and a motel reservation was made. I was off to check out this idea of a new life style. The San Francisco Bay area decided to provide the boat show perfect weather for all four days and I couldn't have had a better time. The sailboats were beautiful, the sky was as clear as I have ever seen it, the temperature was perfect. I hadn't been in a more positive environment since the very early days of snow skiing. Everyone seemed to be enjoying what they were doing and every person I told what Jeanne and I were thinking of doing and what our experience was said it was the one hundred percent right thing to do. You will love it! I came home one hundred percent certain we would.

I had determined through research and at the boat show that one boat stood out as a good one for us, the Hunter Passage 42. It was about the biggest sailboat two people could handle, easy to sail, ranked as one of the most comfortable to live aboard, had headroom clearance for a six foot three me, center line queen berths in both cabins, two heads, efficient galley and comfortable saloon. A center cockpit with an enclosure made for good visibly and comfort. A search on the internet found a number of used ones for sale in the price range we would be comfortable with. It was a sailboat designed for exactly what we wanted to do.

Before we had time to change our minds about any part of this scheme a young couple showed up with their kids and asked for a tour of the house. Within a few days an offer was made and accepted with a closing in mid June. We had time for a big garage sale which was a great success but hardly made a dent in our hoard. A store room was rented and the trips began. Once we had the big stuff moved the Chevy Van was sold and we were down to our Pontiac Bonneville SSE. We made arrangements to rent a home on Lake Loveland for the early summer as Jeanne had a medical operation done that would require a month or so recovery period and I still had a number of things to finish up.

By the end of summer we were ready to start our quest. We had our good byes taken care of with the many good friends we had made over the fifteen years in Loveland, all of whom thought we were crazy. Jeanne's resignation from the Group and retirement was taken care of and her recovery complete. I had all the trophies finished and delivered. A list of all the Hunter Passage 42's for sale in the U.S. had been compiled from YachtWorld.com. We packed up the car and headed for Michigan. Michigan? Well a visit to Jeanne's family was on the must do list and we saw our first Hunter Passage 42 in Kenosha, Wisconsin. I had been aboard a brand new Hunter Passage 42 at the boat show and now Jeanne got her first look at one in Kenosha. She loved it. This one was new and more than we wanted to risk paying, as what if we didn't like life aboard. Also, the Great Lakes are not a year round in the water location and would not make a good place to start out.

Then the serious trip began. The premise of the trip would be to circumnavigate the U.S. coast until the right boat at the right price was found. It turned out to be quite a trip and lasted a bit longer than expected, but was a very good time. After our family visit was over we started a drive around the east side of Lake Erie and then up to Toronto and around Lake Ontario and out along the St. Lawrence. Any time we saw masts sticking up we would pull in and take a look. It was especially nice to arrive at a marina around lunch time and have a picnic. If the docks were open to the public we could walk around and almost always find someone who would want to tell us what a great life living aboard was. Once and a while there would be a boat broker and they would always have a boat to show.

We went into Canada and as far as Quebec City, then down through New Brunswick and into Nova Scotia with a little detour around Cape Breton. By this time October was drawing near and we headed for Maine. In our rush by the Bay of Fundy Jeanne didn't let me witness the peak tidal flow but we did see a boat at a dock near our motel rise overnight by thirty feet.

Our friend John Bush was still in Maine at his small place and we made it there a few days before he left to head south for the winter in Florida. We had the Maine lobster dinner and he said we could stay a few more days to see the leaves start to change. I wanted Jeanne to go to the Annapolis Boat Show which was in the first or second week of October so we headed down there to arrive the day before. That evening we strolled around downtown and could see and hear all the preparations going on behind the fences. The excitement was palpable. We paid extra for the opening day passes and were ready for the morning opening. We awoke to rain, which by the time we were inside had become a downpour. Within the first hour everyone had given up on protocol and bare feet and wet socks were allowed on the boats and quite frankly it was a depressing mess. Only the Swan (very expensive) dealers were able to fight the elements and under their awning one was made to put on the protective booties and enter the boats under held umbrellas. A far cry from my experience in San Francisco Bay area but Jeanne wasn't the least bit deterred in our quest.

The leaves had still to change so we headed north for

one more week's try for color and had to be satisfied with an occasional hill or valley splash. It was then time to head further south. On a Sunday morning we passed the road sign to Kennebunkport and Jeanne said lets go take a look. I had read that morning that President Bush was at the compound and grunted that it would be a mess. She gave me the look and we exited to Kennebunkport. The small town was as pretty as could be but before I could turn around a policeman was telling me that we could drive past the Bush's place as long as we didn't stop or take pictures. There is a grass clearing on the road side of the house and on it were thirty or so young adults, both male and female, all nicely dressed and out enjoying the beautiful fall midday amongst six or seven white vans and three or four black SUVs. As we made the loop returning to the road we had gone in on a helicopter flew over and traffic was stopped. The parade then passed before us as the President and party headed to lunch or golf. The vans, SUVs and an assortment of police and sheriff cars passing one after another. I don't know what the per hour cost of this travel is, but our government was hard at work.

Have you seen the size of Air Force 1? And it requires two of these plus a car hauling cargo plane to get our current President to a fund raiser. By the way, what is the name of the President of Switzerland?

We saw the first possible boat at a private home on Long Island. It was down forty-three steps from the house to the owners private dock. A really nice boat and a very nice owner. Riches to Rags was the boat's name. He spent quite a bit of time with us and we were now convinced the Hunter Passage 42 was the right boat. The price was a bit higher than our comfort level so we expressed our thanks and headed up the stairs and back to the car.

The boat owner suggested trying the motel at nearby Stoney Brook for the night as evening was approaching. When we arrived the associated restaurant was entertaining a very upscale wedding party. The small cubicle at the entrance was also the motel office so we entered and sheepishly inquired as to the availability and rates. The very nicely dressed attendant told us they had a room and it was $145. I said that was a little more than we could afford and started to turn to leave when a older gentleman came up and asked me what I could afford and I said about $90 was tops. He smiled and said that would be fine. He asked for the key and led us up a path to a nice individual unit on a slight hill. I asked if he was sure this would be okay and he replied, "Of course, I own the place." It worked out just fine, especially for New York.

    Heading south we continued our adventure with many looks and still not finding just the right boat at the right price in the right place. We finally arrived in Vero Beach, Florida for a brief second visit. A Morgan 42 was listed in our price range at the City Marina and we made an appointment to see it the next morning. The Morgan is a similar boat to the Hunter but is a little heavier built and a bit harder to sail and steer. The owner met us at the dingy dock, pumped up his half deflated dingy and we motored out to the boat which was on a mooring ball. Not being able to unzip the enclosure he just pulled the zipper apart with little plastic teeth flying everywhere. Inside the instruments were laying about, unconnected to an abundance of wires. The rest of the boat was in equal disarray. The price which had appeared to be a bargain was way too much. "I probably should get this all cleaned up," was the sellers remark as we headed back to the dingy dock.

    One more showing is worth describing before ending this part of our search. In Miami, after seeing several Hunters, I found an ad for a little bigger boat as a finish another man's dream and called the number. A very New Jersey sounding woman answered and gave a few details on the boat and how the owner was fixing up his dream of an around the world cruising yacht and it was about half done. His sudden death had ended his dream and now his wife had the resulting nightmare. A good offer might be accepted. So the appointment was made for the next morning. Now my first impression on the phone of the saleswomen was her being a frumpy, middle aged one, especially when she said to look for the station wagon with a flower decal on the side. She arrived and we followed her through a gate to near where the boat was docked. Out of the dark blue Mercedes Station wagon, with a tiny flower decal on the gas cap cover, appeared a pair of stiletto shoes, followed by shapely legs enclosed in very tight leather pants, with next an very ample pair in a very tight red sweater, and on top of all this a very attractive, young, dark haired head. The voice was the same as on the telephone but one could become accustomed to that, of course. Oh yes, the boat! It was much too big for us. The rigging was complete, high quality and massive, the inside totally unfinished, a disaster, and a major project I wouldn't even consider doing. It was none the less a memorable showing.

    We completed the Atlantic portion of the search by going on down to Key West before heading up and around the Gulf to as far as Corpus Christi, Texas. From there we headed back to Colorado not having found our boat. Janet and family had by this time moved from Salt Lake City to Westminster, a suburb of Denver, and we spent some time with the family. We weren't ask to leave but it was now time to start our Pacific Coast search so we packed up the car, waved good by and hugged and kissed our daughter and grandchildren, I shook Craig's hand leaving the hugs and kiss for Jeanne, and we headed west.

CHAPTER 26

Our plans were to head to Palm Desert and spend a few days with friends Nancy and Richard Williams, who we had met years before through the P.E.O. Bed and Breakfast fund raising project. I would also able to visit one of my best galleries, the Richard Danskin Gallery. A really class act that I was in for a dozen years or more. While we were there Nancy asked if we would like to house sit for a month while they made a trip to England. We said we were set on our quest to find our boat and thought we would have to carry on.

The next day as we were just about to San Diego the cell phone rang and the call was from the mayor's office in Bloomingdale, Illinois. I will elaborate on this as it was not a total surprise. In the Village of Bloomingdale there is a group called the Business Promotion and Cultural Development Committee and my contact with them was through Remo Turano, a very good man and proprietor of Turano's Bakery. He had seen one of my life size golf sculptures at a show and had taken my brochure. The Committee would raise private funds to buy outdoor sculptures to be placed about the Village. They had purchased one piece for the library and choose one of mine in 2001 as their second purchase for the newly renovated golf course. On our trip east we had stopped by to see how they were treating my sculpture and to say hello. In an informal meeting at the mayor's office with Remo, the mayor Bob Iden, and executive Mary Ellen Johnson, they explained that they were looking into their third purchase, a sculpture to honor their police and fire department. I gave them information on several sculptors that had done related sculptures and suggestions on how to approach doing such a project as commissioning a sculpture is much different than buying an existing work.

There was a hint that they may want to contact me later and I was already thinking of the possibility of receiving the commission. We had made arrangements with another couple in Loveland whose house would be available for three months if the commission was to come my way. They were doing the Great Loop trip on their boat. (The Great Loop trip is to circle from a starting point and do the Atlantic Intracoastal Waterway, the canal system in New York into the Great Lakes or the more scenic route into Canadian waters into Ontario and Georgian Bay, then to and down the Mississippi River, around the edge of the Gulf and return to your starting point which can be anywhere on the Loop. If you accomplish this your are a Looper.) We met them in Louisiana for lunch as we were going westward in our car and they were headed eastward to where they had left their boat. It was at lunch we discussed the possibility of renting their house if the timing worked out after our Atlantic and Gulf coast search was done and they started their final leg of the Loop which for them had started in the Great Lakes. They would be starting to complete it in June which would work out good for us.

    The phone call had been made to ask me if I would do the commission and I replied in the affirmative. At this time the house rental in Loveland would be about six weeks away. A quick phone call to our friends in Palm Desert to say we would love to house sit and another to the Loveland couple to secure the rental. This would leave us a few days to visit San Diego and my family before the Williams left for England and we would have a few days after their return to get to Loveland in time to get our instructions for the house rental. Should work out just fine, and it did but just.

    We settled into our house sitting duties. Rising not too early and picking fresh oranges or a grapefruit off their trees, a leisurely breakfast reading the paper, you get the picture. The Palm Desert area in the spring is just about perfect. But I wasn't letting the search for the Hunter Passage 42 go dormant and nearly daily would check YachtWorld.com for any new listings and check other places on the web. On the evening of May 14, 2003 a listing on YachtWorld.com showed up for a 1994 Hunter Passage 42 at a starting bid of $125,000. This was the first time I had seen a listing of this type and I clicked on the link to National Liquidators and there was the boat and the particulars. The next morning I called about seeing the boat and was told they were bringing it to Newport Beach on Friday and would be able to show it on Saturday so I made the appointment. (It is a two hour drive from Palm Desert to Newport Beach if you plan your drive to miss the rush hour.) We had a good showing and although there were a few things needing repair, none were ones I was worried about doing myself.

The procedure was to make an initial offer by Sunday afternoon, the bank would review it on Tuesday, and you would be notified Wednesday by 4:30 pm. We drove back to Palm Desert discussing what we should do. To add to our scheduling conflicts Jeanne's sister and brother-in-law, Jo and Carl Franz, were to arrive in a few days for a weeks stay. I called up Repo Bob at National Liquidators on Sunday and said we would like to make an offer at $90,000. He groaned and said he didn't think the bank would go for it but he would submit it anyway. I thought we were under bid a bit but with the several repairs that needed doing and our time constraints I needed a good price. Wednesday came and no response from the bank At 4:30 pm on Friday Repo Bob calls and says the bank had just countered at $98,000. He can't believe they would come back that low especially since it had been on the market less than a week. I look at Jeanne and she looks at me and I tell Bob we will take it.

They will let us start fixing things before closing as time is running out as we need to be back in Loveland in ten days. Saturday and Sunday the four us trip to Newport Beach and start the fixing up. It is then that I call him Bob, who starts working for us. By days end on Saturday he has our insurance man contacted, a licensed Captain scheduled for lessons, the surveyor scheduled, the off shore closing set up for the closing day, has recommended taking the boat to Ensenada, Baja California for at least three months to avoid California's high sales tax, given us the name of an attorney in San Diego that can do all the paper work, has recommended the Coral Marina in Ensenada, and has found a slip for us to dock the boat at for a few days after we close. I have written a personal check for the down payment and on Monday set up a wire transfer for the balance. On Tuesday the off shore closing is accomplished and Jeanne and I are the owners of a 1994 Hunter Passage 42. We need to learn a lot fast.

Jo and Carl are taken to the Palm Springs Airport and we depart on Friday the 29th of May, with our captain on board, heading for San Diego for the first night. We have two couples near Newport Beach who are both our friends and friends of each other, Terry and Linda Simpkins and Bill and Jennifer Kirwin. We had all known each other from our Aspen days. We left our car at the Kirwin's and the four of them will come down to Ensenada and bring us and the captain back on Sunday. All goes as planned. The entrance into San Diego Harbor was our first big port and went without a hitch. The next day was perfect and other than an exciting docking at the Coral Marina it was a very good trip. The Marina dock master had all the paper work prepared in minutes and we were able to have a drink and a nice dinner at the hotel. The next morning our four saviors showed up early and we made a lazy drive back up the coast doing tourist things along the way. By evening our car was picked up, the captain paid and delivered home and we then spent the night at the Kirwins leaving for Colorado the next day. We actually had a day to spare before assuming our rental house. It would be three months before we saw our new home in the water again but we do get there and start an all new adventure.

But first there was some work for me to get done and as usual all does not go exactly as planned. I propose several poses for the sculpture and start doing a small sculpture of the fireman which is called a maquette, not too detailed but enough to get a visual sense of the pose. The committee in Bloomingdale doesn't show great enthusiasm so a number of sketches are made. I will admit that drawing is not my strong suit but I think they were sufficient for preliminary judgments. By the time the back and forth was done, which is not unexpected in doing a commission of this kind, the first month was pretty well used up. The title for the sculpture was agreed upon to be Everyday Heroes which was fine by me. I then finished the fireman maquette into a finished sculpture, made a mold and cast waxes to have two castings started. I sent a photo of the wax to the committee to see if they might like it better than the sketches. By this time there would not be time to start the life size work before our rental ran out.

The delay was all right with the Bloomingdale group as they were still fund raising and the dedication was planned to be September 11, 2004 which coincided with Septemberfest, a very popular event for the Village of Bloomingdale. With more than a year to go we all could relax a bit. At my suggestion the Committee had one of their fireman and one of their policeman suit up and at the site try a number of poses that might result in exactly what they would like. What a good suggestion it was as they found what they wanted and sent me a good number of photos. I was very satisfied with it. It was left that if they would send me the proposed initial fee I would sculpt the maquette and submit the final proposal which would include the previously agreed to price and a schedule for completion. This I could do on the boat. We found another potential Loveland rental to live in and a work space at one of the finishing shops I had used many times before to do the sculptures. I think the Bloomingdale group also needed more fund raising time. It would work out. So it was back on the road to Ensenada.

CHAPTER 27

The Hotel Coral & Marina is just under one hundred miles south of San Diego and once through the border crossing and clearing the somewhat confusing first few miles it's a very pleasant drive with the last thirty miles quite scenic. The Hotel is gated, upscale with several swimming pools, a good restaurant, workout room and tennis courts. The Marina is excellent and the service is top rate. As we drove down to the parking area nearest the docks we were excited to see our boat as it had been three months since our very rushed purchase and trip down. It was right where we had left her and looked clean and ready to be boarded, which we did. We opened all the hatches to let the Pacific breeze blow through and did a thorough check and all was fine. We were home and it felt just right.

We had brought enough supplies with us so we wouldn't have to go into Esenada for a day or two even though it is just a few miles and is quite easy to get around. In the early 2000s it was just starting to experience a growth spurt as Californians were discovering the value of the real estate, especially when compared to north of the border, and felt confident enough to buy property in Mexico. Within the first week we were feeling very comfortable here and had met a number of boaters who were doing the same thing as we were in keeping our new purchase out of California for the first three months of a six month ownership period. The Marina had the nickname of The Ninety Day Corral.

As I mentioned in the previous chapter we had an exciting docking when we first arrived. The Captain asked me if I wanted to dock the boat stern in which is the best position for having the boat and makes for the easiest exit when taking the boat out. I said I would give it a try and almost made it in when the boat suddenly decided to swing over toward the adjacent boat in our designated slip. He quickly got a foot on both boats pushing us apart and I then drove out into the open area called the turning basin. By this time a crowd had gathered which we later learned was part of a good natured entertainment for the Marina patrons. The Captain took over and made a bigger mess of trying to stern in than I had but recovered immediately and took the boat back to the turning basin and we then went bow in and tied up. I was later informed of the surge in the Marina basin combined with the prevailing winds and the narrowness of the fairways between the boats makes for very difficult docking. Almost all boaters, especially first time visitors, have problems and thus the spectators.

Eventually I learned how to dock my boat under these conditions and since docking here was as difficult as it gets I had very few problems during our later travels. I also developed the habit of helping take lines from other boaters when they came in to dock and met many who became friends, some of whom we still make contact with and visit. It is a very nice community. At the Coral Marina new boats come in almost every week as others leave after they have met the ninety day requirements. It was a fun place to be and we would have the boat here for almost two years.

Most of the Marina staff were Mexican and all were efficient, courteous, helpful and cheerful. There were several that did work on the boats such as bottom cleaning (necessary every sixty days in these waters) and washing who scheduled through the Marina office and were likewise both good and hard workers. A boat yard, Baja Naval, in Ensenada was a top notch yard. It was as good as any I have done business with. Ensenada itself was a very comfortable place to shop and dine and by most measures clean and friendly. Jeanne had some dental work done, as later I would in Puerto Vallarta, and was very satisfied.

There was some downside. There were areas in town you

MY STORY ~ 163

wouldn't want to be in at night and there was some crime. One of the resident boat owners we met owned a number of Pemex gas stations and was quite wealthy by Mexican standards. He expressed concern of the threat of possible kidnapping of his son for ransom and thought he should move to Spain where his wife was from. A year after we left he had moved there taking his boat with him.

I will take a break here to write a few thoughts down on culture and intelligence. Again I skate on thin ice but I first will reiterate that I was brought up to treat every person I met without bias and should only be judged by the content of their character. All the Mexican people we came in contact with in our stay in Ensenada gave us no sense that respect was not deserved. But that is not what I want to discuss here.

In 1974 James Michener's book Centennial was published. Some time later, probably in the late 1980s when we lived in Loveland, I would read and enjoy it as most of the story took place geographically just to the east of Greeley, just east of us. I remember one part where Hans Brumbaugh, the German sugar beet farmer, discussed the cultural differences of his farm hands. Understand this was sugar beet farming and the labor was what is known as stoop labor, hard, menial, backbreaking. He pontified that the European's would do good work exactly what was asked of them and as soon as they saved enough money they would quit and buy their own farm. The East Asian's (mainly Chinese at the time) would do good work exactly what was asked of them and soon would ask if they could grow a few vegetables for themselves and family on a small unused piece of land, only tending it after they had done his farm work. Soon they would have saved enough money, both in pay and extra from vegetable sales, to buy their own land and start a thriving vegetable farm. The Chicano's (Mexicans) would do good work exactly what was asked of them and if provided a place to relax and enjoy their music and food on their days off seemed perfectly contented and had no higher ambitions and were therefore the perfect farm hands.

I am sure Michener at some later date would have

regretted these paragraphs in his thousand plus page book because it would appear to be so politically incorrect, but it does demonstrate cultural differences. In an earlier chapter I wrote of my Grandfather share cropping a small piece of his ranch to a Japanese family just after World War II that ended with that family, through hard work and saving, being able to buy their own land and eventually become one of the biggest strawberry growers in California.

Culture is one important aspect in human endeavor as is intelligence. All men (persons) are not created equal. They should be treated as equals, but they are not all equal. This is obvious in almost any test and is so with regard to intelligence. Environment and culture plays into the achievement of man, but intelligence is such an important part that it cannot be ignored no matter how or why one should try to do so. When you combine a good environment with a culture of achievement and intelligence you can expect good, or even great, results.

It is disheartening to me to witness the Caucasian male being dismissed as the real creator of what we take for granted as the modern western world. In the current fuzzy political and philosophical thought he is being demoted to the average but when looked at through history of just the last few millennium you cannot come to any other conclusion than he has been at the forefront of all we recognize as real achievement.

To be sure this same cultural group, along with others through governments and religions, have created unimaginable weapons of war and caused enormous destruction and misery. One can only wish that this dark side of human nature could be controlled and the creative side be set truly free.

At this time we are entering a period of social disruption not recognizing the influence of technology and globalization is having on both skilled and unskilled labor. Labor is a commodity and what it is valued at is determined by supply and demand. Globalization has reduced the value of labor and technology has replaced a good portion of the need for both skilled and unskilled labor. This leaves the less skilled, especially those

without a cultural work ethic and having below average intelligence, with an enormous gap between the jobs of value available and their numbers. (Technology is of course causing disruption in higher valued jobs, but those in these areas have a much better chance of adjusting to other employment.)
In 1994 the book The Bell Curve by Murray and Herrnstein was published and due to a small section of the book on racial intelligence levels was pillared to the point that the rest of their research and conclusions were lost in the political correctness maelstrom. Somewhere in all this was their warning that as the percentage of the population of the unemployed and unemployable increased the social fabric of our culture would tear and that the results would be dire. I think that this is the place we find ourselves in now and it is a world wide condition. How this situation can be handled is the over riding question of our time. We better find the answer soon.

We quickly got into the rhythm of living aboard a boat. It is a comfortable life style, living in a small space for some reason lends itself to an efficient sense of security. Just before we left the boat to return to Colorado, as we prepared to leave, Linda Simpkins had mentioned to us that this would be an interlude in our life. That sounded just right, so we named the boat Interlude. We had the vinyl letters made and I placed them on the port and starboard sides where a previous name had been removed. I then added the hailing port Loveland, CO on the stern and we were now a legally signed vessel and documented with the U.S. Coast Guard.

It was time to start the maquette sculptures for the Bloomingdale project and I set up so I could work either in the cockpit or in the saloon. It was good to have a definite work to accomplish and in a few weeks I had it done. Photos were taken and I made a brochure showing the best angle in a large picture on the front and a second page showing the views from six angles. Putting this together with a contract that requested payment in three installments. First to start and complete the sculpture in clay, second to finance the bronze casting through completion, and third upon delivery. Also included was an approximate schedule and promise of a delivery date. The package was sent and in a short time the affirmative response was received with the first payment. It was a go and our plans would be firmed up for the next several months.

Again we closed up the boat for an expected 3 months and headed back to Loveland. The house we had rented was for two months and from our storeroom I brought enough of my sculpture equipment and clay to build the armatures for both figures, build the sculpting platforms, and sculpt the heads. I asked Bloomingdale to send me the policeman's cap, badge, and arm patches and the fireman's helmet. I would use both as models and where possible actual make molds to get extra details on the badge and helmet shield.

Once the armatures and sculpting platforms were built (the two platforms were on wheels and shaped so they could placed together for the final positions or separated to make access to each separately) I moved everything over to the rented studio space. My clay heater and about 300 pounds of clay was brought over from the storage room. The real work was now ready to be done. It would take another two months, seven days a week to complete the sculptures. For the last month we lived with our daughter and family and I commuted from their house in Westminster to Loveland each day. Update photos were taken of the work in progress and then the final photos were sent. Approval was given for the casting to be done and the second check was received.

I made the arrangements with the mold maker, wax pourer, wax chasers, the casting foundry, metal chasers, and the patinier. I had used all these craftsmen before and was confident they would do an excellent job for me. We were able to arrange a house sitting for a couple of weeks early in May, in the beautiful home of Ralph and Bobbie Beyersdorf on Lake Loveland, which allowed me to be in on the final assembly and finishing of the bronzes. The patina application was done on May 18 and then Everyday Heroes was left at Dream Chasers who had done the metal work and where I had rented the studio space.

(All went as scheduled and Everyday Heroes was picked up by the good mayor of the Village of Bloomingdale, Bob Iden, and a friend on July 4, 2004. The unveiling was as planned on September 11, 2004 and Jeanne and I were in attendance. Just after the Septemberfest parade had ended and the local dance school performed to The Stars Spangle Banner there was a dedication and then the unveiling was done after a few short speeches, mine being deemed by Jeanne to have been just the right length, if you can believe that. The weather was a perfect mid-western fall day and if Norman Rockwell had been there the scene would have become a painting.)

It was now the end of May, we headed back to Ensenada and back to the boating life. The pressure was now off. It turned out to be my last work although a small storage bin with clay and some tools was always with me. It is at this moment in the garage a few steps from where I write this. In Mexico I had learned the meaning of the word "manyana." Most people think it means tomorrow but it's real meaning is "just not today." Maybe tomorrow is the day?

CHAPTER 28

We finally had a couple of months to really get into the live aboard life. A nice social life with others on the docks, pot lucks, some bridge games, sunsets and trips to town for grocery shopping learning where things were. The tamale ladies came once or twice a week, chicken or beef, one dollar each and they were good. We would take the boat out for afternoon sails and started to think we could actually do this. About eight miles due west was Todas Santos, a small island (technically two islands) which with the prevailing westerly winds was a challenge to sail out to and around before returning. Alas, Interlude under her captain and first mate never made it. Tacking repeatedly into the wind was very slow and after we had made about a mile we would turn to a comfortable beam reach for a few hours of lazy sailing. We did go out under power and as it turned out this would be the way we traveled most of the time, as will be explained later.

Occasionally we had some excitement on the docks. One of the just arrived boats was on our dock and the owners and their captain had just come down from San Francisco, secured the boat and took off for the return trip by rental car. I had met them as they docked and they seemed like people we would like to know. Quick introductions lets Jeanne and me meet Kim and Sharon Barr. They had a Passport sail boat of a few years old and a truly beautiful boat capable of world cruising which was their goal. About two days after they had left I noticed their boat getting lower in the water. I went to the dock master and reported this and he asked if I was sure and I said yes. He then called their number and left the message on their answering machine. "Mr. Barr, call me immediately regarding your vessel!" and hung up. I went back to our boat and left another message, "Kim, don't worry. I have noticed that your boat is about an inch or two lower in the water over the last two days. Give me a call and I will be glad to check on it for you." He called back a few hours later and somewhat reluctantly told me were he hid his emergency key. An inspection showed water half way up the engine crankcase. I couldn't find out why the bilge pump wasn't operating and the manual pump wasn't working. Kim arranged for the local mechanic to check it out the next morning and when he got there he threw the circuit breaker that had inadvertently been turned off and out went the water. (I had looked for it but it was in an unusual spot.) One of the raw water strainer lids had cracked, was letting in the water and was easily repaired. Kim thanked me very much and later he and Sharon took us out for a very nice dinner.

One other time the dock master and several dock hands were standing around a small power boat discussing what they should do as it was obvious the boat was taking on some water. All of a sudden there was some gurgling noise and the boat went to the bottom in about eight feet of water.

You can Google Earth for Coral Hotel Ensenada and see the hotel and marina and get a good sense of the docks. We eventually had the first slip on the fourth dock in from the ocean and the side toward the hotel. These were all two boat slips but being this close to the turning basin made docking and exiting very easy to do. Notice how many of the boats stick out into the fairways beyond the dock ends. Coming into to dock you would see nothing but pulpits, anchors, or sterns on each side. With the surge, which was always present and unpredictable, and the prevailing wind on the beam made for exciting docking. It was not always pretty and it is not a good sound it makes when fiberglass and metal meet.

During this period we made one trip back to Loveland to see my Everyday Heroes sculpture finished in mid-May. We made several trips to Palm Desert to see the Williams and on one of these trips we looked at some real estate thinking maybe that this was a possible place to land. At an open house we met John McKowan. He was my kindred spirit. We were about the same age, he had a Hunter 41 sailboat, had spent a year skiing in Sun Valley about the same time I was in Aspen, and liked to play golf. Later this year when we made our first visit to Puget Sound by car I made a short trip with him on his boat as he relocated it to his home marina. On one of our trips to Palm Desert we played golf and he had one of his best games. His wife Dee was equally likeable, attractive and a good athlete. On another visit the four us played a round of golf, had an excellent dinner at their place and we were guest overnight. Some years later he died from cancer after a long battle. Your sense of mortality is heightened when someone you truly like passes away much too soon in both their life and in your acquaintance.

It was a short trip to San Diego and so it was nice to be able to visit my sister Nancy and join in occasionally for family functions. Nancy was a great cook so there were always good meals and it was good to see my nephews and niece and their kids.

Terry and Linda Simpkins came down for an overnight and we did a great day sail on a good westerly wind. Terry is an experienced sailor and encouraged me to be more aggressive with the sails and we hit some pretty good speeds. When you live aboard the boat is not set up to heel over much and to make faster turns. We secured as best we could and had a really good and exciting sail.

As August approached we decided that as we would be heading north on the boat early the next year maybe it would be not only fun but informative to drive up the coast and visit the marinas we would be stopping at to check on entrances and dock arrangements. There was also a chance to house sit for Dave and Sally Ewald in their super home and vineyard in Sebastopol in the wine country. On the way there we stopped at almost every marina we thought we might stay at and in Marina del Rey we visited the California Yacht Club, one of the most prestigious on the West Coast. It turned out they had an "non-resident" membership at a very reasonable price and belonging to a yacht club has many perks, especially reciprocal privileges at most other nice yacht clubs. So we joined and found later it was a very good decision.

We saw old friends in the Bay Area and then spent two days with Rock and Nancy Hill in Point Richmond just north of Berkley, another of the boaters we met in Ensenada when they brought their new boat down from San Francisco to the Coral Marina. They are bridge players so evenings after Nancy's good dinners were capped off with bridge.

We then spent a week in luxury at the Ewalds, enjoying that beautiful spot in the country and feeding their two cats. It was then on up the coast and we made much faster time as the ports start getting a lot farther apart and there are many fewer marinas to investigate. We had the chance to visit another boating couple Kurt and Terry Schoeder at their home in Squim, Washington. Kurt was a jet aircraft test pilot and he named his trawler Mach Zero. A fun visit as the County Fair was in progress and was everything you would think a county fair should be.

Next was to Anacortes where we visited with friends from Loveland, Ken and Nancy Murphy. Ken is a retired military helicopter pilot who flew many personnel recovery missions in Viet Nam. We met when they were house hunting in Loveland and happened to be able to see them in Vero Beach when we drove through on our East Coast search as Nancy was closing up her mother's home there. They were at this visit having their dream house built up on a hillside overlooking the sound. A very pretty place and their house came out as planned. More good bridge playing.

It was then back down the coast and another brief stay with the Hill's. Some where about this time Jeanne spots an ad for a Crystal Cruise to Alaska leaving from and returning to San Francisco at such a good price we had to go. Not only a good price but the dates were such that our trip to Bloomingdale for the Everyday Heroes dedication would fit in nicely. As soon as Jeanne's sister Jo heard what we were going to do, she and husband Carl decided to join us.

So here is what happened. On September 1 Jeanne and I checked into the El Rancho Inn near the San Francisco Airport with a stay, park and fly package. The next day we flew to Denver to stay with Janet and family. On September 9 we flew to Chicago, rented a car, and spent three nights with our Lake Forest friends Laroy and Lois Meyer. We attended the Everyday Heroes dedication as planned on September 11. The following night finding a motel near the airport and flying back the next day to San Francisco. Our son-in-law's aunt Jane picked us up at the airport and treated us to an overnight at her home. A second night was spent at the El Rancho Inn where Jo and Carl met us. The next morning it was to the Crystal ship and off to Alaska on a wonderful twelve day cruise. Upon return, with an early debarkation, we retrieved the car and did a little sightseeing before dropping off Carl and Jo at the airport. We then headed south to Ensenada, and Interlude, to rest up. And rest up we did.

CHAPTER 29

This brings us to the end of 2004 and the start of 2005. On May 4, 2005 we will return to the U.S. aboard Interlude starting our journey north. Much was to happen before this date and I will just touch on the main points of the period. We will start to know our boat and make a number of improvements to make life aboard more comfortable. New foam mattress for our stateroom, a number of plumbing repairs and replacements, the addition of two more CNG (compressed natural gas) tanks to provide cooking gas for two months usage with some to spare. A small dingy and a 4 horsepower single stroke outboard motor are added. Several chart books and Charlie's Charts for the Pacific Coast which is a guide for cruising that area. A Garmin 152 GPS was added to the instruments which greatly improved the ease of navigation, but would be later followed by a Garmin 182 Chart Plotter which made navigation a very simple task.

Jeanne has become the same great cook in our small galley that she was in her full size kitchen. We both work at learning to be a team at docking and leaving the dock. I am learning more on sail handling and trimming and we are both becoming more comfortable at operating the boat. As May approached we would feel we are ready for the first and easiest leg of the journey.

I am sure that as October and November rolled by we developed the true live aboard boaters life style. Other than a few repairs and upgrades to the boat, we had tradapted to retirement. I have often mentioned to many of my still working Type A friends that it is possible to adjust to retirement. We had time to do nothing and that takes up a lot more time than you would think. Thanksgiving was spent at my sister's in San Diego and we must have made at least one or two trips to Palm Desert.

It is about this time that a forty-six foot Moody sailboat arrives and I may have helped in the initial docking, or met the owner soon there after. This would be one Gil Saul, owner and captain of Wind Rider. He will become a good friend, along with his wife Becky, and Jeanne and I would make the run from Eureka, CA to Annacortes, WA on their boat. How this comes about will be covered in a later chapter along with our meetings along our separate paths. To Introduce you to them I offer the following.

Gil had recently lost his first wife to her passing and had decided to buy a ocean going sailboat as therapy. You see, Gil is a practicing PhD of Psychiatry and one who took his own advice. He had sailed most of his life and the purchase of Wind Rider was to follow his dream of adventure on the oceans. After an accident involving a shoulder separation he met Becky in his physical therapy and I needn't say too much more. She is a delightful Philipino lady, with a degree in engineering, who to the best of my knowledge had never been on a sailboat before she met Gil. The first few trips they took to Ensenada she had a room in the Hotel Coral and Jeanne and I didn't meet her for quite a while. Gil was very private and I would see him take out his boat by himself on a number of long day sails. I offered several times to go with him but he seemed to value his own company. Over the course of the next few months we began to socialize and I helped out on a couple of occasions on doing some minor repairs for and with him on his boat. I will leave you here for now with the fact that in 2011 Gill and Becky crossed the Atlantic for the second time on Wind Rider on their return from Spain and Portugal and during which Gil had his 80th birthday. He is a much tougher man than I and is now currently working full time in his medical practice in the Los Angeles area.

I have left you with a somewhat wrong impression of my retirement situation with regards to my sculpture career. Until 2007 I continued to fulfill orders for my golf trophies with three

golf clubs in Colorado.
This required some hands-on work in Loveland each year and Jeanne and I made one trip just before Christmas to both accomplish the first half of this project and to visit with our daughter and family in Westminster. We had an early Christmas as they arranged to have his family Christmas in Oregon on alternate years and dragged our daughter and granddaughters off to those other grandparents. We house sat their dog for the Holidays. I got my work done and we also got to visit old friends in the area.

We would repeat this trip in late February 2005 to finish up the trophies and then flew to Destin, FL to spend a week with Jeanne's sister and her husband where they spent their winter months away from the cold in Michigan. A little golf, lots of bridge, and too much to eat made for good times. Jeanne's mother would be there and it was always nice to spend time with her if you didn't mind getting beat at pinochle. I would deliver the trophies on the drive back from Denver to Ensenada.

Similar arrangements were made each year until 2007 when I turned over the molds to the Castle Pines Golf Club and the other two Clubs had changed the format of their tournaments and went another direction for trophies. Thus official retirement can be said to have been in 2008.

We continued to prepare for our north bound journey and early on the morning of May 4th we untied the dock lines and headed out of the Coral Marina after almost a two year visit. It had been a very busy and good two years. We left just before sunrise and as I made the familiar turn out of the entrance I suddenly realized it was the first time I had the boat out in the dark. All the marker lights seemed much closer than expected and the radar became a true friend to reinforce my confidence that I was where I thought I was. In an hour the sun came up and the world at sea became familiar and comfortable again.

CHAPTER 30

We arrived in San Diego around 2:00 pm and tied up to the customs dock as instructed. The customs agent boarded Interlude and checked our passports, boat papers, asked a few questions and looked around the boat and welcomed us back to the United States.

The day before we had brought the car up and made arrangements at the San Diego Yacht Club to spend three nights on a reciprocal with our California Yacht Club membership and left the car in their parking lot. A friend from the Coral Marina was in San Diego and met us for lunch and then took us back to Ensenada.

Everything had gone like clockwork and as I headed Interlude down the fairway to the assigned slip I discovered for the first time what it was like to dock a boat where there were no surges, currents, or wind. When I stopped the boat it just sat there. I could step off and have Jeanne hand me the lines. There were many times in the future that was not the case, but only rarely the difficulties of docking at the Coral were exceeded. While at the San Diego Yacht Club Jeanne had the chance to play in the ladies bridge game and won fourteen dollars.

San Diego has a transient dock which is a very nice place to stay. It is first come first served, reasonable, and in a great location adjacent to the police and customs dock right at the entrance to the main channel for Shelter Island. There is a limit to consecutive days you can stay but by altering these with the South Western Yacht Club and the Coronado Yacht Club with our reciprocal CYC membership we were able to stay almost three weeks in great locations and friendly environments in a place of paradise.

Most of my family made visits and I think when they left thought what we were doing wasn't such a crazy idea after all. The Coronado Yacht Club is just across the street from the famous Coronado Hotel and we walked to it and all around the town. The weather as expected was perfect and it was going to be hard to leave but we set the date at May 23rd to head to Oceanside. Again a friend helped us leap frog the car from San Diego to there and we made our arrangement with the Oceanside Yacht Club for a slip. This was working out quite well and would continue to do so until we stopped in San Francisco for an extended stay and would need a more permanent berth

In early June we made a tour to Catalina Island leaving the Alamitos Bay Yacht Club in Long Beach and took a mooring ball at Emerald Bay. Gil and Becky Saul on Wind Rider joined us as they arrived as planned just after we got there. They set anchor just outside the mooring field. The next day, after a bumpy night, we rounded the north end of Catalina and spent the second night at Cat Harbor. It was then around the south end of the island to spend two nights in Avalon Harbor. Gil and Becky peeled off to head home to Newport. We did meet up with Coral Marina boaters Ed and Paula Martin who got us a guest pass to their Catalina Yacht Club which allowed us to park our dingy at the club's dock. No reciprocal with CYC here. We joined the Martins to a movie at the famous Avalon Theater and Casino which was quite a treat.

After our Catalina adventure we headed for Marina Del Rey and the CYC where we would stay, then leave the boat for two weeks, and eventually the car for a longer period. While there we were able to have my cousins Bobbie and Jack Keogh for lunch on the boat for a good visit. Jeanne's nephew Ethan also made a visit as he was teaching mathematics as a temporary hire in nearby colleges and was involved in a theater group and loving life away from his Michigan roots. It is from here that we will restart our trip north and the next major stop would be Santa Barbara.

We entered Santa Barbara Harbor on June 29 and initially

took a side tie on the main dock. This didn't work out in that the only electricity available was 220 volt so we took a slip. This meant an interesting approach as the pilings were the same spacing as Interlude was wide. You gently move the boat into position and then power into place with the appropriately named rub rails pushing the pilings apart enough to let you enter the slip. All went well and we decided to spend a couple of days in Santa Barbara before attempting the Point Conception rounding. Point Conception is considered the West Coast's Cape Horn and our extra day layover set us up for a ten day delay and the hiring of a Captain to take Interlude to San Francisco without us on board. The wind had changed direction and speed and made the Point no place for the inexperienced. Of course immediately after the Captain and crew were hired and paid on July 15th for their evening departure the winds died down and they had a beautiful rounding and trip that we could not only have done with ease but which we had been looking forward to doing.

During our Santa Barbara stay, after it became obvious it would be several days at least, we did a one day car rental and drove to Marina Del Rey and picked up our car at the CYC, dropped off the rental and returned to Santa Barbara. After about a week we thought how bad could Point Conception be and took the car to San Louis Obispo leaving it at the train station and took the train back to Santa Barbara. The train passes right through Vandenberg Air Force base where I had worked for a few months in 1958 and a few of the missile buildings stood about but none I really remembered. The highlight of the trip was that the train stopped directly above Point Conception to allow a north bound to pass and Jeanne and I had the chance to see the Point in full force. No way would we try that rounding. The sea's were white with waves and spray blowing due south. It was a mess and had been for over a week. There is shelter on the south side of the Point to anchor while waiting but even it did not look inviting, even if for only a few hours, not days. It was at that moment we decided to have the boat taken by more experienced hands. But as written above, they had a beautiful trip up. Timing is everything, as the saying goes.

We made arrangements for a slip at the Saint Francis Yacht Club for Interlude and the crew to be berthed on their arrival in San Francisco. It is located at the first marina area after going under the Golden Gate bridge on the south side and is one of the most prestigious of the yacht clubs in the United States. As members of CYC we have a one night guest slip and may stay two more days at forty-two dollars a night for our size boat. Interlude arrived in the early evening on the 17th and we picked the crew up the next morning and rented a big car for their trip back to Santa Barbara. Interlude was in good shape and now safely in San Francisco. As I was tidying up the boat a large Cabin Cruiser pulled up on the opposite side of the dock and I stepped across and took a line to help the owner tie up. Jeanne and I then met Jaren Leet and his girl friend, Kathryn, who was visiting from New Zealand. They were very friendly thanked us for the help.

The next morning Jaren invited us to lunch at the Club as he was giving a presentation on the J-105 sailboat racing and the race that was to be held at the Saint Francis that weekend. Jaren was the commodore of the J-105 fleet and would also be racing his own boat in the event. We of course said we would be delighted as this was an all new experience for us and you can't pass up the chance to have lunch at the Saint Francis. We arrived, about 100 steps from our boat, exactly at 12:00 noon and were greeted by Jaren at the door and escorted to the head table where he and Kathryn were to be seated. Next came a gentleman who was seated between Jeanne and Jaren who was the Commodore of the Saint Francis Yacht Club and then the table was filled by several more dignitaries. I want you to understand that this was the head table and to be seated there is no small honor. All the people we were introduced to wondered who we were to deserve such an honor. Taking a line at the dock to help tie up a boat would never have been considered. As I learned later when I accompanied Jaren taking his boat back to Sausalito, just across the bay after the races were over, he needed no help what so ever in docking his boat.

Jaren's presentation was excellent and accompanied by many slides depicting all facets of J-105 sailboat racing. It had absolutely nothing in common the sailing of Interlude and made me realize that not only I had lots to learn but that I could never ever be a sailboat racer. I am nervous when within a quarter mile of another vessel or fixed object and these characters spend the entire race just avoiding crashes as they jockey for position and advantage. I spent the next two days watching J-105's and their crews do their thing just off the jetty wall. As Jaren repeated many time during his talk, "Fun!, Fun!, Fun!"

The day after the luncheon we moved to a City Marina dock just a few steps away from the Saint Francis dock where we had just been. The fact that I had to wash the sea gull droppings off the dock, the showers and restroom were a long walk away and not very pleasant, the twelve dollars per day, including electricity, was a bargain and we would stay there almost a month.

CHAPTER 31

We would remain in the San Francisco Bay Area until we finally cast off the lines on May 19, 2006 to start our northward trip to Anacortes, WA and beyond. Again many things would happen in our lives during this period. It was in the Bay Area where Jeanne and I first met in Palo Alto in the fall of 1962, were married, had daughter Janet, bought our first house and was home for 9 years. We still had many friends in the area as well as many new ones, and would make even more during our stay. This chapter will cover that period and will end as we head toward the Golden Gate Bridge on the morning of the 19th.

The month of July close to the Golden Gate Bridge is invariable cold and foggy. It was thus for this stay but being able to walk into downtown San Francisco, Fisherman's Warf, and along the waterfront as well the constant activity in the nearby park and the bay made it a very exciting place to be. Our best of friends Dick and Carolyn Brennan made two visits, one for a day sail about the bay with me trying to negotiate the constantly changing currents, tides, and wind directions under sail which made for some good natured ribbing from Dick. They came for a second time to view the Tall Ships Armada on a spectacular sunshiny day which we toured under power with me in total control. Neal and Patty Shea came up for dinner on the boat and were as usual best company. Kim and Sharon Barr invited us to their fantastic home on the Tiburon hillside with sixty steps from top to bottom and unparalleled views of the bay. Rock and Nancy Hill came over in their boat from Point Richmond and docked overnight with dinner and bridge aboard. Life was very good and a fun time was being had.

Some time early in August Gil and Becky Saul stopped by for an overnight on Wind Rider and docked nearby. They were on their way to Alaska, a bit late, or more accurately way too late. We were to get a phone call when they made their next stop in Bodega Bay that he was having some problems with his auto pilot, or navigation lights, and wanted some advice. I am not sure how the subject came up but Jeanne and I volunteered we had the time and would like to have the experience by joining them for the remainder of their trip as far as Anacortes, WA. The offer was accepted and we planned to met them in Eureka, CA on the 18th. We found a slip in Brickyard Cove Marina in Point Richmond to leave Interlude, just a few blocks away from Rock and Nancy's home.

We drove up to Eureka as planned and arranged to leave the car in the Woodley Island Marina where the Sauls had their boat in a slip. What ever it was that needed fixing got fixed in the next day or two, we put on more supplies, and then started our first adventure as crew members heading up the Pacific Coast on it's wilder end. One fun highlight before we left was introducing Becky to a thrift shop in Old Downtown Eureka where she found a perfect fitting, beautiful condition, black mink coat at a ridiculously low price. A little more on this shortly.

Our first day was sixty-four miles to Crescent City followed the next day for an overnight twenty-seven hour run to Newport, OR. At this point a little information is required for you to understand what was happening. First, but not that important, is that Wind Rider is a bigger and higher quality boat than our Interlude. A nice forward stateroom and an almost private head were our quarters. Second, and most important, is that the inlets to most of the harbors are over bars that need to be crossed at the right times with respect to tides and winds and are much farther apart than bay entries south of San Francisco. Unless you want to take undo risks, you motor all the way and plan your crossing time accordingly. Getting there at the wrong time can make for very uncomfortable and even dangerous situations. Some times the entries are simply closed by the Coast

Guard as too dangerous to cross and you just have to stay out in the ocean and continue on or wait it out. This can also be most uncomfortable and scary. The cautious approach is always taken by smart boaters. The other types you sometime read about or see their boats wrecked on the rocks near the entry channels.

We divided the watches between Gil, Becky, and me as Jeanne wasn't quite ready to operate the boat by herself. Since I sleep best early and generally wake up very early I usually took the after midnight watch and would be good until daylight. Becky took the early day portion and Gil the evening. We all three would be about most of the daytime period and this schedule worked out on the three overnight runs we made.

Another schedule is eating meals. Jeanne and I both like breakfast early, lunch around noon and dinner around 6:00 pm. We generally eat light with a main meal at dinner. The Sauls prefer a light or no breakfast, a large meal at noon and a very late dinner. After the first couple of days it was decided the best solution for meals that we would fix our own and eat at our own schedule. I must tell you that when Becky fixed their noonday meal she would retire to the galley and would chop, cut and stir fry up copious amounts of vegetables and meat, or fish, and serve it on large plates of rice. Gil could eat more food for a man his size than any I have ever seen.

Our daughter Janet and the two granddaughters met us in Newport and spent a night there at a nearby motel and then took Jeanne up the coast as the three of us did another overnight up to Gray's Harbor. We left Newport late in the afternoon and the seas were pretty rough for the first few hours. Around ten o'clock the seas quieted down and we made our entrance across the bar on time and with ease. Jeanne rejoined us there and we spent one day doing a little sightseeing with the family and then they headed back towards home and we prepared for the last long leg to Anacortes. We rounded Cape Flattery on my watch about 3:00 am and then into the Straits of Juan de Fuca for a fast with the tide run to Anacortes. It had been a good trip which gave me confidence that Jeanne and I could repeat it on Interlude the next spring by only doing day trips and stopping at more ports.

Gil still wanted to touch Alaska but we talked him out of it. We had done the cruise ship tour the year before and suggested they find one out of Seattle. They found a good deal which would leave in a couple of days and a car rental was arranged for us to take them to the dock and then again to pick them up on their return. They had a wonderful, stress free cruise and if I am not mistaken Becky got to wear her new fur coat. They both thanked us for saving them from what would have been a really long and bad trip of well over a thousand miles much too late in the season. A few things needed to be fixed on Wind Rider and when those were accomplished we did a nice easy tour of the San Juan Islands. Jeanne and I then rented a car and headed south to pick up our car in Eureka and then back to the Bay Area and Interlude. Gil and Becky rented a car and headed out to see Banff and Jasper National Parks and had a great tour before their return to Southern California on Wind Rider.

Upon returning to Point Richmond we secured a slip for the next 6 months at the Brickyard Cove Marina and settle into our live aboard life style again. A few weeks later I get a phone call from Gil Saul telling me he is southbound, is in Bodega Bay, and will reach S.F. the next day and could I find him space near our location as his auto pilot is on the blink again. The dock master OK's the use of one of their loading docks for a couple of days and Gil tells me he will call me when he gets close. He and Becky arrived well after dark on Wind Rider after a harrowing crossing of the Bay, but are safely tied up at about 10:00 pm. The next two days would be spent trying to get the auto pilot up and running. We were unsuccessful and the two of them would head back out hand steering for three days and nights to get home to Newport Beach. Becky had become as tough a sailor as Gil and that was, and will be, a very good thing.

As 2005 closes we have spent the last two months not doing much. One major accomplishment is replacing the holding tank on Interlude. For those of you not knowing what a holding tank is, it is what holds the stuff from the toilets until you can properly dispose of it. Emptying the tank is by pumping out at a proper facility and is required almost universally in all harbors and inland water ways. At sea it can be pumped out through a hull fitting into the water and is perfectly acceptable three miles, or more, off shore. From the day we bought Interlude we could not completely empty the tank and depending on the pump out facilities pump it could be as little as ten of the thirty gallons when full. This was extremely annoying as a trip to the facility was not always an easy one. I finally gave up trying to solve the problem and luckily was able to order a new tank through the original supplier to Hunter. When the old tank was lifted out I found there was a start of a leak in the bottom of the tank so it's replacement was due regardless. The new tank fitted perfectly and all hoses were hooked up. The next pump out was as it should, absolutely no problems. This was probably the very best improvement to Interlude that I would make.

We had several house sitting periods at the Ewalds and I have already discussed what tough duty that was overlooking their vineyard in Sonoma Valley while sitting in the sunshine on their spectacular veranda. Add to this being invited to their annual Thanksgiving dinner makes our life so very good.

Christmas is nearing and we head out to have ours in Colorado with Janet and family. All goes well and the New Year is greeted with anticipation of another good year. We have no complaints.

We hardly get back to Point Richmond than Rock and Nancy want us to spend three weeks in Puerto Vallarta on their sailboat that Rock had taken down there to charter. It seemed like a good idea, so we said sure, and it was. They joined us for a few days and it was good times all around. I had some dental work done and Jeanne had her annual cleaning. It was well done and very reasonable.

Our house sitting chores kept pilling up as both the Ewalds and the Hills kept traveling, the Ewalds to do their annual volunteer officiating at the Pebble Beach golf tournament and the Hills to visit their boat in Puerto Vallarta. Two cats and one dog, respectively, take up our time.

It is suddenly the end of April, my 71st birthday had just occurred and we are now planning our trip north on Interlude. By mid May we are ready. But on May 15th I play in a fund raiser golf tournament organized by Carolyn Brennan at the Stanford University Golf Course and I wouldn't miss out on that opportunity. On the morning of May 19th, 2006 we take in the dock lines at 6:30 am and head for the Golden Gate.

CHAPTER 32

We approach the Golden Gate Bridge about 7:00 am and have been joined by Tom and Barbara Wilkinson on their thirty-six foot Nova trawler Foxtrot to buddy boat the trip up the coast. We met Tom and Barbara in Coronado when we first brought Interlude back to the U.S. They are both in the Coast Guard Auxiliary and were providing boat inspections at the Coronado Yacht Club. The Coast Guard recommends this to be done annually and they can demand an inspection if yours is not current so it is worth while to have it done. We had similar cruising plans and had kept in touch over the past year. They were docked about one hour past Point Richmond and met us as we turned toward the Bridge. Buddy boating is a good way to travel as not only do you have company you can share thoughts on approaches to doing things which makes decisions a little easier.

It is not a bad weather day and we don't expect any bad weather or seas on this first leg to Bodega Bay with an expected travel time of nine and a half hours. All goes as planned and we are safely docked in the marina and feel confident that this will work. It would be a little more than a thousand miles and about one hundred fifty hours under power over a period of twenty-six days to reach our destination of Anacortes, WA. Our longest day would be seventeen hours. We were very cautious and avoided any days at sea that appeared to be too rough. The departure time was always picked by the needed arrival time at the entrance bars and we had only one entry that was a little dicey. I will list the ports in order. Bodega Bay, Ft. Bragg, Eureka, Crescent City, Brookings, Bandon, Coos Bay, Newport, Illwaco, Grays Harbor,

LaPush, Neah Bay, Port Angeles, and Anacortes.

The days of shear beauty of the trip and the enjoyment of the visits to the various ports far over shadowed any of the few unpleasant moments encountered. There are three main routes recommended in the guides, Offshore, Express, and Inshore. The Express keeps you within sight of land and in a lane that is supposed to be a crab pot free zone. We chose this route as entanglement with crab pot bouys and lines can cause major problems. You are far enough offshore to have time to recover if you snag a bouy, or engine or rigging failure were to occur.

In Ft. Bragg Jeanne and I picked a side tie dock that a couple of grizzled old timers said one of the fishing boats used but that they were out for over night. We were awakened about 1:00 am by blasts on a horn and lit up by a search light. A quick exit was made to another dock with apologies to the fishing boat captain. Seeing us scurrying about in our pajamas probably modified his annoyance at us being where we weren't supposed to be. Going into Bandon we hit a rough bar crossing which actually had just one standing wave to get through but caused both of us to rock about a little more than one would like, especially Tom's boat. The Coast Guard had just banned all boats under twenty-six feet from entering or exiting across the bar as we made this approach.

One interesting experience was in Grays Harbor as the big mega yachts by Newport are built there. We heard the sound of power washers approaching down the dock and thought it was a good thing as the docks were pretty soiled. Then the rumble of large boat engines ushered in one of the one hundred thirty foot Newports which tied up directly opposite Interlude. Next came a number of young people neatly dressed with matching Newport Yachts T-shirts. Then the red carpet was rolled out and was followed by caterers carrying trays of finger food and several coolers. A short time later a party of three showed up and were escorted aboard. They were casually dressed, two men in jeans, deck shoes and open shirts and the lady likewise dressed. They were aboard for about an hour and then left as quickly as they had arrived. We later learned these were the new owners of the almost completed Newport and had flown in from the Northeast on their private jet to make the final inspection.

As we approached LaPush Tom contacted the Coast Guard Station and requested information on the bar and they responded it was good to cross. I inquired as to the height of the overhead cables and was assured they were as shown on the chart and then was asked if we had entered LaPush before to which I answered in the negative. Over and out and a short time later out came the Coast Guard in an inflatable and they escorted us in. Tom would later get to go out in one of their big rescue boats for a thrilling ride. He was actually allowed to take the helm for a short time. It pays to be in the Auxiliary.

We enter the Cap Sante Marina in Anacortes on the afternoon of June 13. Jeanne enters in her log, "We Made It," as if there ever had been the slightest doubt.

CHAPTER 33

We spend our week at Cap Sante, a quality marina, which is right in downtown Anacortes. It is a delightful small town with everything we need within walking distance. We have left our car at Brickyard Cove Marina in Point Richmond and won't retrieve it until late September. All we need is right here and in the few times we need help by car our good friends Ken and Nancy Murphy are just minutes away. Our time is spent first recovering from the just completed voyage and preparing for our first thorough visit to the San Juan Islands.

Our time in the Pacific Northwest will be from our arrival on June 13, 2006 in Anacortes until we find ourselves in our trusty, but overloaded, 1996 Pontiac Bonneville SSE heading east out of Seattle, home less and boat less, on the late afternoon of July 17, 2007, one day shy of Jeanne's 69th birthday. We are exhausted and travel only a short distance inland before finding a motel and fall into to bed. Our next plan is formulating and it is now necessary for it's implementation. This is a few chapters away, however, and I now get back to our heading toward the Rosario Resort on Orcas Island. Vero Beach is getting closer but it is not yet even a thought.

I don't want this to be a travelogue so I will summarize our time here. First, although we had no idea of our good fortune at the time, the summer of 2006 was going to be one of the great summers in the Pacific Northwest if you don't mind a small drought. It just refused to rain. The skies were blue most every day, the temperature close to perfect and winds, if any, light. By the time fall had arrived Jeanne and I had decided this was the place. We changed our minds in November, but I again get ahead of my story so will wait for the appropriate time to tell you about that.

    Jeanne has labeled our cruising here as the Wow Cruise. What she means is that every time we come around another point or island the view evokes a Wow. On Interlude we are just a few feet above the clear water, the terrain is covered by forest and vegetation of beautiful greens, the rugged mountains above timberline are snow capped, and the sky is so, so blue. The farther north we go the bigger the Wow becomes. There are places that have a bigger Wow such as Yosemite and the Grand Canyon, but few go on for mile after mile and can be enjoyed in the leisure of being on a boat and traveling at the pace of your choice. For us at this moment nothing could have been finer or provided such a time of peaceful and exciting adventure. It was perfect.

    The San Juan Islands are a cluster of islands in U.S. territory and just above them in Canadian territory are the Gulf Islands. They are bounded to the west by Vancouver Island and to the east by Washington and British Columbia. Almost every island has some habitation and most have marinas or small harbors where docking, mooring, or anchoring is available. Many are associated with quaint towns such as the most famous, Friday Harbor. They make for the most part very safe and relaxing cruising. There is an extensive ferry system for the land bound and the ferries always have the right of way on the water. The cruiser must respect this right of way at all times.

    Our initial cruise would visit Rosario Resort, Friday Harbor, Jones Island, Blind Bay, and Roche Harbor. We returned to Cap Sante in Anacortes and started planning our real cruise to head as far north as we would be comfortable doing.

    Before we can start on the big push north Janet, Craig, Devin and Andie would arrive and we would do a three day tour stopping at Rosario Resort and Roche Harbor and spending midday between these on Jones Island, one of the many wonderful Washington State Marine Parks. On the way back we saw two pods of Orcas fairly close and several others farther out. It was a fun, if short, cruise which I think all enjoyed.

We would start our big trip on July 6th and it would end August 31st when we tied up back in Anacortes. What a trip this was and I will again just list the places visited and will add a few special moments later. Blind Bay, Prevost Bay, Ladysmith (Ganges, Canada), Nanaimo, Schonner Cove, Pender Harbor, Lund, Laura Cove (Desolation Sound), Toba Wilderness Resort, Squirrel Bay, Big Bay, Shoal Bay, Blind Channel, Lagoon Cove, Kwatsi Bay, Shawl Bay, Turnball Cove, Clyton Cove, Sullivan Bay, Shawl Bay, Echo Bay, Lagoon Cove, Shoal Bay, April Point* (Campbell River), Gorge Harbor*, Toba Wilderness Resort*, Laura Cove*, Shut Bay* (Texada Island), Schonner Cove*, Nanaimo*, Montogue, Maple Bay, Sidney, Friday Harbor, Anacortes.

The list of locations doesn't show visits of more than one night of which there were a number. The repeats are second stops along the way. The locations with asterisks designate the cruise with our friends Dick and Carolyn Brennan on board. We had joined the Anacortes Yacht Club by this time and used a number of reciprocals when available. We also started to anchor on occasion where anchorages were good.

The Toba Wilderness Resort has a nice dock, a small cabin and was newly owned by a young Canadian couple with a new baby who were planning to live there full time. Jeanne and I had the chance to be surrogate grandparents for a few hours as we sat around and discussed their plans. It was almost an hour by boat to the nearest town having supplies and medical facilities. Float planes are available for passenger service and emergencies. They have a current web-site. I hope they have made it a success and their dreams continue to be fulfilled.

It warrants as short discussion here about cruising among the islands in that the tidal changes create currents which can attain speeds exceeding your boat speed which is not a good thing. On Interlude our top speed under power is about eight knots. If approaching almost any of the narrows currents of that, and sometimes twice that, can be present. If caught going into the current once it gets faster than your top boat speed you start going backwards. You do have some control but if you lose it your are in serious trouble. In going with the current you can have a thrilling ride but when the current speed exceeds your boat speed you have no control. Disaster is almost guaranteed. Nobody in their right mind messes with Mother Nature here. Your are required to have the manual on tides and currents on board which is a somewhat confusing compilation of information that allows you to figure out when slack, which is a short duration as the tidal currents change direction, occurs. This is the only safe period to make the passage and only last thirty minutes to an hour. Protocol is to arrive a little early and when slack occurs the queue of boats motor through in rapid order, the faster boats generally allowed to go first. Commercial vessels have the right of way. A big tug towing a huge log raft is an awesome sight and in a narrows is always given a lot of space. Things do go wrong and the more space the better. If your timing is off you find a place to anchor and wait until the next slack occurs or maybe try again the next day.

Many of the locations listed above have specialty attractions. Shawl Bay had a pancake breakfast which was a treat and you could order a cake or pie baked for you from their kitchen, a very nice touch. One of the best was Lagoon Cove where each afternoon at cocktail hour Bill would place on the big table in the old shop building a huge bowl of perfectly cooked shrimp caught that very morning and all the boaters were invited to bring a potluck dish and their own drinks. There was a nice deck over looking the docks and this of course easily became dinner each evening. After everyone had their fill, including as many fresh shrimp as you could eat, Bill would tell you one of his bear stories. I think he only had two as we stayed a total of five nights on two passes and heard one of them twice and one three times.

Another event at Lagoon Cove that happened while we were there is worth a mention. There were several floating docks on the opposite side of the lagoon that had small houses on them that some commercial fishermen owned. This was maybe one hundred yards from the boats at the docks. One afternoon a large grizzly bear appeared on one of these docks and was checking things out, swatting at the doors and windows and showing a lot of attention to the big bait tanks. One of Bill's hands went over in a small boat with a air horn and from a safe distance sent a blast or two at the bear which was ignored. Yelling was tried and with no better results they came back to the safe side. About this time the fishermen returned and tried to push the bear off their dock with the anchor pulpit on the bow of their boat and the bear stood up and sparred with them like a boxer and then decided to retreat. The fishermen tied up their boat and were checking things out when here comes the bear swimming back. We now had a large crowd watching this drama when the bear went around to the back side of the house and out of sight. There was an enormous bang, which I was sure was a 44 magnum shot, and a sudden silence. The little lady next to me, with soft brown eyes, asked, "They just scared it away, didn't they?" The bear was not seen again.

Some where up in this area we meet Phil and Kaye Hutchinson on their sailboat. They are from Seattle and have done the cruise up this way many times. We seemed to hit it off so we buddy boat for a number of days. Turnball Cove is one of their favorites and they were willing to share it with us and it was to be our most northern position. Phil is a retired lawyer and Kaye is a PhD and is involved with educational consultant work in the Seattle area. A fun and interesting couple with which we are still very good friends. We have shared a number of visits, dinners and a few parties. They have a group of close friends that reminds Jeanne and me very much of the group of friends we had in the Bay Area and we immediately felt comfortable and accepted into their group.

Another point I want to make was how enjoyable it was to have Dick and Carolyn Brennan join us on the boat for a seven day cruise. They are good company and so enthusiastic about everything, especially new adventure, that the days sped by much too fast. We were able to show them many of the places we liked the best and found a couple of new ones along the way.

I had purchased fishing and crabbing licenses for Washington and British Columbia so I was able to provide some crab, if not fish, for the table. Carolyn put together a slide show on a CD of the cruise and it is the best record we have of our time there.

Jeanne and I found a ritual to follow at each location and that was the search for wild blackberries. This is an easy search as they seemed to be everywhere and locals almost look at them as weeds. Our routine was to take a small plastic container on hikes and when the proper bush was found, first sample a few, then fill it for evening dessert and morning breakfast. As we went north we were following the season so there were no shortage of blackberries. Our last southbound stop was Sidney at the Royal Vick Yacht Club (where we could use our CYC membership for two days reciprocal) and we thought we would get skunked as we were now a long way south. I took a walk down the street facing the club bringing back only three or four sad looking berries. On our way out of the parking lot, as we headed for the bus stop to take a bus to Victoria, there stood a magnificent blackberry bush loaded with berries. We were now one hundred percent as blackberry pickers.

One more moment is worth a few words. On our first stay in Laura Cove, after securing the boat at anchor with a stern line to a tree on the bank, we headed out in our little dingy to explore the area. Just around the corner was a small island having a low spot which at low tide, which it was at this time, looked inviting so we stopped for a look. The low area was covered with oyster shells, big oyster shells. As we carefully stepped about one of them sent a squirt up, then another. I picked one of these up and both halves of the shells were tight together and they were heavy. There were hundreds of them so we picked up a dozen, stuffed them into a satchel we had and carted them back to the boat. Now what do you do? Having a reference library on board told us to thoroughly scrub off the shells and steam until they opened and then five or ten minutes more. Out came the biggest oysters you have seen and they were delicious. It was the next morning on the VHF radio we heard that the Canadian Health Department had just that day lifted the ban on eating wild oysters as they were now deemed safe to eat. Jeanne followed the instructions for preserving in jars the rest of our take and we had oysters for many days.

CHAPTER 34

    I am going to use this chapter examine some thoughts all related to our experiences up to this point but which are about others and only related to us by the fact that we were covering the same ground, albeit in very different circumstances. First be advised that Jeanne and I were aboard a relative modern sailing vessel which was essentially a two bedroom two bath floating condominium, powered by a seventy horsepower diesel engine, and on rare occasions sails, having almost state of the art navigation aids, radar, a very good VHF radio, and all the Coast Guard required safety equipment. It has not always been this way, and in a few cases still isn't. This is what I will write about here.

    About the first thing you will be asked when you are about to cruise the Inside Passage in the Pacific Northwest, or have just cruised it, is have you read The Curve of Time by M. Wylie Blanchet. I think the first one to ask me this was Phil Hutchinson, probably not the first thing after glad to meet you, but soon thereafter. Several others likewise did. It is a very good read as it covers a good portion of the places we cruised. There was this slight difference in that the period was 1920s to 1930s and M. Wylie was a woman, widowed in 1927, in a twenty-five foot power boat and traveling with her five children on board. Of the description of Interlude above, she had none of those amenities. Neither the comfort, the equipment, or the safety gear except for the minimal. It is a very interesting story and quite literally separates the men from the boys, if you correctly interpret my meaning. How she managed is cheerfully described in plenty of details and the many locations she and the kids visited are much the same in appearance now if you can ignore the company you have had upon your own visits. What an extraordinary woman.

    Another good read I found in a thrift shop book section, the catching title Passage to Juneau written by Jonathon Rabin. I picked it up for fifty cents and stowed it on board to read later. Once started I couldn't put it down. It is actually three stories in one combining his relationship with his young daughter he has left behind while on this passage aboard his thirty-five foot sailboat, his trials, observations, and ups and downs as he moves up the Inside Passage, and the overlay of descriptive logs of the European explorers, Vancouver in particular, in the 1790s. The seamanship required of the later is beyond understanding as Jeanne and I would motor through the same areas checking constantly our chart plotter to guide us effortless through even the most dangerous positions. Sailing large, barely manageable ships through the uncharted inlets and passages trying to find routes to the east and continually being frustrated with failure is very hard to imagine. Rabin's research was extensive and his interpretation most informative.

    One particular part that I found most interesting was the cultural divide between the Northwest Indians and the European explorers. In a paragraph or two, if I remember correctly, he describes how the Indians were coastal inhabitants whose whole life was predicated on the sea. They sought its bounty and although recognizing it's dangers were comfortable in it's environment. They were afraid of the dark forest behind them and would seldom venture into it afraid, and rightly so, of the bears and other real and imagined dangers. Even though they could see the snow capped peaks they never ventured to discover what they were like or what was on the other side. The explorers on the other hand looked at the sea as only a means to explore the land. They would see opportunity for logging, mining, game, ranching and farming, and in addition had a great curiosity for what lay beyond the peaks. They were comfortable in the forest and had no fear of it.

The Indians would stand with their backs to the forest and look toward the sea while the Explorers would stand with their backs to the sea and look toward the forests. This cultural difference is what made the Indians vulnerable to the European invasion.

When Jeanne and I had my cousin Bobbie and her husband Jack Keogh on board for lunch in Marina Del Rey they told us of their sailing days in the late 1940s and 50s. They had a very good friend who owned a twenty-six foot Catalina sailboat on which they took many sails. It did have a small outboard to maneuver with in tight spaces but it was primarily a sailboat. On trips to Catalina Island from their base in Long Beach they would load up for camping trips with their friend and their four kids on board and head over. On a clear day the island is visible as the mountains show up despite the twenty-two miles distance. Navigation was by sight and compass. They would pull into a good spot and off load the camping gear, get set up, and then proceed to do what campers do. Jack did describe that on several occasion on their return the fog would roll in, the wind would die down enough to not provide a sense of direction and they would set the compass direction and head east. When they heard the surf they would try to figure out where they were and attempt to complete the passage home.

In the more recent present, while Jeanne and I were just learning to handle Interlude in Esenada, Baja California we met Gary and Spike, father and son, each having their own sailboats docked at the Coral Marina. Spike's was a 1937 wooden boat which he was tenderly restoring, which is no easy task. Gary's was a beautiful steel hull ketch that he had built almost entirely by himself in Port Townsend, WA around 1980. When completed he, his wife and two year old Spike moved aboard. I am not sure of the chronology, but Gary told me once that he had made three trips between Port Townsend and Ensenada and was at this time planning a solo trip to South America. His boat was perfectly crafted. The steel plates that he had formed and welded together into the hull were smoother than any molded fiberglass hull you can find. The wooden masts he had made from scratch starting with the selection of the fir timber and handcrafting for strength and beauty. The wood work both exterior and interior was the best you will see. He had tiller steering and the rigging matched the quality of the rest of the boat. He is a true sailor of the old school. His instrumentation is adequate but not technically modern. He has a chart table on board and uses it. I once asked him when I saw he had no auto pilot, not even the basic wind vane system sometimes found on older boats, how he managed on the long voyages. Did he tie the tiller and keep an eye on the compass? He gave me one of his shy smiles and said, "If you set your sails correctly, the boat will take you where you want to go." Of course he also told me when I asked him about the man overboard technique he would use if that became necessary he offered, "I go to the stern and wave goodbye."

One afternoon Jeanne and I were invited to have dessert on board with he and Spike. We arrived at the appointed time and they had just put two small steaks on the little charcoal hibachi they used for grilling and apologized for being a little late. A tour was given as this was our first visit inboard. The lay out was very basic with a large mattress forward partitioned by a curtain, a small galley starboard and settee opposite, and a "one lung" diesel engine exposed and flanked by a single bunk on either side in the stern. Storage was strategically spaced throughout. The craftsmanship was as expected.

A good dessert was served and good conversation was carried on. These two were true sailors and Jeanne and I were at best boaters. On the way back to Interlude we both asked the same question at the same time, "Where was the head?" I later discreetly found out there wasn't one. Gary, his wife, and Spike had used a portable unit, a bucket, for that purpose for the years of Spike's childhood and his room had been one of the bunks next to the engine.

CHAPTER 35

By the time October 1st arrives we have decided on a sublet at the La Conner Marina for six months and have tied Interlude securely to her dock. La Conner is a great little town and will make a superb home base. In the preceding 30 days we did a lot of traveling by boat to look for dockage for the winter. Cap Sante Marina allows only a very limited number of live aboards and the wait is years in advance so we could only use the weekly rate which is expensive. We visited the Oak Harbor Marina and although nice was not the place for us.

Next was to the Port of Bellingham, Squalicum Harbor, where I make, accidentally, one of my finest dockings. We have made arrangements to stay at the local yacht club and when I contact them on the VHF as we approach I am instructed to enter the harbor and approach the side tie dock which is angled and will be facing me on my entrance. It is there and there is one space that looks big enough between two boats so I cautiously approach and head bow in. The space suddenly looks too small but I have already gone too far. I slip the drive into reverse and turn the wheel hard to kick the stern in and then hit the throttle hard stopping the boat the minute we touch the dock. Perfectly parallel and I can step on the dock and secure the dock lines as Jeanne hands them to me. I then take a breath for the first time since I realized what was about to happen. Jeanne gives me a high five. I had docked a forty-five foot boat (includes the pulpit and anchor) in a forty-nine foot space without touching either boat foreword or stern. The owner of the forward boat shows up sometime later and carefully looks over his boat's stern and when I tell him there was no touch he continues looking but finally gives me a weak smile and goes about his business. I would never again try such a thing and can still visualize that space shrinking before my eyes as I got closer. Bellingham was a nice place, but La Conner was the best of the those visited and won out.

We meet Jim and Peg Jeffries whose boat Nightfall is a Bill Garden Steel Trawler at thirty-eight feet, is a true trawler and really seaworthy. We have kept in touch over the years and very much enjoy their blogs of the many trips to Alaska they have taken on their boat up the Inside Passage each summer. As each year has provided them with so many exciting adventures I often think we should have tried to have done it at least one time.

During the third week of September we rent a one way car and head back down to Point Richmond to pick up our car. As usual we stop to see as many friends as possible and then head back up the coastal highway to home. We will only be there for three weeks as our decision that Puget Sound was the place was changed to not so fast. Not only did it rain, it poured, every day. We were having our cockpit cushions repaired and a new backrest cushion made in Mt. Vernon, just past a highway bridge over the Skagit River. The day we were to pick them up the upholster called and said we should wait a day or two as they might be flooded out. The next day she called and said the river had crested and to come on over. The water was just under the bridge and I estimated thirty feet above its normal level over a very wide river bed. An awful lot of water and not even a hint of sunshine for days.

Another solid week of rain and we packed up and headed south again. We combined a house sitting for Rock and Nancy in Point Richmond with visits to friends in Palo Alto and Sunnyvale and then to the Ewalds for another great Thanksgiving. From there it is down to San Diego for a family visit and an impromptu visit to the Coral Marina in Ensenada where we find Gil and Becky getting their boat ready to head south and through the Panama Canal to the East Coast. Then on to Tubac, Az to see the Diffenbaughs and then to Denver to stay with Janet and family until our flight to Destin, FL on December 15 to do our now annual stay with Jeanne's sister and husband. This year we rented a second condo for over Christmas for Janet and family to join in the family gathering with most of Jeanne's side of her family tree.

    It was on Christmas Eve that my older sister Nancy died. She had a melanoma behind her right eye a few years earlier which had required the removal of the eye for treatment. A prosthetic eye had been fashioned and was controlled by the remaining muscle and was undetectable in both it's look and motion. Unfortunately the melanoma had come back with a vengeance and she died on December 24, 2006. Christmas was her favorite holiday as she loved to shop for and give presents. Even as she knew the prognosis she had gifts for everyone and I am sure she tried valiantly to make through Christmas day. I flew out for her memorial service and the wake at her daughter's home. It was nicely done and celebrated a life well lived.

    We returned to Denver and would stay with our daughter and family until nearly the end of March as I was putting together the sculptures for the golf club trophies. After the first steps in the casting process were completed we had a couple of weeks and since I was a little concerned about our boat in La Conner we took a winter drive to check on Interlude. Jeanne thought I was being overly cautious and as it turned out she was right. Everything was fine and we then had the drive back to Colorado. It did give Janet a break as your parents are not supposed to move in with you, at least not yet.

    The trophies were all finished up and it was now time to get back to boating. We were back on board by early April and as it was still too early to head north we decided to cruise the Pugent Sound and went all the way down and visited Olympia and the neat town of Gig Harbor. Washington State has good number of Marine Parks which usually have a small dock and a number of mooring balls associated with each. For a very small annual fee permit you can stay on a mooring ball and for a few dollars more at the dock if space is available. We had stayed and visited Jones Island in the San Juans and on this trip stopped by

Blake Island and Hat Island. It was a really fun cruise and when the skies were clear Mount Rainier would display itself in all its glory.

Returning to Anacortes we had friends from Loveland, Ralph and Bobbie Beyersdorf, join us for a nice cruise through the San Juan Island and found them just as much fun on the water as on land. Jeanne and I now had enough experience in the area to be comfortable tour guides and this made it very relaxing for us to provide what we hoped was a great on board experience for our guests.

It was now time to plan our northern cruise. Our first must see was the Princess Louisa Inlet which can be somewhat thought of as a water accessible Yosemite Valley. At its head is the famous Chatterbox Falls and to get to this requires a forty-five mile trip up the Jervis Inlet.

But before we even get started to this place, Jeanne and I decided that maybe one more year in the Pacific Northwest on a boat would be adequate and we would like to experience the same life style on the East Coast and a try at cruising the Intracoastal Waterway. This led us to research having Interlude shipped or trucked to the East Coast. The general thinking is that a sailboat in the ICW wasn't the best option and with the cost and potential problems in shipping we decided a sale of Interlude and a purchase of a trawler there would be a better option.

Hunter is a very supportive manufacturer and in addition to always being helpful on all questions, requests for parts, and referrals for custom items (think holding tank replacement) also had a Hunter for sale by owner web site which linked you to SailboatOwners.com. Thus on April 27, 2007 Interlude was listed for sale. We of course thought it would take up to a year, at least, to find a buyer this way so we started our second year of cruising with no plans other than to head toward Princess Louisa Inlet.

CHAPTER 36

Just as we crossed into Canadian waters a good sized inflatable with five dark uniformed men with guns zigzagged up behind us and announced themselves as Canadian officials and requested to board. They said just keep moving on course and coming along side two jumped on board. They were border patrol and checked our passports and papers, looked around and apologized for not having the usual customs official with them so we would have to stop and do our entrance clearance when we made land fall. They would call ahead tell the customs official in Vancouver, our first stop, that we were cleared. Off they jumped and were gone almost as fast as they had appeared. At Vancouver the custom official said no one had called them but welcomed us to Canada and cleared us entry without so much as a look.

Our plan was to spend a couple of nights in Vancouver at the Vancouver Rowing Club, using our Anacortes Yacht Club reciprocal, which is located adjacent to Stanley Park and we did just that. What a great place to be as the Park is fantastic and we were able to take long walks about it. In addition we were able to walk into downtown city center. It was then on to Pender Harbor for the night and a long, long next day to Princess Louisa Inlet, going through the Malibu Rapids without any problems.

The cruise into Princess Louisa is dramatic and as we arrived in the late afternoon the shadows were lengthening, the sky was clear, and the scenery as advertised. Chatterbox Falls was in full glory and all was perfect but the dock was full. There was a mooring field a couple of miles back behind a rather forlorn island and the thought to have to retreat that far was disheartening. Just then a man on one of the docked sailboats hailed us to raft up to him for the night. This is one of those courtesies you will always remember and closed out one of our greatest days in cruising. (I was later able to do a similar courtesy to another boater in a different boat and in a much different place which I will describe to you later.)

We spent our allotted three nights there and on the second and third night was able to get the number one position on the dock as most of the boats had left the next morning. This is the dock position nearest the Falls with an unobstructed view. A float plane did show up the last day and the position just behind us was reserved for it but it was not really a distraction. The Princess Louisa Inlet is truly an almost spiritual place and ranks very high on our list of best memories.

On leaving we time our exit to be slack at Malibu Rapids and made a safe passage. It is a long day out Jervis Inlet and nearing its end the cell phone rings just as we gain a signal. On the other end is a young man in Seattle who has seen our ad and would like to see the boat. We explain where we are and tell him we plan to be in Lund the next night. He asks if he drove up can he see the boat then. He explains he had owned the exact same model before and decided he wanted another one for pleasure boating in Puget Sound. It would be a long drive but we tell him we think we should be in Lund by 2:00 pm. He says he will be there and he is bringing his young son with him.

We contact Egmont Marina for dockage and ask as to the current at the dock because our guide book says it can be very fast and docking difficult. My Tides and Currents book indicates we will be hitting a fairly fast current but the dock master says I should be there at just the right time for slack. I hope he is right and I miss read the book and fortunately he was the one that was right. We dock with no problem and Jeanne fixes dinner and we relax and plan an early departure for the morning to get to Lund by noon. A late comer shows up and makes a successful dockage but only after some bumping and getting stuck on the end of the dock for a brief time. The boat he bumped was his son's, as they were traveling together, but no damage other than to egos was involved.

We made it to Lund but couldn't get onto the land dock for over an hour. Lund has four floating docks but we wanted to be on the main dock with electricity and water so we could clean up the boat a little before the prospective buyer arrived. We were ready by 2:00 pm and he arrived shortly thereafter. His son was about four years old and it had been a ten hour drive with two ferry crossings. (Lund is the northern terminus of Highway 101.) He made about a forty-five minute inspection and then made an almost full price offer. Jeanne and I looked at each other and decided although it was probably earlier than we wanted, a bird in the hand is better than one in the bush and we accepted. As the summer season was just starting he wanted the boat right away and with a deposit check received we agreed to have the boat in Anacortes for the survey and sale in seven days. We shook hands and he started his ten hour drive back to Seattle. His son was as well behaved as your best wishes for a child could be.

Our trip back was as fast as we could make it and we were at the Cap Sante Marina in five days and the race to empty the boat was under way. I can't believe how much stuff you can put on a boat in four plus years, but I can tell you it is a lot. All the equipment and supplies tied to the boat were to be left in place. I made a tour of the docks making offers for sale of a number of items no one really needs but at prices you just couldn't pass up. We took bags of stuff to the local thrift shop, and gave away much more. The car was fully loaded and the boat pretty well cleaned up when the buyer came up. He had made arrangement at a local yard to haul the boat and had the inspector hired. All went smoothly and we were to meet him at his office in Seattle to sign the papers and receive the cashier's check.

As I wrote earlier Jeanne and I left Seattle on the late afternoon of July 17, 2007 exhausted, home less and boat less with an overloaded car heading East. The next day was Jeanne's 69th birthday.

There is more to the story and it is about the new owner of Interlude. It is the kind of story I really like. I think his name was Jeff. In high school Jeff had worked for a plumber who's specialty was domestic water heater sales, installation and service. Through college he continued to work part time for the man and after graduation, with nothing better to do at the time, kept on while he considered his options. His employer decided he wanted to take a long vacation and asked Jeff if he would run the business for three months while he did his thing. About two months into this vacation his boss called him and asked if would like to buy the company as he didn't want to come back. The price was so good that Jeff accepted it and took over. He then managed to get rights to install and service water heaters for Home Depot sold in a large territory including all of Seattle and it's suburbs. I don't know how many water heaters that entails but enough for he and his wife to live in a water front home on Lake Washington and have a sizable power boat and now a very nice 1994 Hunter Passage 42 in excellent condition. Jeff was in the right place, at the right time, and definitely had the right stuff.

CHAPTER 37

With the sale of Interlude completed and a night in a motel not far from where the transaction was accomplished we were ready to start our East Coast boating adventure without a boat and almost three thousand miles from the waters where it would take place. Not a problem for us as it was to take some preparation before we would be ready to really get underway.

In a few hours we had cleared Snoqualmie Pass and were heading to Spokane, Coeur d'Alene and to spend the evening and night with friends from our Aspen days, Roger and Nancy Munro, in Missoula, MT. We were starting to recover slightly from the frantic ten days from our exiting the Princess Louisa Inlet until turning over the keys to Interlude in Seattle. Two hundred fifty miles by water and five hundred miles by land had worn us out but after a relaxing visit with the Munros we felt that we could continue on.

We stopped in Denver at our daughter's for a few days while we reorganized. Left off a few more boxes of stuff in our storeroom in Loveland and got busy on Yachtworld.com looking for trawler prospects. I had thought we could get along with a smaller boat so started looking in the thirty-six to thirty-eight foot size and found quite a few with prices we would be comfortable. We had actually made a profit on Interlude. We had made a good buy when we bought her, added value by having fixed almost everything on board, upgraded her navigation, added a dingy with an outboard motor and a portable generator to the inventory.

By the time we saw our first trawler somewhere just east of Toledo, Ohio I realized I now had a lot more to learn about boats and boating. It only took a couple of showings of trawlers in the thirty-six to thirty-eight foot size to realize for living on they would be much too small. In Baltimore we saw a forty-four footer which was much more like what we would need. There is a lot of variables in design that make up how much space you have in boats of the same overall length. The two main things are beam, the boat width, and space utilization. We found that a sundeck style with fly bridge helm would provide the maximum living comfort at minimum length. This meant two staterooms with a master in the stern with master bathroom. We preferred a down galley, a two entry head forward and a open saloon over the engine room. The covered sundeck provided a nice outdoor space and the fly bridge more space and a good view at the upper helm. A lower helm in the saloon would provide foul weather control.

After following many leads as we ventured down the Chesapeake Bay we still hadn't found the right boat and it was in this area we thought would be a good place to start our next boating adventure. An ad popped up with big red letters about a reduction in price for a forty-three foot boat in Great Bridge, VA listed with Virginia Yacht Brokers at the Atlantic Yacht Basin. It was here we first saw Change O Pace III with Chuck Grice the broker doing the showing. Two things happened that day that were unrelated, but eventful.

First is coincidence. About a month or two earlier, this being mid August, Gil Saul had called me from Isla Mujeres, Mexico just offshore of Cancun. He and Becky had made the trip south on Wind Rider, through the Panama Canal, across the Gulf and were now poised to head north up the Atlantic coastline. As Chuck guided us down the yacht basin toward the barn that held COPIII we were passing a docked sailboat and I remarked "That's a Moody 46 just like....Gil?" There stood Gil looking right at me as I uttered "Gil?" He and Becky had arrived the day before and were going to leave Wind Rider there for a short time to have some work done and would be leaving the next day. Talk about a small world. We spent a great evening at dinner hearing tales of ocean sailing, but both Jeanne and I thought it was much better to hear about it than doing it.

COPIII had the design we had been looking for, so much so that when we made the offer we over looked over a number of things we would have to fix and have fixed later. It was a 1986 Senator 43 built in the Chein Wha boatyard in Taiwan, designed by an outfit in Baltimore. They built a number of thirty-five foot boats under the name Senator but COPIII is the only forty-three foot one we have seen or heard about. To shorten the story, considering a number of other factors with the slow economic recovery and the increase in the price of diesel fuel, we paid too much but in retrospect it was the perfect boat for us to cruise and live on for four years.

Learning to handle a boat of this size with two engines and limited steering control with small rudders takes a bit of time. Another part is running the boat from the upper helm, where you have needed visibility but puts you high above the water. It took some time but I learn quickly so handling the boat didn't pose much of a problem. Learning all the systems with two engines, a big generator for AC power and charging a big bank of house batteries, a windlass and a big anchor with chain, etc. was a little more daunting. We spent the first month just getting COPIII cleaned up, fixing the autopilot (which soon had to be replaced), trying to get the hydraulic steering to work correctly, and in general getting organized.

We planned our first trip to be from Great Bridge into the Chesapeake and then to Horn Harbor to visit friends from Loveland, CO and now in Virginia. I had found Horn Harbor on the chart and estimated our time to get there and we made a date to tie up to their dock and spend a night. But first you must meet our friends Kate and Lael Easterling.

Back when we lived in Loveland one of the sculptors and her husband who had a house just down the street from us decided to move on and put it up for sale. Along comes the fair Kate who has left her job in secret government service in Washington D.C. and her live aboard sailboat companion, to go to work for Hewlett Packard. Her sister lived nearby and she bought the house. We became acquainted and found her fun and interesting. It soon became apparent that she did not find Loveland the most exciting place for a sophisticated and good looking woman to develop a new life style. After about six months she had an invite from a D.C. friend to come to a party there to meet her soul mate just discovered by this same friend. So our fair Kate heads back for the party and comes back with the story of meeting this recently retired Navy man who is indeed her soul mate. Plans are made to return for a second inspection two weeks later. The second inspection is better than the first and on return Kate explains that their wedding will take place within the month and puts her house on the market. As the elder I was asked to be a witness and my signature is on their wedding certificate. The date arrives and the night before the wedding at the party to introduce Lael to his new family. I apparently quizzed, or more accurately grilled, him as to the wisdom of marriage this quickly, etc. and am reminded of this every time we see each other, even some dozen plus years later. Not only this, they sold Lael's thirty-seven foot Tartan and bought a forty-one foot Tartan which they sailed to Australia and have pretty much thoroughly cruised all of Australia, New Zealand and Tasmania and by camper van driven all about all three. The property they bought in Horn Harbor after Kate sold the Loveland house was developed with a dock and small cottage they named the Squirrel Cage.

Now back to Horn Harbor. There are two Horn Harbors on the west side of the Chesapeake and the important one is about fifty miles north of the one I had picked out. I should have used the way-points Kate gave me instead of the ones I chose on the chart. By early after noon we realized my mistake and also discovered the problem with the hydraulic steering was much worse than thought and we made the phone call, admitting stupid me, and turned around to get back to Great Bridge before dark. Later we would get to Horn Harbor, spend a couple of days there and on the way back discover what happens when you don't change your fuel filters often enough. We had planned to be back well before dark and had about four hours to go when the starboard engine quit. A quick look at the chart book showed a marina and boat yard close by and we headed there. Just as we entered the approach with the docks in sight the port engine stopped. Some times luck is with you and a desperate try at restarting the the starboard engine was successful and we were able to make it in. A little ribbing from the boatyard foreman but the needed filters were on hand and I was able to make the change. We spent the night at the marina and had a smooth run home the next day.

CHAPTER 38

Fall has arrived and it is time to leave the Atlantic Yacht Basin for points south joining in the Intracoastal Waterway migration. This is the flotilla of cruising boaters who winter in the southern waters and summer in the northern ones. As November gets underway, so due the cruisers. COPIII is among the throngs. The first thing we find out about our new boat is that the previous owners were quite the party people. Whenever we announced ourselves by the boat name on the VHF we would get responses asking all sorts of how are you, where are you, etc and we would answer that we are the new owners with obvious disappointment from the callers.

Our trip lands us in Beaufort, SC just in time for the Community Thanksgiving Dinner at the St. Helena Episcopal Church. It is an annual combination charity and fund raising event. Dinner is free but donations are accepted and generously made. They feed several hundred families with home delivered meals in the area and a like number at the Church. A wonderful service to the community and very nice place for many others, including a number of us boaters, to have Thanksgiving. The marina is ideally situated right in the heart of historic downtown. Since we were having so much trouble with the steering and with plans to spend the Holidays in Denver with Janet and family we decided to spend the winter in Beaufort. It was a good decision and a fun place to be.

Just before Christmas Jeanne is searching the internet for good things and suddenly says to me,"Look at this!" and shows me an ad for a Norwegian Cruise Line thirteen day relocation cruise going from Miami to Barcelona, Spain with several nice stops at a price that not even I can refuse. So I says, "Do it!" and we are on board for an early March trip to Spain. Spain has been on the list of things to do so we will do it now. Jeanne calls her sister Jo and she immediately talks husband Carl into going so we will be a foursome for the cruise and we make a reservation for an additional four days in Barcelona. Jeanne and I will rent a car for another week and fly back from Madrid. It was Easter week so there were a number of special events going on in most of the larger towns and cities. It was a great cruise, visit, and tour. When we got back we spent a second night at the stay, park and fly motel in Miami. We had met up with Jo and Carl there the night before boarding and had left the car. The next day we drove back to Beaufort. (Stay, park and fly is a great option as the motel cost is about the same as just parking the car at a parking lot.)

     As summer is approaching we decide to head north and go at least as far as the Chesapeake Bay for the season. A stop in Oriental, NC due to a weather pattern makes me attempt a hydraulic steering fix. All my other tries had failed and I found a source for a new pump on line with a three day delivery guarantee. Also on the internet are instruction for disassembly and cleaning so I get started. The one warning was not to loosen the shaft when doing whatever and of course that happens. It only causes a little panic as all the spring loaded parts become unsprung. I can figure this out and actual do after thorough cleaning. When re-assembled and refilled it works much better, not perfect but good enough for the rest of the time we owned COPIII. I didn't have to test the three day delivery promise.

     We end up in Solomons Island, MD for the summer and find a great slip in the Beacon Marina. It is associated with the Comfort Inn and we could partake of the free daily paper provided the motel customers and with moderation could have coffee and occasionally a donut or cookie. The motel swimming pool was also available. The slip was one of the best in the Marina as it backed up to the Calvert Marine Museum and we could sit on our sundeck and view the restored lighthouse and the activities on their docks. The remote controlled sailboat races were held in our backyard. It was also on the bulkhead that fronted a small lawn area with a covered picnic table where a number of parties took place.

It is here we meet the Sveds. They are about ten years our senior and have been doing sailing and boating for years. They had traded in their sailboat a number of years before for a trawler and were on a thirty-six foot Monk named Almada. In our first conversation the game of bridge was mentioned and an immediate invite to dinner and bridge was extended. Our friendship extends to this day and our games of bridge are many and long. Dot is number one and Ed, Jeanne and I are all number two's. Jeanne and I occasional have a good run and beat them, but it is a very tough row to hoe to claim victory from those two. Ed was a navigator on a B-17 in WWII in Europe and later became a dentist and Dot was the medical doctor at Rutgers University. We did a little buddy boating with them and one special trip, not because of the journey but the circumstance, which I will describe in a later chapter.

We did meet up with the Sveds in St. Michaels for a two day stay. We both were anchored out and would meet by dingy, trading evenings for dinner and bridge and they gave us passes to the Marine Museum, of which they are members. It was a real treat. After our visit here we went almost straight across the bay to Horn Harbor, the right one this time, and spent a couple of days with Lael and Kate.

Jeanne found a duplicate bridge group in the little town of Lusby a few miles north of Solomons and so once or twice a week we would play some competitive bridge which Jeanne really likes to do and I enjoy enough to have a good time. She also picked up a guest library card at the library that was just a short way from where the bridge was played so her two things, reading and bridge, were right where they needed to be. Washington D.C. and Annapolis were close enough for day trips by car.

CHAPTER 39

As the Fall of 2008 approached we started to prepare for our trip south. I ordered a new auto-pilot and installed it in COPIII. It had the same controller as the one on Interlude and worked beautifully. The connection to the hydraulic lines was below the upper helm pump and the drive was flawless. We then started heading south in mid-October and swung into the entrance to the Dismal Swamp through the Deep Creek Locks. A few miles farther down the starboard engine starts to overheat and I have to stop the engine and get Jeanne to carefully steer the boat with the port engine at idle. A quick look shows the water pump broken and it will need a major repair. We get the boat turned around, go back through the locks and head for the Atlantic Yacht Basin, only five miles or so, but through the Great Bridge locks. I can run the starboard engine for a few minutes to maneuver but can't use it for very long. We do make it and the mechanic takes a look and the dollar signs in his eyes light up the engine room. This is not really the case this time as the mechanic is employed by the Atlantic Yacht Basin and is not only an excellent one but works fast and efficiently. I found the rates charged reasonable and the service top rate. This is not always the case and some times the dollar signs in the eyes do light up and boat repairs can become very expensive and overcharging rampant.

In a few days we are back in the stream and are entering the Deep Creek locks again, but this time in a steady rain. Jeanne gets a line on one of the cleats and I jump out to tie up the other one and we retreat to the shelter on the sundeck. A beautiful fast trawler, a Saberline, ties up opposite and a attractive lady is tying up and is getting soaked but still has a smile on her face. Jeanne strikes up a conversation and we will soon meet Raymond and Susan Williams of Annapolis, MD and their dog Heathcliff von Severn III. I identify Heathcliff here and will tell you why shortly.

We all get through the Locks successfully and tie up to the free dock just inside. It is about 4:00 pm and a rainy day so no need to continue on as we are in no hurry. Raymond and Susan join us, or we join them. and strike up a friendship which is as close today as it was immediately then. Raymond is a retired attorney and Susan retired from an executive position with Sprint. They are fun and interesting people. They have forsaken their sailing days and this is their first trip on their new trawler and surprisingly their first trip outside the Chesapeake. They look to us as experienced boaters as we have done one partial trip down and back up the ICW. The blind following the blind is the correct expression. None the less we would buddy boat for a good distance and enjoy each others company. After we part ways on this trip we will see each other many times in the future and Jeanne and I will house sit for them a number of times in their little spot of heaven overlooking the Severn River.

Part of our chores when house sitting for the Williams is the care and feeding of the aforementioned Heathcliff. Now I have always been good with dogs and older women and although the older women are now my age the dogs still like me. Heathcliff is a poodle, which is normally way down on my likable dog list, but we bond. He has a personality and sense of humor that matches mine, at least at the dog level. I will site only one situation where I really felt he needed my presence. On one of our house sitting stays Susan has her mobile dog groomer scheduled for the day of their departure and is gone when the grooming is done. The groomer talks with us a few minutes in the house before departing but then I can't find Heathcliff. The search finds him hiding under their bed with the most unhappy dog face you have ever seen. His hair is blow dried into a fluffy puff and he is dowsed in powder and perfume. He, Heathcliff von Severn III, is a girly girl. I talk to him for a while, convince him that he will be a big dog again in a day or two as soon as all the fluff falls and the perfume wears off. That all will be good in his world. Again. I still had to gently pull him out from under the bed and carry him out to the family room to watch some TV. He finally stopped shaking and gave me a confident look that he could make it back.

Now back to Deep Creek. At about 5:00 pm the last opening of the locks is underway and when the outgoing doors are opened a Nordhaven trawler comes through. It is November 5, 2008 and it is still raining. On the Nordhaven is a young woman and a small girl holding dock lines and a worried young man at the helm. The dock is full and as I remember when I was offered a rafting in the Princess Louisa Inlet a few years before I stepped out wave them in to raft up to us. They accept and we get tied up in short order. The boat is Three @ Sea and has on board a young couple and their daughter embarking on the great adventure of touring the world and home schooling their daughter. David, Kathryn, and Ayla Besemer. This is their first experience passing through a lock and their trip is just starting. If you go to their web-site you will find they have just completed the 25,000 mile mark of their journey. Reading through their blogs is worth a little of your time if you have interest in something like this. I like to think that our courtesy at this early point in their adventure was a positive and that when they us told of their plans I told them I thought nothing they could do would be better for their daughter. That we had met a number of families doing the same thing with great results. If you read through a few of their stories I think you will see they have the right stuff and that this is their place and time.

Our trip heading south went smoothly. We had had joined the Marine Trawlers Owners Association and through them had secured a private dock just south of St. Augustine to leave COPIII for the holidays which were spent in Destin for our annual visit. When we returned I decided that it was time to have the bottom painted and set up an appointment at one of the bigger yards. I also felt that there was a little more vibration than there should be when under way and would have that checked out at the same time. This turned out to be a lot of boat fixing which included the bottom painting, straightening the propeller shafts, truing up the struts, and having the props serviced. New house batteries were purchased. All in all a very expensive month, some of which I think was a little more than warranted. But as is always quoted, "It's a boat!"

As January came to an end Jeanne's mother who was in Destin with Jo and Carl fell in the shower and fractured her hip. At ninety years of age her recovery was somewhat doubtful and Carl flew his plane over to St. Augustine and picked up Jeanne to help out with caring for her. One of the condos in their complex was rented and set up with a hospital bed and day nursing was employed. Jeanne and Jo, both nurses, would provide the evening and night care. Dora Bryan passed away peacefully a few days later on January 24, 2009. It had been four weeks earlier that she was her competitive self in family games of pinochle and although in some long term discomfort was still a good companion and family member. It was very sad, but after she fell she was in great pain and never really came back. She had a good life and I think, and hope, her share of happiness.

Once we had the bills paid at the boat yard we continued our south bound trip and made very comfortable cruising with a very smooth and vibration free drive. At anchor our new batteries held up well and required only reasonable charging. Our checking account was somewhat depleted but we were on our way again.

CHAPTER 40

This was to be the year we would make the crossing to the Bahamas. We headed south taking our time and eventually would stage our crossing the gulf stream, from Palm Beach to West End, anchored just south of Peanut Island and the inlet. We have our Homeland Security decal, our $300 in cash for the Bahamas permit, and a fully stocked boat. My fishing gear is ready and we have our snorkeling outfits. This was sometime in February and the north winds blew, and blew, and blew some more. The rule is never try to cross the gulf stream if there is an N in the wind direction. After a couple of weeks of waiting, and one try that beat us back after three hours of almost no progress, we opted to head down to Miami and maybe if things looked better on the way back north we would try once more. We never made it.

It was a good time and we saw and did a lot. But I never dove off COPIII into the clear blue waters, or picked up a lobster for dinner or caught a fish for lunch. We didn't dingy to a deserted beach to lay in the sun and I never saw any of those tall, slender girls in bikini's stroll down the way with music in my ears. College spring break in Miami made up for this last item, but only in a minor way.

At this point I think I need to describe cruising in the ICW in a little more detail. Unlike in the ocean where you are in deep water with very little company, the Atlantic ICW is for the most part a ditch in the center of mostly shallow water and in the season busy with pleasure boats, commercial barges and the like. It is very well marked but a moments lack of attention and you will go aground or be much too close to other boats or very hard objects. You have to keep track of what is in front of you and what maybe approaching from behind. With the exception of several big sounds and a few straight stretches you must hand steer. It is stressful, especially the first few times you navigate it. There are areas that the geography makes it a little less so and for me it was traversing Georgia. The ICW is very crooked and in a few places you travel several miles and come around a bend and can look back and actual see where you were an hour before. There is much less traffic as many boaters, and most of the commercial traffic, goes off shore to avoid the slow pace. Jeanne and I found that fifty miles a day was about maximum for our travels. A bicycle is much faster and we actually were passed by a jogger while underway in the Dismal Swamp.

We then start our trip back north and as we pass through Myrtle Beach, SC we stop at the Coquina Yacht Club in Little River a few miles north. We had stayed here before, decided to take a break and stay a month. That turned into a second month and as summer was approaching it was my turn to ask Jeanne a question.

"Let's make a visit to see Inez and let's drive!" I guess that's a statement more than a question, but please understand that Inez lives in Alaska. Jeanne in her infinite wisdom and knowing that this is something I had always wanted to do (drive the Alaskan Highway) said, "Sure why not." Plans were made and a few days later we were headed somewhat in that direction. Our 1996 Pontiac Bonneville now had about 140,000 miles on it and the decision was made to pack light so if at some point it wanted to go no farther we could leave it there and rent a car, get on a bus or train, and eventually fly back to Little River. Nothing could be simpler, but it was never necessary.

Now Jeanne and I never travel the fastest route to a destination unless required to by time constraints. We have lots of time and no constraints. So we head to Denver to see Janet, Craig and the girls, then a quick pass through Grand Teton and Yellowstone National Parks. Then on to Calgary, Alberta and into Banff and Jasper National Parks, making our way to

Dawson Creek to join the Alaskan Highway. We drove through Whitehorse, Yukon Territory and then on to Fairbanks, Alaska. From Fairbanks it is down the hill through Denali National Park with a 15 minute view of Mt. McKinley, that's all you usually get, and then to Anchorage. Guess who we meet for lunch and a tour of the Natural History Museum, Dick and Carolyn Brennan who have just arrived and will be leaving in the morning for a week in Denali. It is then onto the Kenai Peninsula to stay with Inez Zordel and her daughter Mae. More on our visit with Inez shortly. We then return through Anchorage to Tok and start back home on the Alaskan Highway. Going south smoke from forest fires has blotted out the mountains and at Watson Lake we decide to head for Prince Rupert on the Cassiar Highway to take the ferry to Port Hardy on Vancouver Island. The drive down to Victoria is special and from there it is to Port Angeles and down the east side of the Olympic Range along the Hood Canal and follow Highway 101 down the coast to San Francisco. Finally the last leg east on our favorite Highway 50 across Nevada to Salt Lake, Denver, Michigan (Jeanne's family) and then pretty much the shortest route to COPIII in Little River, SC. Twelve thousand miles in just over seven weeks. I love to drive and Jeanne is a remarkably good sport.

On this trip we did a number of things that made it memorable besides the fantastic scenery. I mentioned before that we often stayed with Jeanne's P.E.O. members who have the Bed & Breakfast service for members as a fund raiser. We have done this a number of times and always found it a treat. Since we had no schedule and would only drive distances that we were comfortable doing we were somewhat limited on how often we could plan in advance enough to make reservations. One stood out and that was in Fairbanks.

We were about two days out of Fairbanks when Jeanne made contact with the P.E.O. that was in charge of reservations for their Chapter's B&B and she said she would set things up for us and call when we got close which we did on arrival. There was no answer so we drove around downtown and wondered if we should find a motel. The phone rang and the young lady said she had been out but had a place for us and it was at her mother's house (also a P.E.O.). She gave us directions and would meet us there. Since I can't remember the names I will just say she showed the room and the rest of the house and told us that her Mom and Dad wouldn't be there till tomorrow afternoon and would we mind feeding the dog and letting him out a couple of times into the fenced yard to save her a couple of trips. This would of course be fine with us.

We stayed three nights as the next day we met some real Alaskans. The father and his younger brother's mother had been in the lumber business in Florida and when the trees ran out she moved to Alaska to see if she could start up another company there, leaving the boys behind. A little while later the boys, 12 and 8, were put on a train and made the trip to Fairbanks by themselves.They eventually started their own business as owners of a site preparation outfit setting up sites for exploration and mining companies. They set up sites all over Alaska and had heavy equipment with trucks, and even tugs and barges, to move the equipment to the required locations. Both were bush pilots and had many stories to tell, a few of which they shared with us. The mother was as would be expected of such a man as the father, a home maker but also a very well educated and intelligent woman. Their two sons were in the process of taking over the business which had expanded into construction. Their home had two large display cases filled with small native art works which had been collected, a few at a time, at every village they had visited. It was a terrific introduction to Alaska. On the morning we left the two brothers, with cups of coffee in hand, were bent over plans for a landing strip they were planning on their own property as the FFA was giving them trouble about their age and a few other things. They would build their own airport. The good wife smiled and told us they are just like little boys having so much fun and they had always been that way. What a great family story.

After our brief visit in Anchorage we headed for the Kenai Peninsula to meet up with Inez Zordel, one of our best friends from Aspen, and her daughter Mae, at their camp along the Kenai River. It is a beautiful day and a fine drive and by mid-afternoon we meet at a cross roads and are guided to where we will spend the next four days. Jeanne and I had only seen Inez once in the last twenty-five years and that was about fifteen years earlier when, at about seventy years of age, she was a passenger in a side car on Mae's husband's motorcycle. The three of them were traveling from Seattle to visit Inez's family in Oklahoma and stopped by our place in Loveland for the night. Quite a sight to see her climb out of the side car all dressed in her black leathers, but with that same shy smile she always showed us. Within the space of a minute or so we were once again in that comfortable sensation of friendship that made it seem that it was just yesterday that we had seen her last.

  The camp was right on the River and had two trailers, a central cooking and dinning cabin, and the guest cottage with a nice bathroom attached. The guest cabin was actually a simply built building constructed like a portable storage unit with half a small room just big enough to hold a double bed and the other housing the small bathroom with toilet, washbasin, shower and laundry unit. Plenty good for a camp but required an outdoor walk to enter the bathroom. A corrugated plastic roof provided light as in July there is almost no night. The cooking and dinning cabin was a fully equipped kitchen as well as the holder of all equipment to process salmon and the equipment to catch them. Owned and used for over thirty years it was old Alaska at its best and the next door neighbors with their modern big log houses looked somewhat out of place, at least in my eyes.

  It was into town to secure my three day fishing license and where we bought a case of cans for canning the expected catch. These come with twenty-three cans and a column of lids in the twenty-fourth spot. At a little over forty dollars it was the most expensive part of the fishing cost but I soon caught the first of a number of big red (sockeye) salmon and had my limit each day. Our cans were expertly filled and cooked and a number of big filets were packaged and frozen for our trip home. A large of amount of salmon was eaten at each meal.

It was the highlight of our trip and we keep in touch on occasions by mail and telephone. Inez's 92th birthday was last year and they still go down to the camp each summer to do a little fishing. Jeanne and I were so glad we got to share some time with Inez and as I mentioned above it was just like our shared time in Aspen.

It was then back on the road and the trip just described back to COPIII in Little River, SC. The only part that seemed the least bit long was from Michigan back to South Carolina, but even that wasn't so bad.

CHAPTER 41

Our plans for the coming fall of 2009 were to head south, then cross over to the gulf side of Florida, through Lake Okeechobee and the locks on either side, to spend some time with the Sveds in Tierra Verde. After the new year head south to the Florida Keyes and back north on the Atlantic side. If all worked out make another try to the Bahamas. We stopped in at St. Simons for a month which was time well spent as this is a very nice place. A bus trip and a car rental got us back to Little River to pick up our car which was later left in St. Simons on our next leg down to Vero Beach.

Our stay at Vero Beach was for several weeks and it was at this time when we started to think of it as being a possible more permanent place to be. The City Marina is nice and very well located within walking distance to the beach and the excellent Vero Beach public bus system has a stop there. One could do without a car but we made another one way rental and fetched our car from St. Simons. It was then time to start for Tierra Verde and we had a good trip through the five locks and across the big lake.

All went very well until we arrived at the draw bridge that crosses from Gasparilla to Boca Grande. The port side raw water pump fails and again I must stop one engine. A decision had to be made and I see entrance bouys to the east so in we go hoping something will be there where we can tie up or anchor. Up pops the Gasparilla Marina and a quick call on the VHF secures me an easy approach to a dock. Help is there and the dock master sets up a mechanic to service the pump. I had just changed the impeller on the starboard raw water pump and was hoping the port side one would last until we got to a dock in Tierra Verde. Close but no cigar as the saying goes. The water pump on the port side is almost unreachable and for me it is unreachable. Four hours at $95/hour and all was good again.

We are fairly close to the Sveds and find the Gasparilla Marina much to our liking so we decided to stay there for a while. Another one way rental and we have our car near our boat. We make several visits to the Sveds for the customary fine dinners and bridge both before and after. On one trip there we continue on to spend Christmas with Jeanne's sister and brother-in-law in Destin and then our life makes an unexpected change and it is my fault.

Back in Gasparilla, on December 31, 2009, after taking the boat to the pump out station to do that chore I find my left foot doesn't want to do what I want it to, not to a great degree but noticeable. The next minute while I am kneeling down to inspect the holding tank I tip over. Jeanne happens to be watching me and sees that the left side of my face is drooping. "You are having a stroke, get up there and sit down!" I am feeling just fine and I can move about but I know something is not quite right so I do what Nurse Jeanne tells me to do. To sum this all up I spend New Years Eve, Day, and the day after in the Port Charlotte Heart and Stroke Center being MRI'd, blood pressured, and all of the other items in the ten step program. It is a bleed stroke and I do what I am told. I feel great. I can think clearly, eat, drink with only a slight dribbling, speak with a slight lisp and have a Harrison Ford smile. I am sent home with instructions and signed up with rehabilitation. After about a month I am doing good except I have serious side effects from the blood pressure medication. After two months it is deemed I don't need any more rehab which, by the way, I knew after one week. The blood pressure dosage was reduced and by April almost all symptoms had cleared up and I felt comfortable driving again. Today the only symptom remaining is the numb left foot and a very mild numbness of skin on my left side. I have no muscle or dexterity problems and my smile is even. A change in BP medication improved my mental comfort. I was very lucky.

In March Jeanne decides I need a recovery cruise, meaning a big ship cruise to the East Caribbean. It was nice but not really necessary. I think Jeanne needed it more than me and she deserved it.

By the first of April we decided to head back to Vero Beach and we coincide our trip to buddy boat with the Sveds as they were starting their trip up to the Chesapeake Bay. It was very comforting to have them along. We met at an anchorage near Ft. Myers and then crossed Okeechobee and part way north together. The evenings were spent together with our usual dinner and bridge. I let Ed lead the entire way and this made it possible for me to not have to make any decisions for most of the trip.

We are then back at the City Marina in Vero Beach and are there until June. We start planning a trip to Denver for a visit to the daughter and family and as Jeanne is having some stomach discomfort and tingling in her feet she wants to visit our family doctor in Loveland. Since during hurricane season the City Marina requires boats to be removed if a named storm is predicted we find a slip at the Grand Harbor Marina, which is deemed a hurricane hole, and take a lease for six months. We are now off to the next advent, an even more serious development in our life.

Jeanne's visit to our doctor, the very good and likable Dr. Danforth, results in his thinking that Jeanne should have x-rays and an MRI of her stomach area but what he is more concerned about is the tingling in her feet and he sets up an appointment with a neurologist. The neurologist does some tests in his office and thinks an MRI of her spine is in order. Jeanne then makes several trips to radiology. In a confusing sequence it is finally determined that her T2 vertebrae has been invaded by a tumor and it is pinching off the spinal cord. Her neurologist is away for three days and his stand-in recommends an immediate trip to the Emergency Room at University of Denver Hospital. This is on a Friday afternoon and Jeanne knows enough about emergency rooms to think this is not such a great idea.

That night and the next morning, thanks to the internet, she finds that the head spinal surgeon at UDH is not only considered one of the best in the country but is also accepting new patients. A telephone call makes contact with his Physicians Assistant and a appointment is made. Jeanne efficiently manages to coordinate the sending of all the reports and MRI's to UDH before the appointment on Monday. She has a seven and one half hour operation on Thursday that completely removes the T2 vertebrae and inserts an expandable metal cage that filled with bone chips that will grow and fuse the T1 and T3 into bone and protect the spinal cord. This is serious stuff and was, with a very minor slip, one hundred percent successful. She was within a short period of being paralyzed from the chest down.

It was also discovered she had a very slow growing tumor on her left kidney and that was surgically removed in another major operation six weeks later. We rented a nice town home in one of the high end extended care facilities in Denver which are set up for the first step for people who wish to have an independent and nice place to live until they require additional help. We had good neighbors and access to a restaurant that served meals at very reasonable cost. With a complete kitchen we mostly ate in and we were also just minutes from Janet's house so life wasn't not all that bad. Jeanne came out of the ordeal in good health and spirits and I was doing just fine. This is now spoken of as our "Medicare Year – 2010."

This is a good place to discuss Medicare and Social Security, two very popular government programs for us older people, and as in all Ponzi schemes are most popular for those who are benefiting from the current payers. Now I know that all of us that are recipients have previously paid into both programs for the benefits promised. My first contribution was in 1952 with a earnings of $475 with eleven years at the maximum and the remaining years at a great variety of taxable earnings. My Medicare contributions only reached maximum for five years. Jeanne reached the maximums less often, but had greater income over the later decades. I don't have the totals as I write *this but as 2010 ended we had received more in benefits than we had paid in even adjusted for inflation and supposed gain in the Social Security investment* strategies. *We are, and have been for a number of years, takers rather than contributors. My last contribution was in 2007 on a small self-employment income which to be offset by my increased benefit will take 30 years to break even. We also pay income tax on a portion of our Social Security income and of course the Part B monthly premium of Medicare, Gap insurance and deductible co-pays. The ratio of takers versus contributors is now becoming unbalanced and this is when the predicable problems with Ponzi schemes become obvious.*

Medicare will be the first to go bankrupt as its business model is the most flawed. As with Social Security we are living too long, the needs of medical care increase with longevity, and the demographics are heading in the wrong direction. Add to this the monies collected are placed in government bonds which at some point will have to be redeemed and our government has of course spent all the money. Governor Dick Lamm, of Colorado, many years ago gained national attention when he said in public that ,"The older generation has a responsibility to die and make way for the next generation." He is of course correct but I would prefer a natural death, which I am sure he meant. Maybe not, however, a number of quadruple by-passes, a variety of knee and hip replacements, and months of end of life support.

This brings me to another problem in Medicare and that is if the reimbursement of the health providers isn't changed we may end up with a shortage of providers. The latest idiocy is The Affordable Care Act which will compound this problem. Most recipients of Medicare pay little or no attention to medical costs and reimbursements of providers. I shall give you a few examples from Jeanne's two surgeries. These will be described as Provider "P", Amount Charged "AC", Medicare Approved "MA", Medicare Paid Provider "MPP", Deductible "D".

P UOD Hospital, AC $170,993.11, MA $170,993.11, MPP $52,084.62, D $1,100.00

P McKee Hospital, C $47,787.50, MA $47,787.50, MPP $11,561.62, D $ 0.00
P Dr. Witt, AC $28,613.00, MA $5,659.98, MPP , 4,527.99, D $1,131.99
P Dr. Eddy, AC $2,500.00, MA $1,551.55, MPP $1,241.2, D $301.31
P Dr. Reese, AC $592.00, MA $157.27, MPP $125.81, D $31.46

    Now these charges go on and on, and if you can make any sense of them you are a better accountant than I, or you work for the government. The hospital deductible is one time a year so on Jeanne's second hospital visit in the same year it had been satisfied. The doctors you may have to pay is part of the Medicare Part D twenty percent co-pay. Unless you request this information from MyMedicare.Gov you will not be able to understand what is going on. If you have Medi-Gap insurance, which is of questionable value, you will get some details.
    The problem here is that what should be the Amount Charged be and what should be the Medicare Paid Provider. Private insurance companies have clout in what is paid but the individual paying cash better get an attorney to act as an arbitrator. This is no way to run a business and it makes our medical system look economically ridiculous. The provider should charge for services in a reasonable and profitable manor and the receiver of those services should pay for what is received. It should be a free market business transaction, not the totally skewed accounting as exampled above. Medicaid I can only imagine. Then there are the indigent in the emergency rooms and hospitals. Of course a lot of this is caused by the providers having to cover the costs of the indigent care in charges to those who pay for care.
    In Jeanne's cases there was no choice for us on what should be done. The spinal surgery prevented almost certain paralysis and the kidney surgery a longer life. We would have paid the costs regardless of what it would have done to our

economic well being and would have found some way to meet our obligations. I think help in this is what Medicare's intention was in the first place, life saving of lives worth saving. Dick Lamm quoted above is correct in that when the time comes we older people should bow out gracefully and not overburden the next generation. If we want another few months then we should pay for them ourselves. If the hip won't let you make a full turn on the golf course and you have lost five strokes a nine, maybe you should pay for that repair yourself.

Christmas 2010 was spent in Destin again with Jeanne's family and Janet and family also joined us. By the time we got back to the boat it was near the start of 2011 and our life was going to slow down a bit, but not too much. We had decided that extensive cruising was pretty much over.

In April I had my 76th birthday and in a few more months Jeanne would be seventy-three. This would be the start of a very busy summer and fall as towards the end of May we headed to Maine spend the month of June in a Vacation Rentals by Owner cabin in New Harbor, which is near Damariscotta and close to East Booth Bay. We meet the owners, Bennett and Pam Brooks, to pick up the key a few days ahead of schedule and offer to open up the cabin for them. Which we do and settle in for a very nice month. Our best friend John Bush is residing near by and we get to spend time socializing with him and his long time friend Nancy Putnam. Always a fun couple to be around. John is in charge of a couple of duplicate bridge groups so there is lots of bridge and we get to know quite a number of the down east folks.

On June 13, 2011 we are notified of the death of Jeanne's youngest sister Janet. She had contracted what was thought to be Alzheimer Disease several years prior and had progressively worsened and died suddenly at age 66. It was later learned that she had Pick's Disease which is a much more aggressive form of dementia and explained her early passing. The memorial service held on July 9 in Flint which we attended with the all the family and a very large and devoted group of school teachers and friends from her 36 years of teaching in the

Flint school system. Dan Pope, her husband and all of our's brother-in-law, after being Janet's full time care giver for all of her illness, some time later found a new love and they are doing many things he and they both like to do. Bicycling, traveling, visiting their children and family, and are of course still very much a part of our family.

After the memorial service we head to Colorado for a visit with daughter and family, a final check up with Jeanne's spine surgeon, a tough tooth extraction for me and a short house sit at a friend's house in Loveland. Then back on the road to get to Carl and Jo's in Michigan in time to play in Carl's member guest golf tournament, which I probably won't be a guest again since it takes two to win. It is then to Annapolis for some long term house sitting for Raymond and Susan Williams as they travel the world. Two three week stays with being guests in between. We were there for the August 23 earthquake and the August 27 arrival of Hurricane Irene. Our daughter Janet and family join us and tours of Washington D.C., Mt. Vernon, and Annapolis are made. Even after a tour of the Naval Academy we couldn't talk Devin into applying. We gave up our house sitting chores after the Williams return from their second trip and head up towards Maine to spend the last 10 days of September at the Brooks cabin to catch some more Maine in the fall. However it then started to rain and get colder so it was time head back to Vero Beach and COPIII to prepare for our next adventure. We did of course make the trip to Destin for Christmas.

CHAPTER 42

We have survived Christmas 2011 and greet the New Year 2012 snug aboard COPIII in Grand Harbor and as usual sound asleep. For some time I have become a bit bored living on board and am starting to think it is time to find a land based residence. Jeanne is still really enjoying the boating life and with a good social life where we are now docked makes life nice. The only time we take the boat out is to make the 300 yard journey to the pump out station and back. My reputation as a helmsman is legend and all come out to wish us good travels and applaud our successful return. Inquires as to the weather and sea conditions are always made and congratulations on our journey given with big, big smiles. I of course embellish the difficulties of this trip and everyone has a good time with the exaggerations. This is actually fun for us but doesn't take the place of cruising.

It is now that I discover the Indian River County (Vero Beach and neighbors) listing of the house foreclosure auctions on a very complete and easy to use web-site. All public records are available and there is more information available than any one person should be able to get their hands on. I now have a quest and quickly start the search for just the right house for us if we decide to make the next big change in lifestyle. Jeanne is a good sport and lets me dominate the laptop.

We meet a real estate agent at an open house that we like and go to a few showings but nothing is working. I find a fixer upper near the beach which is on the market through a Freddie Mac foreclosure. You need to understand that trying to buy a property through the foreclosure auction is a bit tricky and in general the mortgage holder almost always is the high bidder.

The total claimed in the foreclosure is not only the unpaid mortgage balance, but interest, taxes, and a number of other costs. The mortgage is usually guaranteed by either Freddie Mac or Fannie Mae so the banks get their money back with I am sure other compensation. An offer is made on the fixer upper with Jeanne cringing in the background about my thinking I could handle the amount of work that would be needed to make it habitable and much to her relief, and later mine, we are out bid.

It is here that 1390 River Ridge Drive shows up on the IRC Auction Calendar. We drive by and the property looks nice but just a little unkempt. The neighborhood is very good and the location is what we are looking for. The bank wins the auction and the house disappears. I did not bid as first you can't get inside for an inspection and the requirements for bidding are such that you had better know what you are doing before committing. Three months later the house is listed as a Fannie Mae sale by a local Coldwell Banker agent and we go to the first open house. Jeanne is honest in that she didn't see exactly what I saw when we walked in the front door the first time. The agent was not too helpful when she found out we had another helping us look for a property and felt we should honor him as our agent. But none the less the inspection is made and I think that this is the one. We started our debate on whether to proceed.

I had about convinced Jeanne I could do the obviously needed modifications inside. A removal of a very large bar and a partition that had been added separating the dinning area from the living room, We see a notice of a further $15,000 price reduction had been made. I suggested that this was too good a property to pass on and that at the new price we should just go ahead and make a full price offer. Jeanne, still with some doubts, agreed as we had managed to get this far together and things had gone along just fine. What could go wrong here and nothing really wrong did.

Our real estate agent got to write up our offer without every having seen the property. Not a bad thing for him as it would be a good commission. With some additional help from the listing agent the offer was submitted and accepted on May 18, 2012. I will point out that the additional help by the listing agent was that this was an offer to Fannie Mae and as she explained at the time every i had to be dotted and every t crossed. Every blank accounted for and no exceptions no matter how unimportant they were. She was right and what came next was a lesson in what is wrong with our Government.

Closing was to be on June 18 and we had a major family organizational plan to implement. Craig, the son-in-law, had been transferred to a job near Kansas City, KS and Janet had post phoned the move until the girls finished that years school. They had purchased a house in Overland Park which was about half way between Kansas City and Craig's job site and were able to sell their house in Westminster. All was set up to make the move such that Jeanne and I could pickup our belongings in Loveland, everything would be packed and the moves would take place at the same time. We spent the last night in their house and left, Janet a few hours after we did, for the trip to our new homes.

There is of course a little more to this part of the story before Jeanne and I can move off the boat on to land. First is buying a house from Fannie Mae is not a logical procedure. To start with we were going to put one half down and secure a seven year ARM from my beloved bank of more than twenty-five years that held all our accounts, checking, savings, securities, and both IRAs. Should be a piece of cake. I went on line and clicked on the banks mortgage link and the process started immediately. For the ARM I supplied expected documents such as the last two year's Form 1040, Social Security, etc and we were underway. Then there was a little bit of this and a little bit of that to the point of minor annoyance. There was then some discussion that maybe the closing date was a bit too soon but I explained that a lot of things were being scheduled to coincide with this date and that I would be much more than a little annoyed if that date wasn't met.

I am sitting on Janet's backyard porch when the cell phone rings and a sweet young female voice introduces herself as from the bank's mortgage office and that she needs to know where the funds for the down payment have come from. All of the funds were moved from our securities account to our savings account and the overnight wire transfer would be from there and that their bank had all the records on all our available assets and what had been transferred and from where. I didn't explain all this in a very pleasant manor as I had just finished loading a small moving van that morning emptying our store room in Loveland, was very tired, and we would be leaving the next day on the trip back to Florida. I think she said something like, "Yes I understand," followed by, "Goodbye."

As we were pushing hard to make it back to Vero Beach before dark on the Friday before the Monday closing we still hadn't got the final statement for the down payment amount. After several calls an answer was obtained that it was about $37,000 more than the week before estimate and no explanation was given. Fortunately when we were in Loveland we had stopped in to see our friends and securities adviser at the bank and met their new office manager who I think was wearing a spiked collar, or maybe it was just her demeanor. In any case when she heard the problems we were encountering with the loan and closing schedule she said she would take care of things. It was several days later on that Friday just mentioned that I called her back and she went into full power mode. Around 6:00 pm we received the last call and the number was straightened out and the amount was what had been expected. I won't describe what had happened, but it was in the you wouldn't believe category.

Monday Jeanne and I had the wire transfer done and by 10:00 am the sending was verified and the afternoon closing was scheduled. We went through more papers than any transaction should have, initialing page after page until our hands hurt, things we never read. At about 3:00 pm we finished and then in almost the final straw to thirty days of near insanity the closing agent said she couldn't give us the key as the closing's most important document from Fannie Mae was indeed signed but the signature had not been notarized as required and new one would have to be sent overnight express. At 10:00 am on June 19, 2012 we owned our new home and had our key. We then unloaded and returned the rental truck on schedule, and went back to the boat and collapsed.

I later found out what was going on. My bank was merely acting as a loan broker and mortgage server and the mortgage was sold to Freddie Mac thirty days later. If the bank had held the mortgage I was informed that with fifty percent down and the appraisal at more than the purchase price it would have taken about one hour to have set up the loan. We were being treated as first time home buyers and every i had to be dotted, every t crossed and every blank filled in to meet Freddie Mac's requirements.

CHAPTER 43

After about four weeks of concentrated labor the large bar has been removed as well as the partition wall, the tile floor laid under the bar area, and the dry wall details completed. We had the three bedrooms carpeted and had a few pieces of furniture purchased including a king size bed for our bedroom. The agent for Fannie Mae had the entire interior of the house painted and the painters had done a good job. The kitchen had been left with high end appliances which all worked. The decision was made as Jeanne made up the bed that we would sleep here tonight. We did and never went back on the boat to spend the night. Our boating days were over and Change O Pace III was put up for sale.

The next few months, and then on a regular basis which is still going on, the search for furniture was conducted and was a fun recreation. You should know that as the years went by Janet managed to take some of the furniture from our store room as her needs occurred and when we decided to live in south Florida our Loveland furniture wasn't going to fit and we gave her the rest of it. Fortunately it looks and functions very nicely in her house in Kansas. The few pieces that she couldn't use were either sold or donated to the Goodwill and therefore we had a 2700 square foot house to fill. Since all of Jeanne and my previous furniture shopping had been on very limited budgets and almost all had been purchased used from garage and yard sales, personal ads, or thrift and second hand shops, we adopted this same strategy here. Vero Beach is terrific hunting grounds and we were very successful. Besides the search is half the fun and you might say we are hunter-gatherers in that respect.

We are now ready to unpack and the boxes are brought in one by one and it is like Christmas everyday for weeks. All our possessions have been packed away for over ten years and each box yields at least one surprise. Our art collections is especially good to see again and hanging the paintings in this almost perfect house for display is most gratifying. We have a nice built in display case for our small collectibles and many places to exhibit a large amount of sculpture, much of which is of course mine. I find a large bookcase at Habitat for Humanity which needs some work and build a smaller matching one to house my big collection of books. One of our best surprises is when Jeanne finds the fire place screen my Grandmother Willisford had carved for a wedding present for my parents which had been stored for over fifty years and when she placed it in front of our fireplace it had finally found a perfect home.

A yard service was hired to cut back the jungle on our half acre with nine large oak trees, thirteen palms, and practically every other plant, bush and small tree that will grow in Florida. My promise to myself after selling our house in Loveland was that I would never again own any yard equipment was broken. Now with a garage full of a complete array of garden equipment and coupled with remaining boxes, tools, golf and fishing equipment, and miscellaneous leaves the car parked outside.

In late September we drove up to Annapolis to house sit for the Williams, to enjoy some cooler weather and to take a break from getting our new home in shape. Christmas is celebrated in our new home and almost every day as Jeanne walks about she declares, "I love my house!"

The first half of 2013 is busy doing nothing which we are becoming quite good at doing. But that can't last too long, and at the same time as COPIII sells, finally and ouch, we take a short trip to Hilton Head to visit Raymond and Susan Williams in one of their new homes as they have sold their big property in Annapolis. They have a smaller home there have this one as their get away retreat. It would be my last visit with my four legged pal Heathcliff.

This is followed in September by a ten day tour of

Ireland highlighted by a three day stay with boating friends Chris and Claire Ogilvie-White at Cuan-na-Mara, their little place with their own designed nine hole golf course, near Waterford. We met Chris and Claire in Grand Harbor where they keep their boat a few slips from where we had COPIII. Chris is an Englishman who at a young age as an employee went to Africa and then shortly after started a business with a partner which became very successful. The fair Claire is a very attractive red haired Irish girl and the pair are a delight to know and a pleasure to visit. Chris is a wood turner when time permits and proudly displays his large and fully equipped shop which now contains enough beautiful wood to last his lifetime ten times over. Jeanne and I were presented one of his small works, a wonderful bowl turned in Irish Yew, engraved on the bottom with Art & Jeanne Ireland 2013 Chris & Claire. Turned by Chris O-W. It has a place of honor on our mantle.

After a jet lag recovery from our trip to Ireland and taking care of the homestead, we are off to Destin for the Holidays. 2014 starts of with enjoying home, a little golf and fishing are interspersed with the yard work, and this and that. In late June we visit our friends the Sveds in a small place they are renting for the summers in western North Carolina for a few days and return via Pinehurst for a three day stay and I get the chance to play Pinehurst #7. A most enjoyable trip. September finds us flying to San Diego to attend the wedding of the son of one of my nephews. It is a grand California wedding and provides Jeanne and me a chance to see all my relatives at one time in one place. Janet and Andie fly in too and it makes for a fun, if short visit. Jeanne and I then rent a car and make our San Francisco run to see all our friends in the area and fly back from there.

We now come to this day which I have promised you and that as in a few short months I will have my 80th birthday and will officially be an old man living in Southern Florida.

This is THE END of MY STORY,

        but not yet for me.

            AM

www.ingramcontent.com/pod-product-compliance
Lightning Source LLC
Chambersburg PA
CBHW071811080526
44589CB00012B/757